HBase Administration Cookbook

Master HBase configuration and administration for optimum database performance

Yifeng Jiang

[PACKT] open source ✳
PUBLISHING   community experience distilled

BIRMINGHAM - MUMBAI

HBase Administration Cookbook

Copyright © 2012 Packt Publishing

First published: August 2012

Production Reference: 1080812

Published by Packt Publishing Ltd.
Livery Place
35 Livery Street
Birmingham B3 2PB, UK..

ISBN 978-1-84951-714-0

www.packtpub.com

Cover Image by Asher Wishkerman (a.wishkerman@mpic.de)

Credits

Author

Yifeng Jiang

Reviewers

Masatake Iwasaki

Tatsuya Kawano

Michael Morello

Shinichi Yamashita

Acquisition Editor

Sarah Cullington

Lead Technical Editor

Pramila Balan

Technical Editors

Merin Jose

Kavita Raghavan

Manmeet Singh Vasir

Copy Editors

Brandt D'Mello

Insiya Morbiwala

Project Coordinator

Yashodhan Dere

Proofreader

Aaron Nash

Indexer

Hemangini Bari

Graphics

Manu Joseph

Valentina D'silva

Production Coordinator

Arvindkumar Gupta

Cover Work

Arvindkumar Gupta

About the Author

Yifeng Jiang is a Hadoop and HBase Administrator and Developer at Rakuten—the largest e-commerce company in Japan. After graduating from the University of Science and Technology of China with a B.S. in Information Management Systems, he started his career as a professional software engineer, focusing on Java development.

In 2008, he started looking over the Hadoop project. In 2009, he led the development of his previous company's display advertisement data infrastructure using Hadoop and Hive.

In 2010, he joined his current employer, where he designed and implemented the Hadoop- and HBase-based, large-scale item ranking system. He is also one of the members of the Hadoop team in the company, which operates several Hadoop/HBase clusters.

Acknowledgement

Little did I know, when I was first asked by Packt Publishing whether I would be interested in writing a book about HBase administration on September 2011, how much work and stress (but also a lot of fun) it was going to be.

Now that the book is finally complete, I would like to thank those people without whom it would have been impossible to get done.

First, I would like to thank the HBase developers for giving us such a great piece of software. Thanks to all of the people on the mailing list providing good answers to my many questions, and all the people working on tickets and documents.

I would also like to thank the team at Packt Publishing for contacting me to get started with the writing of this book, and providing support, guidance, and feedback.

Many thanks to Rakuten, my employer, who provided me with the environment to work on HBase and the chance to write this book.

Thank you to Michael Stack for helping me with a quick review of the book.

Thank you to the book's reviewers—Michael Morello, Tatsuya Kawano, Kenichiro Hamano, Shinichi Yamashita, and Masatake Iwasaki.

To Yotaro Kagawa: Thank you for supporting me and my family from the very start and ever since.

To Xinping and Lingyin: Thank you for your support and all your patience—I love you!

About the Reviewers

Masatake Iwasaki is a Software Engineer at NTT DATA CORPORATION, providing technical consultation for open source softwares such as Hadoop, HBase, and PostgreSQL.

Tatsuya Kawano is an HBase contributor and evangelist in Japan. He has been helping the Japanese Hadoop and HBase community to grow since 2010.

He is currently working for Gemini Mobile Technologies as a Research & Development software engineer. He is also developing Cloudian, a fully S3 API-complaint cloud storage platform, and Hibari DB, an open source, distributed, key-value store.

He has co-authored a Japanese book named "Basic Knowledge of NOSQL" in 2012, which introduces 16 NoSQL products, such as HBase, Cassandra, Riak, MongoDB, and Neo4j to novice readers.

He has studied graphic design in New York, in the late 1990s. He loves playing with 3D computer graphics as much as he loves developing high-availability, scalable, storage systems.

Michael Morello holds a Masters degree in Distributed Computing and Artificial Intelligence. He is a Senior Java/JEE Developer with a strong Unix and Linux background. His areas of research are mostly related to large-scale systems and emerging technologies dedicated to solving scalability, performance, and high availability issues.

I would like to thank my wife and my little angel for their love and support.

Shinichi Yamashita is a Chief Engineer at the OSS Professional Service unit in NTT DATA Corporation, in Japan. He has more than 7 years of experience in software and middleware (Apache, Tomcat, PostgreSQL, Hadoop eco system) engineering.

Shinicha has written a few books on Hadoop in Japan.

I would like to thank my colleagues.

www.PacktPub.com

Support files, eBooks, discount offers and more

You might want to visit www.PacktPub.com for support files and downloads related to your book.

Did you know that Packt offers eBook versions of every book published, with PDF and ePub files available? You can upgrade to the eBook version at www.PacktPub.com and as a print book customer, you are entitled to a discount on the eBook copy. Get in touch with us at service@packtpub.com for more details.

At www.PacktPub.com, you can also read a collection of free technical articles, sign up for a range of free newsletters and receive exclusive discounts and offers on Packt books and eBooks.

http://PacktLib.PacktPub.com

Do you need instant solutions to your IT questions? PacktLib is Packt's online digital book library. Here, you can access, read and search across Packt's entire library of books.

Why Subscribe?

- ▶ Fully searchable across every book published by Packt
- ▶ Copy and paste, print and bookmark content
- ▶ On demand and accessible via web browser

Free Access for Packt account holders

If you have an account with Packt at www.PacktPub.com, you can use this to access PacktLib today and view nine entirely free books. Simply use your login credentials for immediate access.

Table of Contents

Preface

As an open source, distributed, big data store, HBase scales to billions of rows, with millions of columns and sits on top of the clusters of commodity machines. If you are looking for a way to store and access a huge amount of data in real time, then look no further than HBase.

HBase Administration Cookbook provides practical examples and simple step-by-step instructions for you to administrate HBase with ease. The recipes cover a wide range of processes for managing a fully distributed, highly available HBase cluster on the cloud. Working with such a huge amount of data means that an organized and manageable process is key, and this book will help you to achieve that.

The recipes in this practical cookbook start with setting up a fully distributed HBase cluster and moving data into it. You will learn how to use all the tools for day-to-day administration tasks, as well as for efficiently managing and monitoring the cluster to achieve the best performance possible. Understanding the relationship between Hadoop and HBase will allow you to get the best out of HBase; so this book will show you how to set up Hadoop clusters, configure Hadoop to cooperate with HBase, and tune its performance.

What this book covers

Chapter 1, Setting Up HBase Cluster: This chapter explains how to set up an HBase cluster, from a basic standalone HBase instance to a fully distributed, highly available HBase cluster on Amazon EC2.

Chapter 2, Data Migration: In this chapter, we will start with the simple task of importing data from MySQL to HBase, using its Put API. We will then describe how to use the importtsv and bulk load tools to load TSV data files into HBase. We will also use a MapReduce sample to import data from other file formats. This includes putting data directly into an HBase table and writing to HFile format files on Hadoop Distributed File System (HDFS). The last recipe in this chapter explains how to precreate regions before loading data into HBase.

This chapter ships with several sample sources written in Java. It assumes that you have basic Java knowledge, so it does not explain how to compile and package the sample Java source in the recipes.

Chapter 3, Using Administration Tools: In this chapter, we describe the usage of various administration tools such as HBase web UI, HBase Shell, HBase hbck, and others. We explain what the tools are for, and how to use them to resolve a particular task.

Chapter 4, Backing Up and Restoring HBase Data: In this chapter, we will describe how to back up HBase data using various approaches, their pros and cons, and which approach to choose depending on your dataset size, resources, and requirements.

Chapter 5, Monitoring and Diagnosis: In this chapter, we will describe how to monitor and diagnose HBase cluster with Ganglia, OpenTSDB, Nagios, and other tools. We will start with a simple task to show the disk utilization of HBase tables. We will install and configure Ganglia to monitor an HBase metrics and show an example usage of Ganglia graphs. We will also set up OpenTSDB, which is similar to Ganglia, but more scalable as it is built on the top of HBase.

We will set up Nagios to check everything we want to check, including HBase-related daemon health, Hadoop/HBase logs, HBase inconsistencies, HDFS health, and space utilization.

In the last recipe, we will describe an approach to diagnose and fix the frequently asked hot spot region issue.

Chapter 6, Maintenance and Security: In the first six recipes of this chapter we will learn about the various HBase maintenance tasks, such as finding and correcting faults, changing cluster size, making configuration changes, and so on.

We will also look at security in this chapter. In the last three recipes, we will install Kerberos and then set up HDFS security with Kerberos, and finally set up secure HBase client access.

Chapter 7, Troubleshooting: In this chapter, we will look through several of the most confronted issues. We will describe the error messages of these issues, why they happen, and how to fix them with the troubleshooting tools.

Chapter 8, Basic Performance Tuning: In this chapter, we will describe how to tune HBase to gain better performance. We will also include recipes to tune other tuning points such as Hadoop configurations, the JVM garbage collection settings, and the OS kernel parameters.

Chapter 9, Advanced Configurations and Tuning: This is another chapter about performance tuning in the book. The previous chapter describes some recipes to tune Hadoop, OS setting, Java, and HBase itself, to improve the overall performance of the HBase cluster. These are general improvements for many use cases. In this chapter, we will describe more specific recipes, some of which are for write-heavy clusters, while some are aimed at improving the read performance of the cluster.

What you need for this book

Everything you need is listed in each recipe.

The basic list of software required for this book are as follows:

- Debian 6.0.1 (squeeze)
- Oracle JDK (Java Development Kit) SE 6
- HBase 0.92.1
- Hadoop 1.0.2
- ZooKeeper 3.4.3

Who this book is for

This book is for HBase administrators, developers, and will even help Hadoop administrators. You are not required to have HBase experience, but are expected to have a basic understanding of Hadoop and MapReduce.

Conventions

In this book, you will find a number of styles of text that distinguish between different kinds of information. Here are some examples of these styles, and an explanation of their meaning.

Code words in text are shown as follows: "HBase can be stopped using its `stop-hbase.sh` script."

A block of code is set as follows:

```
nameserver 10.160.49.250 #private IP of ns
search hbase-admin-cookbook.com #domain name
```

When we wish to draw your attention to a particular part of a code block, the relevant lines or items are set in bold:

```
MAJOR_COMPACTION_KEY = \x00
MAX_SEQ_ID_KEY = 96573
TIMERANGE = 1323026325955....1323026325955
hfile.AVG_KEY_LEN = 31
hfile.AVG_VALUE_LEN = 4
hfile.COMPARATOR = org.apache.hadoop.hbase.KeyValue$KeyComparator
```

Any command-line input or output is written as follows:

```
$ bin/ycsb load hbase -P workloads/workloada -p columnfamily=f1 -p
recordcount=1000000 -p threadcount=4 -s | tee -a workloada.dat
YCSB Client 0.1

Command line: -db com.yahoo.ycsb.db.HBaseClient -P workloads/workloada -p
columnfamily=f1 -p recordcount=1000000 -p threadcount=4 -s -load

Loading workload...
```

New terms and **important words** are shown in bold. Words that you see on the screen, in menus or dialog boxes for example, appear in the text like this: " Verify the startup from **AWS Management Console**".

 Warnings or important notes appear in a box like this.

 Tips and tricks appear like this.

Reader feedback

Feedback from our readers is always welcome. Let us know what you think about this book— what you liked or may have disliked. Reader feedback is important for us to develop titles that you really get the most out of.

To send us general feedback, simply send an e-mail to feedback@packtpub.com, and mention the book title through the subject of your message.

If there is a topic that you have expertise in and you are interested in either writing or contributing to a book, see our author guide on www.packtpub.com/authors.

Customer support

Now that you are the proud owner of a Packt book, we have a number of things to help you to get the most from your purchase.

Downloading the example code

You can download the example code files for all Packt books you have purchased from your account at http://www.packtpub.com. If you purchased this book elsewhere, you can visit http://www.packtpub.com/support and register to have the files e-mailed directly to you.

Errata

Although we have taken every care to ensure the accuracy of our content, mistakes do happen. If you find a mistake in one of our books—maybe a mistake in the text or the code—we would be grateful if you would report this to us. By doing so, you can save other readers from frustration and help us improve subsequent versions of this book. If you find any errata, please report them by visiting http://www.packtpub.com/support, selecting your book, clicking on the **errata submission form** link, and entering the details of your errata. Once your errata are verified, your submission will be accepted and the errata will be uploaded to our website, or added to any list of existing errata, under the Errata section of that title.

Piracy

Piracy of copyright material on the Internet is an ongoing problem across all media. At Packt, we take the protection of our copyright and licenses very seriously. If you come across any illegal copies of our works, in any form, on the Internet, please provide us with the location address or website name immediately so that we can pursue a remedy.

Please contact us at copyright@packtpub.com with a link to the suspected pirated material.

We appreciate your help in protecting our authors, and our ability to bring you valuable content.

Questions

You can contact us at questions@packtpub.com if you are having a problem with any aspect of the book, and we will do our best to address it.

1
Setting Up HBase Cluster

In this chapter, we will cover:

- ▶ Quick start
- ▶ Getting ready on Amazon EC2
- ▶ Setting up Hadoop
- ▶ Setting up ZooKeeper
- ▶ Changing the kernel settings
- ▶ Setting up HBase
- ▶ Basic Hadoop/ZooKeeper/HBase configurations
- ▶ Setting up multiple **High Availability** (**HA**) masters

Introduction

This chapter explains how to set up HBase cluster, from a basic standalone HBase instance to a fully distributed, highly available HBase cluster on Amazon EC2.

According to Apache HBase's home page:

> *HBase is the Hadoop database. Use HBase when you need random, real-time, read/write access to your Big Data. This project's goal is the hosting of very large tables—billions of rows X millions of columns—atop clusters of commodity hardware.*

HBase can run against any filesystem. For example, you can run HBase on top of an EXT4 local filesystem, **Amazon Simple Storage Service** (**Amazon S3**), and **Hadoop Distributed File System** (**HDFS**), which is the primary distributed filesystem for Hadoop. In most cases, a fully distributed HBase cluster runs on an instance of HDFS, so we will explain how to set up Hadoop before proceeding.

Apache ZooKeeper is an open source software providing a highly reliable, distributed coordination service. A distributed HBase depends on a running ZooKeeper cluster.

HBase, which is a database that runs on Hadoop, keeps a lot of files open at the same time. We need to change some Linux kernel settings to run HBase smoothly.

A fully distributed HBase cluster has one or more master nodes (HMaster), which coordinate the entire cluster, and many slave nodes (RegionServer), which handle the actual data storage and request. The following diagram shows a typical HBase cluster structure:

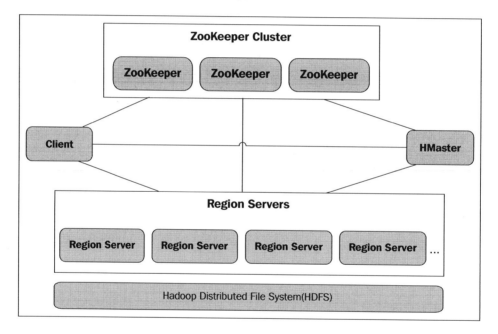

HBase can run multiple master nodes at the same time, and use ZooKeeper to monitor and failover the masters. But as HBase uses HDFS as its low-layer filesystem, if HDFS is down, HBase is down too. The master node of HDFS, which is called NameNode, is the **Single Point Of Failure** (**SPOF**) of HDFS, so it is the SPOF of an HBase cluster. However, NameNode as a software is very robust and stable. Moreover, the HDFS team is working hard on a real HA NameNode, which is expected to be included in Hadoop's next major release.

The first seven recipes in this chapter explain how we can get HBase and all its dependencies working together, as a fully distributed HBase cluster. The last recipe explains an advanced topic on how to avoid the SPOF issue of the cluster.

We will start by setting up a standalone HBase instance, and then demonstrate setting up a distributed HBase cluster on Amazon EC2.

Quick start

HBase has two run modes—standalone mode and distributed mode. Standalone mode is the default mode of HBase. In standalone mode, HBase uses a local filesystem instead of HDFS, and runs all HBase daemons and an HBase-managed ZooKeeper instance, all in the same JVM.

This recipe describes the setup of a standalone HBase. It leads you through installing HBase, starting it in standalone mode, creating a table via HBase Shell, inserting rows, and then cleaning up and shutting down the standalone HBase instance.

Getting ready

You are going to need a Linux machine to run the stack. Running HBase on top of Windows is not recommended. We will use Debian 6.0.1 (Debian Squeeze) in this book, because we have several Hadoop/HBase clusters running on top of Debian in production at my company, Rakuten Inc., and 6.0.1 is the latest **Amazon Machine Image** (**AMI**) we have, at http://wiki.debian.org/Cloud/AmazonEC2Image.

As HBase is written in Java, you will need to have Java installed first. HBase runs on Oracle's JDK only, so do not use OpenJDK for the setup. Although Java 7 is available, we don't recommend you to use Java 7 now because it needs more time to be tested. You can download the latest Java SE 6 from the following link: http://www.oracle.com/technetwork/java/javase/downloads/index.html.

Execute the downloaded bin file to install Java SE 6. We will use /usr/local/jdk1.6 as JAVA_HOME in this book:

```
root# ln -s /your/java/install/directory /usr/local/jdk1.6
```

We will add a user with the name hadoop, as the owner of all HBase/Hadoop daemons and files. We will have all HBase files and data stored under /usr/local/hbase:

```
root# useradd hadoop
root# mkdir /usr/local/hbase
root# chown hadoop:hadoop /usr/local/hbase
```

How to do it...

Get the latest stable HBase release from HBase's official site, `http://www.apache.org/dyn/closer.cgi/hbase/`. At the time of writing this book, the current stable release was 0.92.1.

You can set up a standalone HBase instance by following these instructions:

1. Download the tarball and decompress it to our root directory for HBase. We will set an `HBASE_HOME` environment variable to make the setup easier, by using the following commands:

   ```
   root# su - hadoop
   hadoop$ cd /usr/local/hbase
   hadoop$ tar xfvz hbase-0.92.1.tar.gz
   hadoop$ ln -s hbase-0.92.1 current
   hadoop$ export HBASE_HOME=/usr/local/hbase/current
   ```

2. Set `JAVA_HOME` in HBase's environment setting file, by using the following command:

   ```
   hadoop$ vi $HBASE_HOME/conf/hbase-env.sh
       # The java implementation to use. Java 1.6 required.
       export JAVA_HOME=/usr/local/jdk1.6
   ```

3. Create a directory for HBase to store its data and set the path in the HBase configuration file (`hbase-site.xml`), between the `<configuration>` tag, by using the following commands:

   ```
   hadoop$ mkdir -p /usr/local/hbase/var/hbase
   hadoop$ vi /usr/local/hbase/current/conf/hbase-site.xml

     <property>
       <name>hbase.rootdir</name>
       <value>file:///usr/local/hbase/var/hbase</value>
     </property>
   ```

4. Start HBase in standalone mode by using the following command:

   ```
   hadoop$ $HBASE_HOME/bin/start-hbase.sh
   starting master, logging to /usr/local/hbase/current/logs/hbase-
   hadoop-master-master1.out
   ```

5. Connect to the running HBase via HBase Shell, using the following command:

    ```
    hadoop$ $HBASE_HOME/bin/hbase shell
    ```

    ```
    HBase Shell; enter 'help<RETURN>' for list of supported commands.
    Type "exit<RETURN>" to leave the HBase Shell
    Version 0.92.1, r1298924, Fri Mar  9 16:58:34 UTC 2012
    ```

6. Verify HBase's installation by creating a table and then inserting some values. Create a table named `test`, with a single column family named `cf1`, as shown here:

    ```
    hbase(main):001:0> create 'test', 'cf1'
    ```

    ```
    0 row(s) in 0.7600 seconds
    ```

    i. In order to list the newly created table, use the following command:

        ```
        hbase(main):002:0> list
        TABLE
        test
        1 row(s) in 0.0440 seconds
        ```

    ii. In order to insert some values into the newly created table, use the following commands:

        ```
        hbase(main):003:0> put 'test', 'row1', 'cf1:a', 'value1'
        0 row(s) in 0.0840 seconds
        hbase(main):004:0> put 'test', 'row1', 'cf1:b', 'value2'
        0 row(s) in 0.0320 seconds
        ```

7. Verify the data we inserted into HBase by using the `scan` command:

    ```
    hbase(main):003:0> scan 'test'
    ROW                          COLUMN+CELL
    row1         column=cf1:a, timestamp=1320947312117, value=value1
    row1         column=cf1:b, timestamp=1320947363375, value=value2
    1 row(s) in 0.2530 seconds
    ```

8. Now clean up all that was done, by using the `disable` and `drop` commands:

    i. In order to disable the table test, use the following command:

        ```
        hbase(main):006:0> disable 'test'
        0 row(s) in 7.0770 seconds
        ```

    ii. In order to drop the the table test, use the following command:

        ```
        hbase(main):007:0> drop 'test'
        0 row(s) in 11.1290 seconds
        ```

9. Exit from HBase Shell using the following command:

   ```
   hbase(main):010:0> exit
   ```

10. Stop the HBase instance by executing the `stop` script:

    ```
    hadoop$ /usr/local/hbase/current/bin/stop-hbase.sh
    stopping hbase.......
    ```

How it works...

We installed HBase 0.92.1 on a single server. We have used a symbolic link named `current` for it, so that version upgrading in the future is easy to do.

In order to inform HBase where Java is installed, we will set `JAVA_HOME` in `hbase-env. sh`, which is the environment setting file of HBase. You will see some Java heap and HBase daemon settings in it too. We will discuss these settings in the last two chapters of this book.

In step 1, we created a directory on the local filesystem, for HBase to store its data. For a fully distributed installation, HBase needs to be configured to use HDFS, instead of a local filesystem. The HBase master daemon (HMaster) is started on the server where `start-hbase.sh` is executed. As we did not configure the region server here, HBase will start a single slave daemon (HRegionServer) on the same JVM too.

As we mentioned in the *Introduction* section, HBase depends on ZooKeeper as its coordination service. You may have noticed that we didn't start ZooKeeper in the previous steps. This is because HBase will start and manage its own ZooKeeper ensemble, by default.

Then we connected to HBase via HBase Shell. Using HBase Shell, you can manage your cluster, access data in HBase, and do many other jobs. Here, we just created a table called `test`, we inserted data into HBase, scanned the `test` table, and then disabled and dropped it, and exited the shell.

HBase can be stopped using its `stop-hbase.sh` script. This script stops both HMaster and HRegionServer daemons.

Getting ready on Amazon EC2

Amazon Elastic Compute Cloud (**EC2**) is a web service that provides resizable computer capacity in the cloud. By using Amazon EC2, we can practice HBase on a fully distributed mode easily, at low cost. All the servers that we will use to demonstrate HBase in this book are running on Amazon EC2.

This recipe describes the setup of the Amazon EC2 environment, as a preparation for the installation of HBase on it. We will set up a name server and client on Amazon EC2. You can also use other hosting services such as Rackspace, or real servers to set up your HBase cluster.

Getting ready

You will need to sign up, or create an **Amazon Web Service** (**AWS**) account at `http://aws.amazon.com/`.

We will use EC2 command-line tools to manage our instances. You can download and set up the tools by following the instructions available at the following page:

`http://docs.amazonwebservices.com/AWSEC2/latest/UserGuide/index.html?SettingUp_CommandLine.html`.

You need a public/private key to log in to your EC2 instances. You can generate your key pairs and upload your public key to EC2, using these instructions:

`http://docs.amazonwebservices.com/AWSEC2/latest/UserGuide/generating-a-keypair.html`.

Before you can log in to an instance, you must authorize access. The following link contains instructions for adding rules to the default security group:

`http://docs.amazonwebservices.com/AWSEC2/latest/UserGuide/adding-security-group-rules.html`.

After all these steps are done, review the following checklist to make sure everything is ready:

▶ **X.509 certificates**: Check if the X.509 certificates are uploaded. You can check this at your account's **Security Credentials** page.

▶ **EC2 key pairs**: Check if EC2 key pairs are uploaded. You can check this at **AWS Management Console | Amazon EC2 | NETWORK & SECURITY | Key Pairs**.

▶ **Access**: Check if the access has been authorized. This can be checked at **AWS Management Console | Amazon EC2 | NETWORK & SECURITY | Security Groups | Inbound**.

▶ **Environment variable settings**: Check if the environment variable settings are done. As an example, the following snippet shows my settings; make sure you are using the right `EC2_URL` for your region:

```
$ cat ~/.bashrc
export EC2_HOME=~/opt/ec2-api-tools-1.4.4.2
export PATH=$PATH:$EC2_HOME/bin
export EC2_PRIVATE_KEY=~/.ec2/pk-OWRHNWUG7UXIOPJXLOBC5UZTQBOBCVQY.pem
```

```
export EC2_CERT=~/.ec2/cert-OWRHNWUG7UXIOPJXLOBC5UZTQBOBCVQY.pem
export JAVA_HOME=/Library/Java/Home
export EC2_URL=https://ec2.us-west-1.amazonaws.com
```

We need to import our EC2 key pairs to manage EC2 instances via EC2 command-line tools:

```
$ ec2-import-keypair your-key-pair-name --public-key-file ~/.ssh/id_rsa.
pub
```

Verify the settings by typing the following command:

```
$ ec2-describe-instances
```

If everything has been set up properly, the command will show your instances similarly to how you had configured them in the previous command.

Downloading the example code

You can download the example code files for all Packt books you have purchased from your account at `http://www.packtpub.com`. If you purchased this book elsewhere, you can visit `http://www.packtpub.com/support` and register to have the files e-mailed directly to you.

The last preparation is to find a suitable AMI. An AMI is a preconfigured operating system and software, which is used to create a virtual machine within EC2. We can find a registered Debian AMI at `http://wiki.debian.org/Cloud/AmazonEC2Image`.

For the purpose of practicing HBase, a 32-bit, EBS-backed AMI is the most cost effective AMI to use. Make sure you are choosing AMIs for your region. As we are using US-West (us-west-1) for this book, the AMI ID for us is `ami-77287b32`. This is a 32-bit, small instance of EC2. A small instance is good for practicing HBase on EC2 because it's cheap. For production, we recommend you to use at least High-Memory Extra Large Instance with EBS, or a real server.

How to do it...

Follow these instructions to get your EC2 instances ready for HBase. We will start two EC2 instances; one is a DNS/NTP server, and the other one is the client:

1. Start a micro instance for the mentioned server. We will use `ns1.hbase-admin-cookbook.com` (`ns1`) as its **Fully Qualified Domain Name** (**FQDN**), in a later section of this book:

   ```
   $ ec2-run-instances ami-77287b32 -t t1.micro -k your-key-pair
   ```

2. Start a small instance for the client. We will use `client1.hbase-admin-cookbook.com` (`client1`) as its FQDN, later in this book:

```
$ ec2-run-instances ami-77287b32 -t m1.small -k your-key-pair
```

3. Verify the startup from **AWS Management Console**, or by typing the following command:

```
$ ec2-describe-instances
```

You should see two instances from the output of the command. From the output of the `ec2-describe-instances` command, or **AWS Management Console**, you can find the public DNS of the instances that have already started. The DNS shows a value such as `ec2-xx-xx-xxx-xx.us-west-1.compute.amazonaws.com`:

| ☑ | ns | 🖥 i-d3853894 | ami-77287b32 | ebs | t1.micro | ⬤ running |
| ☐ | slave1 | 🖥 i-b99f20fe | ami-77287b32 | ebs | m1.small | ⬤ stopped |

Root Device:			Root
Tenancy:	default		Lifec
Block Devices:	sda		
Public DNS:	ec2-50-18-172-92.us-west-1.compute.amazonaws.com		
Private DNS:	ip-10-160-49-250.us-west-1.compute.internal		

4. Log in to the instances via `SSH`, using the following command:

```
$ ssh root@ec2-xx-xx-xxx-xx.us-west-1.compute.amazonaws.com
```

5. Update the package index files before we install packages on the server, by using the following command:

```
root# apt-get update
```

6. Change your instances' time zone to your local timezone, using the following command:

```
root# dpkg-reconfigure tzdata
```

7. Install the NTP server daemon on the DNS server, using the following command:

```
root@ns# apt-get install ntp ntp-server ntpdate
```

8. Install the NTP client on the client/server, using the following command:

```
root@client1# apt-get install ntp ntpdate
```

9. Configure `/etc/ntp.conf` on ns1 to run as an NTP server, and `client1` to run as an NTP client, using ns1 as its server.

Because there is no HBase-specific configuration for the NTP setup, we will skip the details. You can find the sample `ntp.conf` files for both the server and client, from the sample source of this book.

10. Install BIND9 on `ns1` to run as a DNS server, using the following command:

```
root@ns# apt-get install bind9
```

You will need to configure BIND9 to run as a primary master server for internal lookup, and run as a caching server for external lookup. You also need to configure the DNS server, to allow other EC2 instances to update their record on the DNS server.

We will skip the details as this is out of the scope of this book. For sample BIND9 configuration, please refer to the source, shipped with this book.

11. For `client1`, just set it up using `ns1` as its DNS server:

```
root@client1# vi /etc/resolv.conf
```

```
nameserver 10.160.49.250 #private IP of ns
search hbase-admin-cookbook.com #domain name
```

12. Update the DNS hostname automatically. Set up hostname to the EC2 instance's user data of the client. From the **My Instances** page of **AWS Management Console**, select `client1` from the instances list, stop it, and then click **Instance Actions | View | Change User Data**; enter the `hostname` of the instance you want to use (here `client1`) in the pop-up page:

View/Change User Data   Cancel ☒

Instance ID: i-8f1384c8 (client1)

User Data:
client1

13. Create a script to update the client's record on the DNS server, using user data:

```
root@client1# vi ec2-hostname.sh
```

```
#!/bin/bash
#you will need to set up your DNS server to allow update from this
key
DNS_KEY=/root/etc/Kuser.hbase-admin-cookbook.com.+157+44141.
private
DOMAIN=hbase-admin-cookbook.com

USER_DATA=`/usr/bin/curl -s http://169.254.169.254/latest/user-
data`
HOSTNAME=`echo $USER_DATA`
#set also the hostname to the running instance
hostname $HOSTNAME

#we only need to update for local IP
```

```
LOCIP=`/usr/bin/curl -s http://169.254.169.254/latest/meta-data/
local-ipv4`
cat<<EOF | /usr/bin/nsupdate -k $DNS_KEY -v
server ns.$DOMAIN
zone $DOMAIN
update delete $HOSTNAME.$DOMAIN A
update add $HOSTNAME.$DOMAIN 60 A $LOCIP
send
EOF
```

14. Finally, to run this at boot time from `rc.local`, add the following script to the `rc.local` file:

root@client1# vi /etc/rc.local

```
sh /root/bin/ec2-hostname.sh
```

How it works...

First we started two instances, a micro instance for DNS/NTP server, and a small one for client. To provide a name service to other instances, the DNS name server has to be kept running. Using micro instance can reduce your EC2 cost.

In step 3, we set up the NTP server and client. We will run our own NTP server on the same DNS server, and NTP clients on all other servers.

 Note: Make sure that the clocks on the HBase cluster members are in basic alignment.

EC2 instances can be started and stopped on demand; we don't need to pay for stopped instances. But, restarting an EC2 instance will change the IP address of the instance, which makes it difficult to run HBase. We can resolve this issue by running a DNS server to provide a name service to all EC2 instances in our HBase cluster. We can update name records on the DNS server every time other EC2 instances are restarted.

That's exactly what we have done in steps 4 and 5. Step 4 is a normal DNS setup. In step 5, we stored the instance name in its user data property at first, so that when the instance is restarted, we can get it back using EC2 API. Also, we will get the private IP address of the instance via EC2 API. With this data, we can then send a DNS update command to our DNS server every time the instance is restarted. As a result, we can always use its fixed hostname to access the instance.

We will keep only the DNS instance running constantly. You can stop all other instances whenever you do not need to run your HBase cluster.

Setting up Hadoop

A fully distributed HBase runs on top of HDFS. As a fully distributed HBase cluster installation, its master daemon (HMaster) typically runs on the same server as the master node of HDFS (NameNode), while its slave daemon (HRegionServer) runs on the same server as the slave node of HDFS, which is called DataNode.

Hadoop MapReduce is not required by HBase. MapReduce daemons do not need to be started. We will cover the setup of MapReduce in this recipe too, in case you like to run MapReduce on HBase. For a small Hadoop cluster, we usually have a master daemon of MapReduce (JobTracker) run on the NameNode server, and slave daemons of MapReduce (TaskTracker) run on the DataNode servers.

This recipe describes the setup of Hadoop. We will have one master node (master1) run NameNode and JobTracker on it. We will set up three slave nodes (slave1 to slave3), which will run DataNode and TaskTracker on them, respectively.

Getting ready

You will need four small EC2 instances, which can be obtained by using the following command:

```
$ec2-run-instances ami-77287b32 -t m1.small -n 4 -k your-key-pair
```

All these instances must be set up properly, as described in the previous recipe, *Getting ready on Amazon EC2*. Besides the NTP and DNS setups, Java installation is required by all servers too.

We will use the hadoop user as the owner of all Hadoop daemons and files. All Hadoop files and data will be stored under /usr/local/hadoop. Add the hadoop user and create a /usr/local/hadoop directory on all the servers, in advance.

We will set up one Hadoop client node as well. We will use client1, which we set up in the previous recipe. Therefore, the Java installation, hadoop user, and directory should be prepared on client1 too.

How to do it...

Here are the steps to set up a fully distributed Hadoop cluster:

1. In order to SSH log in to all nodes of the cluster, generate the hadoop user's public key on the master node:

    ```
    hadoop@master1$ ssh-keygen -t rsa -N ""
    ```

    This command will create a public key for the hadoop user on the master node, at ~/.ssh/id_rsa.pub.

2. On all slave and client nodes, add the `hadoop` user's public key to allow SSH login from the master node:

```
hadoop@slave1$ mkdir ~/.ssh
hadoop@slave1$ chmod 700 ~/.ssh
hadoop@slave1$ cat >> ~/.ssh/authorized_keys
```

3. Copy the `hadoop` user's public key you generated in the previous step, and paste to `~/.ssh/authorized_keys`. Then, change its permission as following:

```
hadoop@slave1$ chmod 600 ~/.ssh/authorized_keys
```

4. Get the latest, stable, HBase-supported Hadoop release from Hadoop's official site, `http://www.apache.org/dyn/closer.cgi/hadoop/common/`. While this chapter was being written, the latest HBase-supported, stable Hadoop release was 1.0.2. Download the tarball and decompress it to our `root` directory for Hadoop, then add a symbolic link, and an environment variable:

```
hadoop@master1$ ln -s hadoop-1.0.2 current
hadoop@master1$ export HADOOP_HOME=/usr/local/hadoop/current
```

5. Create the following directories on the master node:

```
hadoop@master1$ mkdir -p /usr/local/hadoop/var/dfs/name
hadoop@master1$ mkdir -p /usr/local/hadoop/var/dfs/data
hadoop@master1$ mkdir -p /usr/local/hadoop/var/dfs/namesecondary
```

6. You can skip the following steps if you don't use MapReduce:

```
hadoop@master1$ mkdir -p /usr/local/hadoop/var/mapred
```

7. Set up JAVA_HOME in Hadoop's environment setting file (`hadoop-env.sh`):

```
hadoop@master1$ vi $HADOOP_HOME/conf/hadoop-env.sh
export JAVA_HOME=/usr/local/jdk1.6
```

8. Add the `hadoop.tmp.dir` property to `core-site.xml`:

```
hadoop@master1$ vi $HADOOP_HOME/conf/core-site.xml
  <property>
    <name>hadoop.tmp.dir</name>
    <value>/usr/local/hadoop/var</value>
  </property>
```

9. Add the `fs.default.name` property to `core-site.xml`:

```
hadoop@master1$ vi $HADOOP_HOME/conf/core-site.xml
  <property>
    <name>fs.default.name</name>
    <value>hdfs://master1:8020</value>
  </property>
```

10. If you need MapReduce, add the `mapred.job.tracker` property to `mapred-site.xml`:

hadoop@master1$ vi $HADOOP_HOME/conf/mapred-site.xml

```
  <property>
    <name>mapred.job.tracker</name>
    <value>master1:8021</value>
  </property>
```

11. Add a slave server list to the `slaves` file:

hadoop@master1$ vi $HADOOP_HOME/conf/slaves

```
slave1
slave2
slave3
```

12. Sync all Hadoop files from the master node, to client and slave nodes. Don't sync `${hadoop.tmp.dir}` after the initial installation:

hadoop@master1$ rsync -avz /usr/local/hadoop/ client1:/usr/local/hadoop/

hadoop@master1$ for i in 1 2 3

do   rsync -avz /usr/local/hadoop/ slave$i:/usr/local/hadoop/

sleep 1

done

13. You need to format NameNode before starting Hadoop. Do it only for the initial installation:

hadoop@master1$ $HADOOP_HOME/bin/hadoop namenode -format

14. Start HDFS from the `master` node:

hadoop@master1$ $HADOOP_HOME/bin/start-dfs.sh

15. You can access your HDFS by typing the following command:

hadoop@master1$ $HADOOP_HOME/bin/hadoop fs -ls /

You can also view your HDFS admin page from the browser. Make sure the `50070` port is opened. The HDFS admin page can be viewed at `http://master1:50070/dfshealth.jsp`:

16. Start MapReduce from the master node, if needed:

```
hadoop@master1$ $HADOOP_HOME/bin/start-mapred.sh
```

Now you can access your MapReduce admin page from the browser. Make sure the `50030` port is opened. The MapReduce admin page can be viewed at `http://master1:50030/jobtracker.jsp`:

17. To stop HDFS, execute the following command from the master node:

```
hadoop@master1$ $HADOOP_HOME/bin/stop-dfs.sh
```

18. To stop MapReduce, execute the following command from the master node:

```
hadoop@master1$ $HADOOP_HOME/bin/stop-mapred.sh
```

How it works...

To start/stop the daemon on remote slaves from the master node, a passwordless SSH login of the `hadoop` user is required. We did this in step 1.

HBase must run on a special HDFS that supports a durable `sync` implementation. If HBase runs on an HDFS that has no durable `sync` implementation, it may lose data if its slave servers go down. Hadoop versions later than 0.20.205, including Hadoop 1.0.2 which we have chosen, support this feature.

HDFS and MapReduce use local filesystems to store their data. We created directories required by Hadoop in step 3, and set up the path to the Hadoop's configuration file in step 5.

In steps 9 to 11, we set up Hadoop so it could find HDFS, JobTracker, and slave servers. Before starting Hadoop, all Hadoop directories and settings need to be synced with the slave servers. The first time you start Hadoop (HDFS), you need to format NameNode. Note that you should only do this at the initial installation.

At this point, you can start/stop Hadoop using its start/stop script. Here we started/stopped HDFS and MapReduce separately, in case you don't require MapReduce. You can also use `$HADOOP_HOME/bin/start-all.sh` and `stop-all.sh` to start/stop HDFS and MapReduce using one command.

Setting up ZooKeeper

A distributed HBase depends on a running ZooKeeper cluster. All HBase cluster nodes and clients need to be able to access the ZooKeeper ensemble.

This recipe describes how to set up a ZooKeeper cluster. We will only set up a standalone ZooKeeper node for our HBase cluster, but in production it is recommended that you run a ZooKeeper ensemble of at least three nodes. Also, make sure to run an odd number of nodes.

We will cover the setting up of a clustered ZooKeeper in the *There's more...* section of this recipe.

Getting ready

First, make sure Java is installed in your ZooKeeper server.

We will use the `hadoop` user as the owner of all ZooKeeper daemons and files. All the ZooKeeper files and data will be stored under `/usr/local/ZooKeeper`; you need to create this directory in advance. Our ZooKeeper will be set up on `master1` too.

We will set up one ZooKeeper client on `client1`. So, the Java installation, `hadoop` user, and directory should be prepared on `client1` as well.

How to do it...

To set up a standalone ZooKeeper installation, follow these instructions:

1. Get the latest stable ZooKeeper release from ZooKeeper's official site, `http://ZooKeeper.apache.org/releases.html#download`.

2. Download the tarball and decompress it to our root directory for ZooKeeper. We will set a `ZK_HOME` environment variable to make the setup easier. As of this writing, ZooKeeper 3.4.3 is the latest stable version:

   ```
   hadoop@master1$ ln -s ZooKeeper-3.4.3 current
   ```

   ```
   hadoop@master1$ export ZK_HOME=/usr/local/ZooKeeper/current
   ```

3. Create directories for ZooKeeper to store its snapshot and transaction log:

   ```
   hadoop@master1$ mkdir -p /usr/local/ZooKeeper/data
   ```

   ```
   hadoop@master1$ mkdir -p /usr/local/ZooKeeper/datalog
   ```

4. Create the `$ZK_HOME/conf/java.env` file and put the Java settings there:

   ```
   hadoop@master1$ vi $ZK_HOME/conf/java.env
   ```

   ```
   JAVA_HOME=/usr/local/jdk1.6
   export PATH=$JAVA_HOME/bin:$PATH
   ```

5. Copy the sample ZooKeeper setting file, and make the following changes to set where ZooKeeper should store its data:

   ```
   hadoop@master1$ cp $ZK_HOME/conf/zoo_sample.cfg $ZK_HOME/conf/zoo.cfg
   ```

   ```
   hadoop@master1$ vi $ZK_HOME/conf/zoo.cfg
   ```

   ```
   dataDir=/usr/local/ZooKeeper/var/data
   dataLogDir=/usr/local/ZooKeeper/var/datalog
   ```

6. Sync all files under `/usr/local/ZooKeeper` from the master node to the client. Don't sync `${dataDir}` and `${dataLogDir}` after this initial installation.

7. Start ZooKeeper from the master node by executing this command:

```
hadoop@master1$ $ZK_HOME/bin/zkServer.sh start
```

8. Connect to the running ZooKeeper, and execute some commands to verify the installation:

```
hadoop@client1$ $ZK_HOME/bin/zkCli.sh -server master1:2181
```

```
[zk: master1:2181(CONNECTED) 0] ls /
[ZooKeeper]
[zk: master1:2181(CONNECTED) 1] quit
```

9. Stop ZooKeeper from the master node by executing the following command:

```
hadoop@master1$ $ZK_HOME/bin/zkServer.sh stop
```

How it works...

In this recipe, we set up a basic standalone ZooKeeper instance. As you can see, the setting is very simple; all you need to do is to tell ZooKeeper where to find Java and where to save its data.

In step 4, we created a file named `java.env` and placed the Java settings in this file. You must use this filename as ZooKeeper, which by default, gets its Java settings from this file.

ZooKeeper's settings file is called `zoo.cfg`. You can copy the settings from the sample file shipped with ZooKeeper. The default setting is fine for basic installation. As ZooKeeper always acts as a central role in a cluster system, it should be set up properly to gain the best performance.

To connect to a running ZooKeeper ensemble, use its command-line tool, and specify the ZooKeeper server and port you want to connect to. The default client port is `2181`. You don't need to specify it, if you are using the default port setting.

All ZooKeeper data is called a **Znode**. Znodes are constructed like a filesystem hierarchy. ZooKeeper provides commands to access or update Znode from its command-line tool; type `help` for more information.

There's more...

As HBase relays ZooKeeper as its coordination service, the ZooKeeper service must be extremely reliable. In production, you must run a ZooKeeper cluster of at least three nodes. Also, make sure to run an odd number of nodes.

The procedure to set up a clustered ZooKeeper is basically the same as shown in this recipe. You can follow the previous steps to set up each cluster node at first. Add the following settings to each node's `zoo.cfg`, so that every node knows about every other node in the ensemble:

```
hadoop@node{1,2,3}$ vi $ZK_HOME/conf/zoo.cfg
    server.1=node1:2888:3888
    server.2=node2:2888:3888
    server.3=node3:2888:3888
```

Also, you need to put a `myid` file under `${dataDir}`. The `myid` file consists of a single line containing only the node ID. So `myid` of `node1` would contain the text `1` and nothing else.

 Note that clocks on all ZooKeeper nodes must be synchronized. You can use **Network Time Protocol** (**NTP**) to have the clocks synchronized.

Start ZooKeeper from each node of your cluster respectively. Then, you can connect to the cluster from your client, by using the following command:

```
$ zkCli.sh -server node1,node2,node3
```

ZooKeeper will function as long as more than half of the nodes in the ZooKeeper cluster are alive. This means, in a three node cluster, only one server can die.

Changing the kernel settings

HBase is a database running on Hadoop, and just like other databases, it keeps a lot of files open at the same time. Linux limits the number of file descriptors that any one process may open; the default limits are 1024 per process. To run HBase smoothly, you need to increase the maximum number of open file descriptors for the user, who started HBase. In our case, the user is called `hadoop`.

You should also increase Hadoop's `nproc` setting. The `nproc` setting specifies the maximum number of processes that can exist simultaneously for the user. If `nproc` is too low, an `OutOfMemoryError` error may happen.

We will describe how to show and change the kernel settings, in this recipe.

Getting ready

Make sure you have `root` privileges on all of your servers.

How to do it...

You will need to make the following kernel setting changes to all servers of the cluster:

1. To confirm the current open file limits, log in as the `hadoop` user and execute the following command:

```
hadoop$ ulimit -n
1024
```

2. To show the setting for maximum processes, use the `-u` option of the `ulimit` command:

```
hadoop$ ulimit -u
unlimited
```

3. Log in as the `root` user to increase open file and `nproc` limits. Add the following settings to the `limits.conf` file:

```
root# vi /etc/security/limits.conf
hadoop soft nofile 65535
hadoop hard nofile 65535
hadoop soft nproc 32000
hadoop hard nproc 32000
```

4. To apply the changes, add the following line into the `/etc/pam.d/common-session` file:

```
root# echo "session required  pam_limits.so" >>  /etc/pam.d/
common-session
```

5. Log out and back in again, as the `hadoop` user, and confirm the setting values again; you should see the above changes have been applied:

```
hadoop$ ulimit -n
65535
hadoop$ ulimit -u
32000
```

How it works...

The previous setting changes the `hadoop` user's open file limit to `65535`. It also changes the `hadoop` user's max processes number to `32000`. With this change of the kernel setting, HBase can keep enough files open at the same time and also run smoothly.

See also

▸   *Chapter 8, Basic Performance Tuning*

Setting up HBase

A fully distributed HBase instance has one or more master nodes (HMaster), and many slave nodes (RegionServer) running on HDFS. It uses a reliable ZooKeeper ensemble to coordinate all the components of the cluster, including masters, slaves, and clients.

It's not necessary to run HMaster on the same server of HDFS NameNode, but, for a small cluster, it's typical to have them run on the same server, just for ease of management. RegionServers are usually configured to run on servers of HDFS DataNode. Running RegionServer on the DataNode server has the advantage of **data locality** too. Eventually, DataNode running on the same server, will have a copy on it of all the data that RegionServer requires.

This recipe describes the setup of a fully distributed HBase. We will set up one HMaster on `master1`, and three region servers (`slave1` to `slave3`). We will also set up an HBase client on `client1`.

Getting ready

First, make sure Java is installed on all servers of the cluster.

We will use the `hadoop` user as the owner of all HBase daemons and files, too. All HBase files and data will be stored under `/usr/local/hbase`. Create this directory on all servers of your HBase cluster, in advance.

We will set up one HBase client on `client1`. Therefore, the Java installation, `hadoop` user, and directory should be prepared on `client1` too.

Make sure HDFS is running. You can ensure it started properly by accessing HDFS, using the following command:

```
hadoop@client1$ $HADOOP_HOME/bin/hadoop fs -ls /
```

MapReduce does not need to be started, as HBase does not normally use it.

We assume that you are managing your own ZooKeeper, in which case, you can start it and confirm if it is running properly. You can ensure it is running properly by sending the `ruok` command to its client port:

```
hadoop@client1$ echo ruok | nc master1 2181
```

How to do it...

To set up our fully distributed HBase cluster, we will download and configure HBase on the master node first, and then sync to all slave nodes and clients.

Get the latest stable HBase release from HBase's official site, `http://www.apache.org/dyn/closer.cgi/hbase/`.

At the time of writing this book, the current stable release was 0.92.1.

1. Download the tarball and decompress it to our `root` directory for HBase. Also, set an `HBASE_HOME` environment variable to make the setup easier:

   ```
   hadoop@master1$ ln -s hbase-0.92.1 current
   hadoop@master1$ export HBASE_HOME=/usr/local/hbase/current
   ```

2. We will use `/usr/local/hbase/var` as a temporary directory of HBase on the local filesystem. Remove it first if you have created it for your standalone HBase installation:

   ```
   hadoop@master1$ mkdir -p /usr/local/hbase/var
   ```

3. To tell HBase where the Java installation is, set `JAVA_HOME` in the HBase environment setting file (`hbase-env.sh`):

   ```
   hadoop@master1$ vi $HBASE_HOME/conf/hbase-env.sh
   # The java implementation to use.  Java 1.6 required.
   export JAVA_HOME=/usr/local/jdk1.6
   ```

4. Set up HBase to use the independent ZooKeeper ensemble:

   ```
   hadoop@master1$ vi $HBASE_HOME/conf/hbase-env.sh
   # Tell HBase whether it should manage it's own instance of
   ZooKeeper or not.
   export HBASE_MANAGES_ZK=false
   ```

5. Add these settings to HBase's configuration file (`hbase-site.xml`):

   ```
   hadoop@master1$ vi $HBASE_HOME/conf/hbase-site.xml
   <configuration>
     <property>
       <name>hbase.rootdir</name>
       <value>hdfs://master1:8020/hbase</value>
     </property>
     <property>
       <name>hbase.cluster.distributed</name>
       <value>true</value>
     </property>
     <property>
   ```

```
    <name>hbase.tmp.dir</name>
    <value>/usr/local/hbase/var</value>
  </property>
  <property>
    <name>hbase.ZooKeeper.quorum</name>
    <value>master1</value>
  </property>
</configuration>
```

6. Configure the slave nodes of the cluster:

   ```
   hadoop@master1$ vi $HBASE_HOME/conf/regionservers
   ```

   ```
   slave1
   slave2
   slave3
   ```

7. Link the HDFS configuration file (`hdfs-site.xml`) to HBase's configuration folder (`conf`), so that HBase can see the HDFS's client configuration on your Hadoop cluster:

   ```
   hadoop@master1$ ln -s $HADOOP_HOME/conf/hdfs-site.xml $HBASE_HOME/
   conf/hdfs-site.xml
   ```

8. Copy the `hadoop-core` and `Zookeeper` JAR file, and their dependencies, from your Hadoop and ZooKeeper installation:

   ```
   hadoop@master1$ rm -i $HBASE_HOME/lib/hadoop-core-*.jar
   ```

   ```
   hadoop@master1$ rm -i $HBASE_HOME/lib/ZooKeeper-*.jar
   ```

   ```
   hadoop@master1$ cp -i $HADOOP_HOME/hadoop-core-*.jar $HBASE_HOME/
   lib/
   ```

   ```
   hadoop@master1$ cp -i $HADOOP_HOME/lib/commons-configuration-
   1.6.jar $HBASE_HOME/lib/
   ```

   ```
   hadoop@master1$ cp -i $ZK_HOME/ZooKeeper-*.jar $HBASE_HOME/lib/
   ```

9. Sync all the HBase files under `/usr/local/hbase` from `master`, to the same directory as client and slave nodes.

10. Start the HBase cluster from the master node:

    ```
    hadoop@master1 $HBASE_HOME/bin/start-hbase.sh
    ```

11. Connect to your HBase cluster from the client node:

    ```
    hadoop@client1$ $HBASE_HOME/bin/hbase shell
    ```

You can also access the HBase web UI from your browser. Make sure your master server's `60010` port is opened. The URL is `http://master1:60010/master.jsp`:

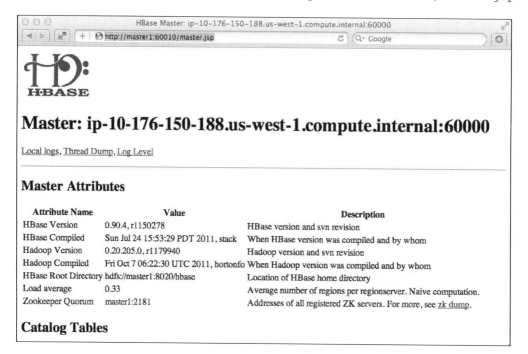

12. Stop the HBase cluster from the master node:

    ```
    hadoop@master1$ $HBASE_HOME/bin/stop-hbase.sh
    ```

How it works...

Our HBase cluster is configured to use `/hbase` as its root directory on HDFS, by specifying the `hbase.rootdir` property. Because it is the first time HBase was started, it will create the directory automatically. You can see the files HBase created on HDFS from the client:

```
hadoop@client1$ $HADOOP_HOME/bin/hadoop fs -ls /hbase
```

We want our HBase to run on distributed mode, so we set `hbase.cluster.distributed` to `true` in `hbase-site.xml`.

We also set up the cluster to use an independent ZooKeeper ensemble by specifying `HBASE_MANAGES_ZK=false` in `hbase-env.sh`. The ZooKeeper ensemble is specified by the `hbase.ZooKeeper.quorum` property. You can use clustered ZooKeeper by listing all the servers of the ensemble, such as `zoo1,zoo2,zoo3`.

All region servers are configured in the $HBASE_HOME/conf/regionservers file. You should use one line per region server. When starting the cluster, HBase will SSH into each region server configured here, and start the HRegionServer daemon on that server.

By linking hdfs-site.xml under the $HBASE_HOME/conf directory, HBase will use all the client configurations you made for your HDFS in hdfs-site.xml, such as the dfs.replication setting.

HBase ships with its prebuilt hadoop-core and ZooKeeper JAR files. They may be out of date, compared to what you used in your Hadoop and ZooKeeper installation. Make sure HBase uses the same version of .jar files with Hadoop and ZooKeeper, to avoid any unexpected problems.

Basic Hadoop/ZooKeeper/HBase configurations

There are some basic settings we should tune, before moving forward. These are very basic and important Hadoop (HDFS), ZooKeeper, and HBase settings that you should consider to change immediately after setting up your cluster.

Some of these settings take effect due to data durability or cluster availability, which must be configured, while some are recommended configurations for running HBase smoothly.

Configuration settings depend on your hardware, data, and cluster size. We will describe a guideline in this recipe. You may need to change the settings to fit your environment.

Every time you make changes, you need to sync to all clients and slave nodes, then restart the respective daemon to apply the changes.

How to do it...

The configurations that should be considered for change are as follows:

1. Turn on dfs.support.append for HDFS. The dfs.support.append property determines whether HDFS should support the append (sync) feature or not. The default value is false. It must be set to true, or you may lose data if the region server crashes:

   ```
   hadoop$ vi $HADOOP_HOME/conf/hdfs-site.xml

     <property>
       <name>dfs.support.append</name>
       <value>true</value>
     </property>
   ```

2. Increase the `dfs.datanode.max.xcievers` value to have DataNode keep more threads open, to handle more concurrent requests:

   hadoop$ vi $HADOOP_HOME/conf/hdfs-site.xml

   ```
   <property>
     <name>dfs.datanode.max.xcievers</name>
     <value>4096</value>
   </property>
   ```

3. Increase ZooKeeper's heap memory size so that it does not swap:

   hadoop$ vi $ZK_HOME/conf/java.env

   ```
   export JAVA_OPTS="-Xms1000m -Xmx1000m"
   ```

4. Increase ZooKeeper's maximum client connection number to handle more concurrent requests:

   hadoop$ echo "maxClientCnxns=60" >> $ZK_HOME/conf/zoo.cfg

5. Increase HBase's heap memory size to run HBase smoothly:

   hadoop$ vi $HBASE_HOME/conf/hbase-env.sh

   ```
   export HBASE_HEAPSIZE=8000
   ```

6. Decrease the `zookeeper.session.timeout` value so that HBase can find the crashed region server fast, and recover it in a short time:

   hadoop$ vi $HBASE_HOME/conf/hbase-site.xml

   ```
   <property>
     <name>zookeeper.session.timeout</name>
     <value>60000</value>
   </property>
   ```

7. To change Hadoop/ZooKeeper/HBase log settings, edit the `log4j.properties` file and the `hadoop-env.sh/hbase-env.sh` file under the `conf` directory of the Hadoop/ZooKeeper/HBase installation. It's better to change the log directory out of the installation folder. For example, the following specifies HBase to generate its logs under the `/usr/local/hbase/logs` directory:

   hadoop$ vi $HBASE_HOME/conf/hbase-env.sh

   ```
   export HBASE_LOG_DIR=/usr/local/hbase/logs
   ```

How it works...

In step 1, by turning on `dfs.support.append`, the HDFS flush is enabled. With this feature enabled, a writer of HDFS can guarantee that data will be persisted by invoking a `flush` call. So, HBase can guarantee that when a region server dies, data can be recovered and replayed on other region servers using its **Write-Ahead Log** (**WAL**).

To verify if the HDFS append is supported or not, see your HMaster log of the HBase startup. If the append is not turned to `on`, you will find a log like the following:

```
$ grep -i "HDFS-200" hbase-hadoop-master-master1.log
...syncFs -- HDFS-200 -- not available, dfs.support.append=false
```

For step 2, we configured the `dfs.datanode.max.xcievers` setting, which specifies the upper bound on the number of files HDFS DataNode will serve at any one time.

 Note that the name is `xcievers`—it's a misspelled name. Its default value is `256`, which is too low for running HBase on HDFS.

Steps 3 and 4 are about ZooKeeper settings. ZooKeeper is very sensitive to swapping, which will seriously degrade its performance. ZooKeeper's heap size is set in the `java.env` file. ZooKeeper has an upper bound on the number of connections it will serve at any one time. Its default is `10`, which is too low for HBase, especially when running MapReduce on it. We would suggest setting it to `60`.

In step 5, we configured HBase's heap memory size. HBase ships with a heap size of 1 GB, which is too low for modern machines. A reasonable value for large machines is 8 GB or larger, but under 16 GB.

In step 6, we changed the ZooKeeper's session timeout to a lower value. Lower timeout means HBase can find crashed region servers faster, and thus, recover the crashed regions on other servers in a short time. On the other hand, with a very short session timeout, there is a risk that the HRegionServer daemon may kill itself when the cluster is in heavy load, because it may not be able to send a heartbeat to the ZooKeeper before getting a timeout.

See also

- Chapter 8, *Basic Performance Tuning*
- Chapter 9, *Advanced Configurations and Performance Tuning*

Setting up multiple High Availability (HA) masters

Hadoop and HBase are designed to handle the failover of their slave nodes automatically. Because there may be many nodes in a large cluster, a hardware failure of a server or shut down of a slave node are considered as normal in the cluster.

For the master nodes, HBase itself has no SPOF. HBase uses ZooKeeper as its central coordination service. A ZooKeeper ensemble is typically clustered with three or more servers; as long as more than half of the servers in the cluster are online, ZooKeeper can provide its service normally.

HBase saves its active master node, root region server location, and other important running data in ZooKeeper. Therefore, we can just start two or more `HMaster` daemons on separate servers and the one started first will be the active master server of the HBase cluster.

But, NameNode of HDFS is the SPOF of the cluster. NameNode keeps the entire HDFS's filesystem image in its local memory. HDFS cannot function anymore if NameNode is down, as HBase is down too. As you may notice, there is a Secondary NameNode of HDFS. Note that Secondary NameNode is not a standby of NameNode, it just provides a checkpoint function to NameNode. So, the challenge of a highly available cluster is to make NameNode highly available.

In this recipe, we will describe the setup of two highly available master nodes, which will use **Heartbeat** to monitor each other. Heartbeat is a widely used HA solution to provide communication and membership for a Linux cluster. Heartbeat needs to be combined with a **Cluster Resource Manager** (**CRM**) to start/stop services for that cluster. Pacemaker is the preferred cluster resource manager for Heartbeat. We will set up a **Virtual IP** (**VIP**) address using Heartbeat and Pacemaker, and then associate it with the active master node. Because EC2 does not support static IP addresses, we cannot demonstrate it on EC2, but we will discuss an alternative way of using **Elastic IP** (**EIP**) to achieve our purpose.

We will focus on setting up NameNode and HBase; you can simply use a similar method to set up two JobTracker nodes as well.

Getting ready

You should already have HDFS and HBase installed. We will set up a standby master node (`master2`), as you need another server ready to use. Make sure all the dependencies have been configured properly. Sync your Hadoop and HBase root directory from the active master (`master1`) to the standby master.

We will need NFS in this recipe as well. Set up your NFS server, and mount the same NFS directory from both `master1` and `master2`. Make sure the `hadoop` user has write permission to the NFS directory. Create a directory on NFS to store Hadoop's metadata. We assume the directory is `/mnt/nfs/hadoop/dfs/name`.

We will set up VIP for the two masters, and assume you have the following IP addresses and DNS mapping:

- ▶ `master1`: This has its IP address as 10.174.14.11.
- ▶ `master2`: This has its IP address as 10.174.14.12.
- ▶ `master`: This has its IP address as 10.174.14.10. It is the VIP that will be set up later.

How to do it...

The following instructions describe how to set up two highly available master nodes.

Install and configure Heartbeat and Pacemaker

First, we will install Heartbeat and Pacemaker, and make some basic configurations:

1. Install Heartbeat and Pacemaker on `master1` and `master2`:

   ```
   root# apt-get install heartbeat cluster-glue cluster-agents
   pacemaker
   ```

2. To configure Heartbeat, make the following changes to both `master1` and `master2`:

   ```
   root# vi /etc/ha.d/ha.cf
   ```

   ```
   # enable pacemaker, without stonith
   crm yes
   # log where ?
   logfacility local0
   # warning of soon be dead
   warntime 10
   # declare a host (the other node) dead after:
   deadtime 20
   # dead time on boot (could take some time until net is up)
   initdead 120
   # time between heartbeats
   keepalive 2
   # the nodes
   node master1
   node master2
   # heartbeats, over dedicated replication interface!
   ucast eth0 master1 # ignored by master1 (owner of ip)
   ucast eth0 master2 # ignored by master2 (owner of ip)
   # ping the name server to assure we are online
   ping ns
   ```

3. Create an `authkeys` file. Execute the following script as a `root` user on `master1` and `master2`:

   ```
   root# ( echo -ne "auth 1\n1 sha1 "; \
     dd if=/dev/urandom bs=512 count=1 | openssl md5 ) \
     > /etc/ha.d/authkeys
   ```

   ```
   root# chmod 0600 /etc/ha.d/authkeys
   ```

Create and install a NameNode resource agent

Pacemaker depends on a resource agent to manager the cluster. A resource agent is an executable that manages a cluster resource. In our case, the VIP address and the HDFS NameNode service is the cluster resource we want to manage, using Pacemaker. Pacemaker ships with an `IPaddr` resource agent to manage VIP, so we only need to create our own `namenode` resource agent:

1. Add environment variables to the `.bashrc` file of the `root` user on `master1` and `master2`. Don't forget to apply the changes:

   root# vi /root/.bashrc

   ```
   export JAVA_HOME=/usr/local/jdk1.6
   export HADOOP_HOME=/usr/local/hadoop/current
   export OCF_ROOT=/usr/lib/ocf
   ```

   Invoke the following command to apply the previous changes:

   root# source /root/.bashrc

2. Create a standard **Open Clustering Framework** (**OCF**) resource agent file called `namenode`, with the following content.

   The `namenode` resource agent starts with including standard OCF functions such as the following:

   root# vi namenode

   ```
   #!/bin/sh
   : ${OCF_FUNCTIONS_DIR=${OCF_ROOT}/resource.d/heartbeat}
   . ${OCF_FUNCTIONS_DIR}/.ocf-shellfuncs
   usage() {
      echo "Usage: $0 {start|stop|status|monitor|meta-data|validate-
   all}"
   }
   ```

3. Add a `meta_data()` function as shown in the following code. The `meta_data()` function dumps the resource agent metadata to standard output. Every resource agent must have a set of XML metadata describing its own purpose and supported parameters:

   root# vi namenode

   ```
   meta_data() {cat <<END
   <?xml version="1.0"?>
   <!DOCTYPE resource-agent SYSTEM "ra-api-1.dtd">
   <resource-agent name="namenode">
   <version>0.1</version>
   <longdesc lang="en">
   This is a resource agent for NameNode. It manages HDFS namenode
   daemon.
   ```

```
</longdesc>
<shortdesc lang="en">Manage namenode daemon.</shortdesc>
<parameters></parameters>
<actions>
<action name="start" timeout="120" />
<action name="stop" timeout="120" />
<action name="status" depth="0" timeout="120" interval="120" />
<action name="monitor" depth="0" timeout="120" interval="120" />
<action name="meta-data" timeout="10" />
<action name="validate-all" timeout="5" />
</actions>
</resource-agent>
END
}
```

4. Add a `namenode_start()` function. This function is used by Pacemaker to actually start the NameNode daemon on the server. In the `namenode_start()` function, we firstly check whether NameNode is already started on the server; if it is not started, we invoke `hadoop-daemon.sh` from the `hadoop` user to start it:

root# vi namenode

```
namenode_start() {
  # if namenode is already started on this server, bail out early
    namenode_status
  if [ $? -eq 0 ]; then
    ocf_log info "namenode is already running on this server,
skip"
    return $OCF_SUCCESS
  fi

    # start namenode on this server
    ocf_log info "Starting namenode daemon..."
    su - hadoop -c "${HADOOP_HOME}/bin/hadoop-daemon.sh start name
      node"
    if [ $? -ne 0 ]; then
      ocf_log err "Can not start namenode daemon."
      return $OCF_ERR_GENERIC;
    fi
    sleep 1
    return $OCF_SUCCESS
}
```

5. Add a `namenode_stop()` function. This function is used by Pacemaker to actually stop the NameNode daemon on the server. In the `namenode_stop()` function, we first check whether NameNode is already stopped on the server; if it is running, we invoke `hadoop-daemon.sh` from the `hadoop` user to stop it:

root# vi namenode

```
namenode_stop () {
  # if namenode is not started on this server, bail out early
    namenode_status
  if [ $? -ne 0 ]; then
    ocf_log info "namenode is not running on this server, skip"
      return $OCF_SUCCESS
  fi

  # stop namenode on this server
  ocf_log info "Stopping namenode daemon..."
  su - hadoop -c "${HADOOP_HOME}/bin/hadoop-daemon.sh stop name
    node"
    if [ $? -ne 0 ]; then
      ocf_log err "Can not stop namenode daemon."
      return $OCF_ERR_GENERIC;
    fi
    sleep 1
    return $OCF_SUCCESS
}
```

6. Add a `namenode_status()` function. This function is used by Pacemaker to monitor the status of the NameNode daemon on the server. In the `namenode_status()` function, we use the `jps` command to show all running Java processes owned by the `hadoop` user, and the `grep` name of the NameNode daemon to see whether it has started:

root# vi namenode

```
namenode_status () {
  ocf_log info "monitor namenode"
  su - hadoop -c "${JAVA_HOME}/bin/jps" | egrep -q "NameNode"
    rc=$?
  # grep will return true if namenode is running on this machine
  if [ $rc -eq 0 ]; then
    ocf_log info "Namenode is running"
    return $OCF_SUCCESS  else
    ocf_log info "Namenode is not running"      return $OCF_NOT_
RUNNING

  fi
}
```

7. Add a `namenode_validateAll()` function to make sure the environment variables are set properly before we run other functions:

root# vi namenode

```
namenode_validateAll () {
   if [ -z "$JAVA_HOME" ]; then
     ocf_log err "JAVA_HOME not set."
     exit $OCF_ERR_INSTALLED
   fi
   if [ -z "$HADOOP_HOME" ]; then
     ocf_log err "HADOOP_HOME not set."
     exit $OCF_ERR_INSTALLED
   fi
   # Any subject is OK
     return $OCF_SUCCESS
}
```

8. Add the following main routine. Here, we will simply call the previous functions to implement the required standard OCF resource agent actions:

root# vi namenode

```
# See how we were called.
if [ $# -ne 1 ]; then
  usage
  exit $OCF_ERR_GENERIC
fi

namenode_validateAll

case $1 in
    meta-data) meta_data
    exit $OCF_SUCCESS;;
   usage) usage
    exit $OCF_SUCCESS;;
   *);;
   esac

case $1 in
    status|monitor) namenode_status;;
    start) namenode_start;;
    stop) namenode_stop;;
    validate-all);;
    *)usage
    exit $OCF_ERR_UNIMPLEMENTED;;
   esac
exit $?
```

9. Change the `namenode` file permission and test it on `master1` and `master2`:

```
root# chmod 0755 namenode

root# ocf-tester -v -n namenode-test /full/path/of/namenode
```

10. Make sure all the tests are passed before proceeding to the next step, or the HA cluster will behave unexpectedly.

11. Install the `namenode` resource agent under the `hac` provider on `master1` and `master2`:

```
root# mkdir ${OCF_ROOT}/resource.d/hac

root# cp namenode ${OCF_ROOT}/resource.d/hac

root# chmod 0755 ${OCF_ROOT}/resource.d/hac/namenode
```

Configure highly available NameNode

We are ready to configure highly available NameNode using Heartbeat and Pacemaker. We will set up a VIP address and configure Hadoop and HBase to use this VIP address as their master node. NameNode will be started on the active master where VIP is assigned. If active master has crashed, Heartbeat and Pacemaker will detect it and assign the VIP address to the standby master node, and then start NameNode there.

1. Start Heartbeat on `master1` and `master2`:

```
root# /etc/init.d/heartbeat start
```

2. Change the default `crm` configuration. All resource-related commands are only executed once, from `master1` or `master2`:

```
root# crm configure property stonith-enabled=false

root# crm configure property default-resource-stickiness=1
```

3. Add a VIP resource using our VIP address:

```
root# crm configure primitive VIP ocf:heartbeat:IPaddr params
ip="10.174.14.10" op monitor interval="10s"
```

4. Make the following changes to configure Hadoop to use our VIP address. Sync to all masters, clients, and slaves after you've made the changes:

```
hadoop$ vi $HADOOP_HOME/conf/core-site.xml

  <property>
    <name>fs.default.name</name>
    <value>hdfs://master:8020</value>
  </property>
```

5. Make the following changes to configure HBase to use our VIP address. Sync to all masters, clients, and slaves after you've made the changes:

```
hadoop$ vi $HBASE_HOME/conf/hbase-site.xml
```

```
<property>
  <name>hbase.rootdir</name>
  <value>hdfs://master:8020/hbase</value>
</property>
```

6. To configure Hadoop to write its metadata to a local disk and NFS, make the following changes and sync to all masters, clients, and slaves:

hadoop$ vi $HADOOP_HOME/conf/hdfs-site.xml

```
<property>
  <name>dfs.name.dir</name>
  <value>/usr/local/hadoop/var/dfs/name,/mnt/nfs/hadoop
    /dfs/name</value>
</property>
```

7. Add the `namenode` resource agent we created in step 5 to Pacemaker. We will use NAMENODE as its resource name:

root# crm configure primitive NAMENODE ocf:hac:namenode op monitor interval="120s" timeout="120s" op start timeout="120s" op stop timeout="120s" meta resource-stickiness="1"

8. Configure the VIP resource and the NAMENODE resource as a resource group:

root# crm configure group VIP-AND-NAMENODE VIP NAMENODE

9. Configure `colocation` of a VIP resource and the NAMENODE resource:

root# crm configure colocation VIP-WITH-NAMENODE inf: VIP NAMENODE

10. Configure the resource order of the VIP resource and the NAMENODE resource:

root# crm configure order IP-BEFORE-NAMENODE inf: VIP NAMENODE

11. Verify the previous Heartbeat and resource configurations by using the `crm_mon` command. If everything is configured properly, you should see an output like the following :

root@master1 hac$ crm_mon -1r

============

Last updated: Tue Nov 22 22:39:11 2011

Stack: Heartbeat

Current DC: master2 (7fd92a93-e071-4fcb-993f-9a84e6c7846f) - partition with quorum

Version: 1.0.9-74392a28b7f31d7ddc86689598bd23114f58978b

2 Nodes configured, 1 expected votes

1 Resources configured.

============

```
Online: [ master1 master2 ]


Full list of resources:


Resource Group: VIP-AND-NAMENODE
     VIP (ocf::heartbeat:IPaddr): Started master1
     NAMENODE (ocf::hac:namenode): Started master1
```

12. Make sure that the VIP and NAMENODE resources are started on the same server.

13. Now stop Heartbeat from master1; VIP-AND-NAMENODE should be started at master2 after several seconds.

14. Restart Heartbeat from master1; VIP-AND-NAMENODE should remain started at master2. Resources should NOT failback to master1.

Start DataNode, HBase cluster, and backup HBase master

We have confirmed that our HA configuration works as expected, so we can start HDFS and HBase now. Note that NameNode has already been started by Pacemaker, so we need only start DataNode here:

1. If everything works well, we can start DataNode now:

```
hadoop@master$ for i in 1 2 3
do
  ssh slave$i "$HADOOP_HOME/bin/hadoop-daemon.sh start datanode"
  sleep 1
done
```

2. Start your HBase cluster from master, which is the active master server where the VIP address is associated:

```
hadoop@master$ $HBASE_HOME/bin/start-hbase.sh
```

3. Start standby HMaster from the standby master server, master2 in this case:

```
hadoop@master2$ $HBASE_HOME/bin/hbase-daemon.sh start master
```

How it works...

The previous steps finally leave us with a cluster structure like the following diagram:

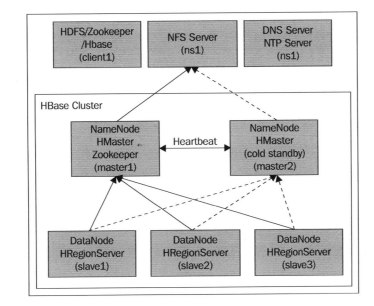

At first, we installed Heartbeat and Pacemaker on the two masters and then configured Heartbeat to enable Pacemaker.

In step 2 of the *Create and install a NameNode resource agent* section, we created the namenode script, which is implemented as a standard OCF resource agent. The most important function of the namenode script is namenode_status, which monitors the status of the NameNode daemon. Here we use the jps command to show all running Java processes owned by the hadoop user, and the grep name of the NameNode daemon to see if it has started. The namenode resource agent is used by Pacemaker to start/stop/monitor the NameNode daemon. In the namenode script, as you can see in the namenode_start and namenode_stop methods, we actually start/stop NameNode by using hadoop-daemon.sh, which is used to start/stop the Hadoop daemon on a single server. You can find a full list of the code from the source shipped with this book.

We started Heartbeat after our namenode resource agent was tested and installed. Then, we made some changes to the default crm configurations. The default-resource-stickiness=1 setting is very important as it turns off the automatic failback of a resource.

We added a VIP resource to Pacemaker and configured Hadoop and HBase to use it in steps 3 to 5 of the *Configure highly available NameNode* section. By using VIP in their configuration, Hadoop and HBase can switch to communicate with the standby master if the active one is down.

In step 6 of the same section, we configured Hadoop (HDFS NameNode) to write its metadata to both the local disk and NFS. If an active master is down, NameNode will be started from the standby master. Because they were mounted on the same NFS directory, NameNode started from the standby master can apply the latest metadata from NFS, and restore HDFS to the status before the original active master is down.

In steps 7 to 10, we added the NAMENODE resource using the namenode resource agent we created in step 2 of the *Create and install a NameNode resource agent* section, then we set up VIP and NAMENODE resources as a group (step 8), and made sure they always run on the same server (step 9), with the right start-up order (step 10). We did this because we didn't want VIP running on master1, while NameNode was running on master2.

Because Pacemaker will start NameNode for us via the namenode resource agent, we need to start DataNode separately, which is what we did in step 1 of the *Start DataNode, HBase cluster, and backup HBase master* section.

After starting HBase normally, we started our standby HBase master (HMaster) on the standby master server. If you check your HBase master log, you will find output like the following, which shows itself as a standby HMaster:

```
2011-11-21 23:38:55,168 INFO org.apache.hadoop.hbase.master.
ActiveMasterManager: Another master is the active master, ip-10-174-
14-15.us-west-1.compute.internal:60000; waiting to become the next
active master
```

Finally, we got NameNode and HMaster running on two servers with an active-standby configuration. The single point of failure of the cluster was avoided.

However, it leaves us with lots of works to do in production. You need to test your HA cluster in all rare cases, such as a server power off, unplug of a network cable, shut down of network switch, or anything else you can think of.

On the other hand, SPOF of the cluster may not be as critical as you think. Based on our experience, almost all of the downtime of the cluster is due to an operational miss or software upgrade. It's better to make your cluster simple.

There's more...

It is more complex to set up a highly available HBase cluster on Amazon EC2 because EC2 does not support static IP addresses, and so we can't use VIP on EC2. An alternative way is to use an Elastic IP address. An Elastic IP address is the role of a static IP address on EC2 while it is associated with your account, not a particular instance. We can use Heartbeat to associate EIP to the standby master automatically, if the active one is down. Then, we configure Hadoop and HBase to use an instance's public DNS associated with EIP, to find an active master. Also, in the `namenode` resource agent, we have to start/stop not only NameNode, but also all DataNodes. This is because the IP address of an active master has changed, but DataNode cannot find the new active master unless it is restarted.

We will skip the details because it's out of the scope of this book. We created an `elastic-ip` resource agent to achieve this purpose. You can find it in the source shipped with this book.

2
Data Migration

In this chapter, we will cover:

- ▸ Importing data from MySQL using a single client
- ▸ Importing data from TSV files using the bulk load tool
- ▸ Writing your own MapReduce job to import data
- ▸ Precreating regions before moving data into HBase

Introduction

There are several ways to move data into HBase:

- ▸ Using the HBase Put API
- ▸ Using the HBase bulk load tool
- ▸ Using a customized MapReduce job

The HBase **Put** API is the most straightforward method. Its usage is not difficult to learn. For most situations however, it is not always the most efficient method. This is especially true when a large amount of data needs to be transferred into HBase within a limited time period. The volume of data to be taken care of is usually huge, and that's probably why you will be using HBase rather than another database. You have to think about how to move all that data into HBase carefully at the beginning of your HBase project; otherwise you might run into serious performance problems.

HBase has the bulk load feature to support loading of huge volumes of data efficiently into HBase. The bulk load feature uses a MapReduce job to load data into a specific HBase table by generating HBase's internal HFile data format files and then loading the data files directly into a running cluster. The easiest way to use this bulk load feature is to use the `importtsv` tool. `importtsv` is a built-in tool to load data from TSV files into HBase. It will run MapReduce jobs to read data from TSV files and will then write output directly into either HBase tables or HBase internal data format files.

Although the `importtsv` tool can be very useful if you are going to load textual data into HBase, there are cases, such as importing data from other formats, where you might want to generate data programmatically. MapReduce is the most efficient way to process a huge amount of data. It might be the only practical way to load a large amount of data into HBase. We can, of course, use MapReduce to import data into HBase. However, the MapReduce job might be very heavy, as the data set is huge. If you don't treat it properly, the heavy MapReduce job might run with poor throughput.

Data migration is a write-heavy task over HBase, unless we generate the internal data files and load them directly into HBase. Even though HBase writes are always fast, writes can be blocked often during the migration process if it is not configured properly. Another issue with write-heavy tasks is that all writes may go to the same region server, this is especially true when loading a large amount of data into a new HBase installation. As all loads go to the same server, the cluster is unbalanced and writing speed will slow down significantly.

We are going to address these issues in this chapter. We will start with the simple task of importing data from MySQL to HBase, using its Put API. We will then describe how to use the `importtsv` and bulk load tools to load TSV data files into HBase. We will also have a MapReduce sample to import data from other file formats. This includes putting data directly into an HBase table and writing to HFile format files on **Hadoop Distributed File System** (**HDFS**). The last recipe in this chapter explains how to precreate regions before loading data into HBase.

This chapter ships with several sample sources written in Java. We assume you have basic Java knowledge, so we will skip explaining how to compile and package the sample Java source in the recipes, but we will put an introduction in the sample source.

Importing data from MySQL via single client

The most usual case of data migration might be importing data from an existing RDBMS into HBase. For this kind of task, the most simple and straightforward way could be to fetch the data from a single client and then put it into HBase, using the HBase Put API. It works well if there is not too much data to transfer.

This recipe describes importing data from MySQL into HBase using its Put API. All the operations will be executed on a single client. MapReduce is not included in this recipe. This recipe leads you through creating an HBase table via HBase Shell, connecting to the cluster from Java, and then putting data into HBase.

Getting ready

Public data sets are an ideal data source to practice HBase data migration. There are many public data sets available on the internet. We will use the NOAA'S 1981-2010 CLIMATE NORMALS public data set in this book. You can access it at http://www1.ncdc.noaa. gov/pub/data/normals/1981-2010/.

This is climate statistics data generated by the **National Oceanic and Atmospheric Administration (NOAA)**.

 In this recipe, we will use its hourly temperature data under **products | hourly**, which you will find at the aforementioned link. Download hly-temp-normal.txt from the directory.

A running MySQL installation is required for this recipe. Create an hly_temp_normal table in your MySQL database, using the following SQL statements:

```
create table hly_temp_normal (
    id INT NOT NULL AUTO_INCREMENT PRIMARY KEY,
    stnid CHAR(11),
    month TINYINT,
    day TINYINT,
    value1 VARCHAR(5),
    value2 VARCHAR(5),
    value3 VARCHAR(5),
    value4 VARCHAR(5),
    value5 VARCHAR(5),
    value6 VARCHAR(5),
    value7 VARCHAR(5),
    value8 VARCHAR(5),
    value9 VARCHAR(5),
    value10 VARCHAR(5),
    value11 VARCHAR(5),
    value12 VARCHAR(5),
    value13 VARCHAR(5),
    value14 VARCHAR(5),
    value15 VARCHAR(5),
    value16 VARCHAR(5),
    value17 VARCHAR(5),
```

```
        value18  VARCHAR(5),
        value19  VARCHAR(5),
        value20  VARCHAR(5),
        value21  VARCHAR(5),
        value22  VARCHAR(5),
        value23  VARCHAR(5),
        value24  VARCHAR(5)
    );
```

This book ships with some scripts to help you load data into your MySQL table. You can use `insert_hly.py` to load hourly NOAA data. You will need to change your host, user, password, and database name, in the script. After you have changed these, insert the data from the downloaded `hly-temp-normal.txt` file into the `hly_temp_normal` table, using:

$ python insert_hly.py -f hly-temp-normal.txt -t hly_temp_normal

To compile the Java source that will be mentioned in the following section, you will need the following libraries:

- `hadoop-core-1.0.2.jar`
- `hbase-0.92.1.jar`
- `mysql-connector-java-5.1.18.jar`

You can add them to your classpath manually, or you can use the sample source available with this book.

Before starting to import data, make sure your HDFS, ZooKeeper, and HBase clusters are running properly. Log in to your HBase's client node.

How to do it...

To import data from MySQL to HBase via a single client:

1. Connect to your HBase cluster through HBase Shell, from your HBase client server:

   hadoop$ $HBASE_HOME/bin/hbase shell

2. Create an `hly_temp` table in HBase:

   hbase> create 'hly_temp', {NAME => 'n', VERSIONS => 1}

3. Write a Java source to import data from MySQL into HBase. Package it as a JAR file. The following steps are to import data using Java source:

    i. Create a `connectHBase()` method to connect to a specific HBase table from Java:

```
$ vi Recipe1.java
  private static HTable connectHBase(String tablename) \
  throws IOException {
    HTable table = null;
    Configuration conf = HBaseConfiguration.create();
    table = new HTable(conf, tablename);
    return table;
  }
```

    ii. Create a `connectDB()` method to connect to MySQL from Java:

```
$ vi Recipe1.java
  private static Connection connectDB() \
  throws Exception {
    String userName = "db_user";
    String password = "db_password";
    String url = "jdbc:mysql://db_host/database";
    Class.forName("com.mysql.jdbc.Driver").newInstance();
    Connection conn = DriverManager.getConnection(url,
    userName, password);
    return conn;
  }
```

Here is the `main()` method of the Java class. In this method, we get data from MySQL and put this data into HBase:

```
$ vi Recipe1.java
public class Recipe1 {
  public static void main(String[] args) {
    Connection dbConn = null;
    HTable htable = null;
    Statement stmt = null;
    String query = "select * from hly_temp_normal";
    try {
      dbConn = connectDB();
      htable = connectHBase("hly_temp");
      byte[] family = Bytes.toBytes("n");
      stmt = dbConn.createStatement();
      ResultSet rs = stmt.executeQuery(query);
      // time stamp for all inserted rows
      long ts = System.currentTimeMillis();
```

```
      while (rs.next()) {
        String stationid = rs.getString("stnid");
        int month = rs.getInt("month");
        int day = rs.getInt("day");
        String rowkey = stationid + Common.lpad(String.
        valueOf(month), 2,
        '0') + Common.lpad(String.valueOf(day), 2, '0');
        Put p = new Put(Bytes.toBytes(rowkey));
        // get hourly data from MySQL and put into hbase
        for (int i = 5; i < 29; i++) {
          String columnI = "v" + Common.lpad
          (String.valueOf(i - 4), 2, '0');
          String valueI = rs.getString(i);
          p.add(family, Bytes.toBytes(columnI), ts,
          Bytes.toBytes(valueI));
        }
        htable.put(p);
      }
    } catch (Exception e) {
      e.printStackTrace();
    } finally {
      try {
        if (stmt != null) {
          stmt.close();
        }
        if (dbConn != null) {
          dbConn.close();
        }
        if (htable != null) {
          htable.close();
        }
      } catch (Exception e) {
        // ignore
      }
    }
  }
}
```

4. Run the import job. The script to run the JAR file looks as follows:

```
#/bin/bash
bin=`dirname $0`
bin=`cd $bin;pwd`
cp=$HBASE_HOME/conf:$HBASE_HOME/hbase-0.92.1.jar:$bin/build/hac-
chapter2.jar
for jar in $bin/lib/*.jar
```

```
do
    cp=$cp:$jar
done
for jar in $HBASE_HOME/lib/*.jar
do
    cp=$cp:$jar
done

$JAVA_HOME/bin/java -classpath $cp "hac.chapter2.Recipe1"
```

5. To verify the data imported in HBase, connect to the running HBase instance via HBase Shell:

    hadoop$ $HBASE_HOME/bin/hbase shell

6. Verify if the data has been imported to the target table in HBase:

    hbase> count 'hly_temp'

    95630 row(s) in 8.9850 seconds

    hbase> scan 'hly_temp', {LIMIT => 10}

    ...

    AQW000617050110   column=n:v23,
    timestamp=1322958813521, value=814S

    AQW000617050110   column=n:v24,
    timestamp=1322958813521, value=811C

    10 row(s) in 0.6730 seconds

How it works...

In steps 1 and 2, we created the target table in HBase to insert data into. The table name is hly_temp, and it has a single column family n. The reason we gave it a name one character long is that the column family name will be stored in every Key/Value in HBase. Using a very short name makes storing and caching of data efficient. We only need one version of our data, which is specified by the VERSION property for the column family.

In the Java source, to connect to HBase, we first create a Configuration object and then use it with the table name to create an HTable instance. The HTable object will handle all client API calls. As you can see, we don't set any ZooKeeper or HBase connection configurations in the source. So how does it find the proper running HBase cluster? This is possible because we added the $HBase/conf directory to the classpath, in step 4. By doing this, the HBase client API will load configurations from the file hbase-site.xml from classpath. The connection setting is specified in the hbase-site.xml file.

After fetching data from MySQL using JDBC, we looped through the result set and mapped one row in MySQL to one row in the HBase table. Here, we use `stationid`, `month`, and `day`, to compose the row key of the HBase data. We also added a left padding of `0` to the month and day data. This is important because the HBase row key sorts in lexicographical order, which means 12 stands before 2; this is of course not our expected result.

We created one `Put` object for one row using the row key. Hourly data is set by calling `Put.add()`, which takes column family, qualifier, timestamp, and value, as parameters. Again, we took a very short column name here to make the stored data efficient. After all data has been set, calling `HTable.put()` will put the data into the table.

Finally, all opened resources need to be closed manually. We closed the MySQL and HBase connections in the final block of the source to make sure it will be called even if an exception occurs during the importing.

You can verify the importing by comparing the row counts of MySQL and HBase tables. As you can see in the scan result, data was accurately imported into HBase.

Importing data from TSV files using the bulk load tool

HBase has an `importtsv` tool to support importing data from TSV files into HBase. Using this tool to load text data into HBase is very efficient, because it runs a MapReduce job to perform the importing. Even if you are going to load data from an existing RDBMS, you can dump data into a text file somehow and then use `importtsv` to import dumped data into HBase. This approach works well when importing a huge amount of data, as dumping data is much faster than executing SQL on RDBMS.

The `importtsv` tool does not only load data directly into an HBase table, it also supports generating HBase internal format (HFile) files, so that you can use the HBase bulk load tool to load generated files directly into a running HBase cluster. This way, you reduce network traffic that was generated from the data transfers and your HBase load, during the migration.

This recipe describes usage of the `importtsv` and bulk load tools. We first demonstrate loading data from TSV files into the HBase table, using the `importtsv` tool. We will also cover how to generate HBase internal format files and how to load generated files into HBase directly.

Getting ready

We will use the NOAA CLIMATE NORMALS data in this recipe. The data is available at the following link:

`http://www1.ncdc.noaa.gov/pub/data/normals/1981-2010/`

Download the `hly-temp-10pctl.txt` file, which can be found under the **products | hourly** directory.

The downloaded data cannot be loaded directly from the `importtsv` tool, as its format is not supported. We provide scripts to help you convert the data into TSV files. Besides the actual data, the TSV file to be loaded must contain a field representing the row key of the HBase table row. The `to_tsv_hly.py` script shipped with this book reads data from an hourly NOAA data file and generates the row key and output data to a TSV file on the local file system:

```
$ python to_tsv_hly.py -f hly-temp-10pctl.txt -t  hly-temp-10pctl.tsv
```

As the `importtsv` tool runs a MapReduce job to perform the importing, we need to get MapReduce running on our cluster. Start the MapReduce daemons by executing the following command from your master node:

```
hadoop$ $HADOOP_HOME/bin/start-mapred.sh
```

We will add a `hac` user on the client server to run the job; this is desirable for production. To run the MapReduce job from a client, you need to give write permission for the `${hadoop.tmp.dir}` directory to the `hac` user on the client. We assume that the `${hadoop.tmp.dir}` directory is set as `/usr/local/hadoop/var`:

```
root@client1# usermod -a -G hadoop hac
root@client1# chmod -R 775 /usr/local/hadoop/var
```

On HDFS, create the home directory for the `hac` user:

```
hadoop@client1$ $HADOOP_HOME/bin/hadoop fs -mkdir /user/hac
hadoop@client1$ $HADOOP_HOME/bin/hadoop fs -chown hac /user/hac
```

Also make sure the `hac` user has write permission to the MapReduce temporary directory on HDFS:

```
hadoop@client1$ $HADOOP_HOME/bin/hadoop fs -chmod -R 775 /usr/local/hadoop/var/mapred
```

How to do it...

To load data from the TSV file into the HBase table using MapReduce, carry out the following steps:

1. Create a directory on HDFS and copy the TSV file from the local file system to HDFS:

    ```
    hac@client1$ $HADOOP_HOME/bin/hadoop fs -mkdir /user/hac/input/2-1
    hac@client1$ $HADOOP_HOME/bin/hadoop fs -copyFromLocal hly-temp-10pctl.tsv /user/hac/input/2-1
    ```

2. Add the target table in HBase. Connect to HBase and add the `hly_temp` table to it:

```
hac@client1$ $HBASE_HOME/bin/hbase shell
hbase> create 'hly_temp', {NAME => 't', VERSIONS => 1}
```

3. If the table exists (we created it in the first recipe of this chapter), add a new column family to it:

```
hbase> disable 'hly_temp'
hbase> alter 'hly_temp', {NAME => 't', VERSIONS => 1}
hbase> enable 'hly_temp'
```

4. Add the `hbase-site.xml` file to the Hadoop classpath by linking it under the Hadoop configuration directory:

```
hac@client1$ ln -s $HBASE_HOME/conf/hbase-site.xml $HADOOP_HOME/
conf/hbase-site.xml
```

5. Add HBase dependency JARs to the Hadoop classpath by editing the `hadoop-env.sh` file under the `$HADOOP_HOME/conf` directory on the client server:

```
hadoop@client1$ vi $HADOOP_HOME/conf/hadoop-env.sh
export HADOOP_CLASSPATH=/usr/local/zookeeper/current/zookeeper-
3.4.3.jar:/usr/local/hbase/current/lib/guava-r09.jar
```

6. Run the `importtsv` tool by running the following script by the `hac` user:

```
hac@client1$ $HADOOP_HOME/bin/hadoop jar $HBASE_HOME/hbase-
0.92.1.jar importtsv \
    -Dimporttsv.columns=HBASE_ROW_KEY,t:v01,t:v02,t:v03,t:v04,t:v0
5,t:v06,t:v07,t:v08,t:v09,t:v10,t:v11,t:v12,t:v13,t:v14,t:v15,t:v1
6,t:v17,t:v18,t:v19,t:v20,t:v21,t:v22,t:v23,t:v24 \
    hly_temp \
    /user/hac/input/2-1
```

7. Check the job status via the MapReduce admin page—`http://master1:50030/jobtracker.jsp`:

8. Verify the data imported in the target table in HBase. Here, we get row count in the `hly_temp` table and we also scan some sample data in the table. The row count should be equal to the number of lines in the TSV file. The row key in the table should be equal to the first field in the file. There will be `t:v01`, `t:v02`, ..., `t:v24` cells in each row, and the value of each cell should be equal to the relative field in the TSV file:

```
hbase> count 'hly_temp'

95630 row(s) in 12.2020 seconds

hbase> scan 'hly_temp', {COLUMNS => 't:', LIMIT => 10}

AQW000617050110                              column=t:v23,
timestamp=1322959962261, value=781S
AQW000617050110                              column=t:v24,
timestamp=1322959962261, value=774C

10 row(s) in 0.1850 seconds
```

How it works...

The `importtsv` tool will only read data from HDFS, so we started by copying the TSV files from the local file system to HDFS, using the `hadoop fs -copyFromLocal` command.

In step 2, we create the target table (`hly_temp`) and column family (`t`) in HBase. If the table already exists, we can alter it to just add our column family to it. All data will be loaded into the newly added column family; data in the existing column family will not be touched.

In order to run the MapReduce job, the JAR file containing the class files needs to be executed by the `hadoop jar` command. In order to pass our HBase configuration to the command, we link `hbase-site.xml` under the `$HADOOP_HOME/conf` directory; all files under this directory will be added to the classpath of the Java processes that are kicked by the `hadoop` command.

In step 5, runtime dependencies are added by setting `HADOOP_CLASSPATH` in `hadoop-env.sh`. Besides the ZooKeeper library, the `guava-r09.jar` file is required by the `importtsv` tool. It is a library to parse the TSV files.

The `importtsv` tool itself is a Java class included in the HBase JAR file. In step 6, we run the tool by executing the `hadoop jar` command. This command will start the Java process for us and add all dependencies to it. The JAR to run is specified by the first parameter of the `hadoop jar` command; here it is `hbase-0.92.1.jar`.

The following parameters are passed to the main class of `hbase-0.92.1.jar`:

- ▶ The mapping information for a field index of the TSV file to an HBase table column is set by the `-Dimporttsv.columns` parameter. In our case, the TSV file format is `(rowkey, value1, value2, …, value24)`. We put the data in the HBase `t` column family, using `v01` as `value1`, `v02` as `value2`, and so on. `HBASE_ROW_KEY` is a constant word specifying the row key field.

- ▶ Following the `-Dimporttsv.columns` parameter, we specified the table name (`hly_temp`) and input the TSV file path (`/user/hac/input/2-1`) for the command.

There are several other options that may be specified. Running `importtsv` with no arguments prints brief usage information:

```
hac@client1$ $HADOOP_HOME/bin/hadoop jar $HBASE_HOME/hbase-0.92.1.jar
importtsv

Usage: importtsv -Dimporttsv.columns=a,b,c <tablename> <inputdir>


Imports the given input directory of TSV data into the specified table.
...
```

Other options that may be specified with `-D` include:

```
  -Dimporttsv.skip.bad.lines=false - fail if encountering an invalid line
  '-Dimporttsv.separator=|' - eg separate on pipes instead of tabs
  -Dimporttsv.timestamp=currentTimeAsLong - use the specified timestamp
for the import
  -Dimporttsv.mapper.class=my.Mapper - A user-defined Mapper to use
instead of org.apache.hadoop.hbase.mapreduce.TsvImporterMapper
```

The tool starts the MapReduce job for us. In the map phase of the job, it reads and parses rows from TSV files under the specified input directory, and puts rows into the HBase table using the column mapping information. The `Read` and `Put` operations are executed in parallel on multiple servers, so it is much faster than loading data from a single client. There is no reduce phase in the job, by default. We can check the job progress, counters, and other MapReduce information on the Admin page of MapReduce.

To view data inserted in the table, we can use the `scan` command of HBase Shell. We specified `COLUMNS => 't:'` to only scan the `t` column family in the table.

There's more...

The `importtsv` tool, by default, uses the HBase Put API to insert data into the HBase table using `TableOutputFormat` in its map phase. But when the `-Dimporttsv.bulk.output` option is specified, it instead generates HBase internal format (HFile) files on HDFS, by using `HFileOutputFormat`. Therefore, we can then use the `completebulkload` tool to load the generated files into a running cluster. The following steps are to use the bulk output and load tools:

1. Create a directory on HDFS to put the generated files in:

   ```
   hac@client1$ $HADOOP_HOME/bin/hadoop fs -mkdir /user/hac/output
   ```

2. Run `importtsv` with the bulk output option:

   ```
   hac@client1$ $HADOOP_HOME/bin/hadoop jar $HBASE_HOME/hbase-
   0.92.1.jar importtsv \
       -Dimporttsv.bulk.output=/user/hac/output/2-1 \
       -Dimporttsv.columns=HBASE_ROW_KEY,t:v01,t:v02,t:v03,t:v04,
       t:v05,t:v06,t:v07,t:v08,t:v09,t:v10,t:v11,t:v12,t:v13,t:v14,
       t:v15,t:v16,t:v17,t:v18,t:v19,t:v20,t:v21,t:v22,t:v23,t:v24 \
       hly_temp \
       /user/hac/input/2-1
   ```

3. Complete the bulk load:

   ```
   hac@client1$ $HADOOP_HOME/bin/hadoop jar $HBASE_HOME/hbase-
   0.92.1.jar completebulkload \
       /user/hac/output/2-1 \
       hly_temp
   ```

The `completebulkload` tool looks through the generated files, determines the regions in which they belong, and then contacts the appropriate region server. The region server will move the adopted HFile into its storage directories and create the data online for clients.

Writing your own MapReduce job to import data

Although the `importtsv` tool is very useful for loading text files into HBase, in many cases, for full control of the loading process you may want to write your own MapReduce job to import data into HBase. For example, the `importtsv` tool does not work if you are going to load files of other formats.

HBase provides `TableOutputFormat` for writing data into an HBase table from a MapReduce job. You can also generate its internal HFile format files in your MapReduce job by using the `HFileOutputFormat` class, and then load the generated files into a running HBase cluster, using the `completebulkload` tool we described in the previous recipe.

In this recipe, we will explain the steps for loading data using your own MapReduce job. We will first describe how to use `TableOutputFormat`. In the *There's more...* section, we will explain how to generate HFile format files in a MapReduce job.

Getting ready

We will use the raw NOAA `hly-temp-normal.txt` file in this recipe. You don't need to do any formatting to the downloaded data file. We will load the raw data from MapReduce directly.

We assume your environment is already prepared for running MapReduce on HBase. If it still isn't, you can refer to the *Importing from TSV files using the bulk load tool* recipe for details.

How to do it...

Follow these instructions to load data into HBase using your own MapReduce job:

1. Copy the raw data file from the local file system to HDFS:

   hac@client1$ $HADOOP_HOME/bin/hadoop fs -mkdir /user/hac/input/2-3

   hac@client1$ $HADOOP_HOME/bin/hadoop fs -copyFromLocal hly-temp-normal.tsv /user/hac/input/2-3

2. Edit `hadoop-env.sh` on the client server, and add the HBase JAR file to the Hadoop classpath:

   hadoop@client1$ vi $HADOOP_HOME/conf/hadoop-env.sh

   export HADOOP_CLASSPATH=/usr/local/hbase/current/hbase-0.92.1.jar

3. Write your MapReduce Java source and then package it as a JAR file. The Java source should look as follows:

   ```
   $ vi Recipe3.java
   public class Recipe3 {
     public static Job createSubmittableJob
       (Configuration conf, String[] args)
       throws IOException {
       String tableName = args[0];
       Path inputDir = new Path(args[1]);
       Job job = new Job (conf, "hac_chapter2_recipe3");
       job.setJarByClass(HourlyImporter.class);
       FileInputFormat.setInputPaths(job, inputDir);
   ```

```
    job.setInputFormatClass(TextInputFormat.class);
    job.setMapperClass(HourlyImporter.class);

// ++++ insert into table directly using TableOutputFormat ++++
    TableMapReduceUtil.initTableReducerJob(tableName, null, job);
    job.setNumReduceTasks(0);
    TableMapReduceUtil.addDependencyJars(job);
    return job;
  }

  public static void main(String[] args)
    throws Exception {
    Configuration conf =
      HBaseConfiguration.create();
    Job job = createSubmittableJob(conf, args);
    System.exit (job.waitForCompletion(true) ? 0 : 1);
  }
}
```

4. Add an inner class (HourlyImporter) in Recipe3.java. This class is the mapper class of the MapReduce job:

$ vi Recipe3.java

```
static class HourlyImporter extends
Mapper<LongWritable, Text, ImmutableBytesWritable, Put> {

    private long ts;
    static byte[] family = Bytes.toBytes("n");

    @Override
    protected void setup(Context context) {
        ts = System.currentTimeMillis();
    }

    @Override
    public void map(LongWritable offset, Text value, Context
context)throws IOException {
        try {
          String line = value.toString();
          String stationID = line.substring(0, 11);
          String month = line.substring(12, 14);
          String day = line.substring(15, 17);
          String rowkey = stationID + month + day;
          byte[] bRowKey = Bytes.toBytes(rowkey);
          ImmutableBytesWritable rowKey =
```

```
          new ImmutableBytesWritable(bRowKey);
        Put p = new Put(bRowKey);
        for (int i = 1; i < 25 ; i++) {
            String columnI =
                "v" + Common.lpad(String.valueOf(i), 2, '0');
            int beginIndex = i * 7 + 11;
            String valueI =
                line.substring(beginIndex, beginIndex + 6).trim();
            p.add(family, Bytes.toBytes(columnI),
                ts, Bytes.toBytes(valueI));
        }
        context.write(rowKey, p);
    }
    catch (InterruptedException e) {
        e.printStackTrace();
    }
  }
 }
}
```

5. In order to run the MapReduce job, package the Java source into a JAR file, and run it from the client by using the `hadoop jar` command:

```
hac@client1$ $HADOOP_HOME/bin/hadoop jar hac-chapter2.jar hac.
chapter2.Recipe3 \
    hly_temp \
    /user/hac/input/2-3
```

Check the result. The output of the MapReduce job should be as shown in the following screenshot:

```
11/12/03 20:49:38 INFO mapred.JobClient:    Map-Reduce Framework
11/12/03 20:49:38 INFO mapred.JobClient:     Map input records=95630
11/12/03 20:49:38 INFO mapred.JobClient:     Physical memory (bytes) snapshot=52543488
11/12/03 20:49:38 INFO mapred.JobClient:     Spilled Records=0
11/12/03 20:49:38 INFO mapred.JobClient:     CPU time spent (ms)=37400
11/12/03 20:49:38 INFO mapred.JobClient:     Total committed heap usage (bytes)=16318464
11/12/03 20:49:38 INFO mapred.JobClient:     Virtual memory (bytes) snapshot=376438784
11/12/03 20:49:38 INFO mapred.JobClient:     Map output records=95630
11/12/03 20:49:38 INFO mapred.JobClient:     SPLIT_RAW_BYTES=118
```

Map input records should be equal to the total lines of files under your input path; the **Map output records** value is supposed to be equal to the input record count. You can also check the result using the HBase `count/scan` command.

How it works...

To run a MapReduce job, we first create a `Job` instance in `createSubmittableJob()`. After the instance is created, we set an input path, input format, and mapper class to the job. After that, we call `TableMapReduceUtil.initTableReducerJob()` to set up the job appropriately for us. The setup includes adding HBase configurations, setting up `TableOutputFormat`, and adding dependencies to the job. `TableMapReduceUtil` is a useful utility class for writing a MapReduce program over HBase.

The `job.waitForCompletion()` call in the `main` method submits the job to the MapReduce framework and waits for it to be completed before exiting. The running job will read all files under the input path and pass the data line by line to the specified mapper class (`HourlyImporter`).

In the `map` method of the class, we parse the line, compose a row key, create the `Put` object, and then add parsed data to the corresponding column by calling `Put.add()`. Finally, we write the data into the HBase table by calling `context.write()`. There is no reduce phase needed in this case.

As you can see, writing a customized MapReduce job to insert data into HBase is very simple. The program is similar to the one using HBase API from a single client, which we described in the *Importing data from MySQL using a single client* recipe. For a large amount of data, we recommend that you use MapReduce to load the data into HBase.

There's more...

Using a customized MapReduce job to load data into HBase makes sense for many situations. However, if your data is voluminous, this approach might be not efficient enough. There are ways to make the data migration more efficient.

Generating HFile files in MapReduce

Instead of writing data directly into an HBase table, we can also generate the internal HFile format files in our MapReduce job and then load them into our cluster using the `completebulkload` tool that we described in the second recipe. This approach will use less CPU and network resources than simply using the `TableOutputFormat` API:

1. Change the job configuration. To generate HFile files, find the following two lines of the `createSubmittableJob()` method:

    ```
    TableMapReduceUtil.initTableReducerJob
        (tableName, null, job);
    job.setNumReduceTasks(0);
    ```

2. Replace them with the following code:

```
HTable table = new HTable(conf, tableName);
job.setReducerClass(PutSortReducer.class);
Path outputDir = new Path(args[2]);
FileOutputFormat.setOutputPath
   (job, outputDir);
job.setMapOutputKeyClass
   (ImmutableBytesWritable.class);
job.setMapOutputValueClass(Put.class);
HFileOutputFormat.configureIncrementalLoad (job, table);
```

3. Add the output path to the command-line argument. Compile and package the source, and then add the output path to the command of running the job:

```
hac@client1$ $HADOOP_HOME/bin/hadoop jar hac-chapter2.jar hac.
chapter2.Recipe3 \
    hly_temp \
    /user/hac/input/2-3 \
    /user/hac/output/2-3
```

4. Complete the bulk load:

```
hac@client1$ $HADOOP_HOME/bin/hadoop jar $HBASE_HOME/hbase-
0.92.1.jar completebulkload \
    /user/hac/output/2-3 \
    hly_temp
```

In step 1, we changed the source of the job configuration. We set the job to use the PutSortReducer reducer class, which is provided by HBase. This class will sort columns of a row before writing them out. The HFileOutputFormat.configureIncrementalLoad() method will take care of setting the appropriate configurations for the job to generate HFile files.

After the job completes running in step 2, the internal HFile format files are generated under the output path we specified. Files under 2-3/n, which is the column family directory, will be loaded by the completebulkload tool into our HBase cluster.

```
hac@client1 java$ hadoop fs -lsr /user/hac/output/2-3
Warning: $HADOOP_HOME is deprecated.

-rw-r--r--   2 hac supergroup          0 2011-12-04 11:20 /user/hac/output/2-3/_SUCCESS
drwxr-xr-x   - hac supergroup          0 2011-12-04 11:18 /user/hac/output/2-3/_logs
drwxr-xr-x   - hac supergroup          0 2011-12-04 11:18 /user/hac/output/2-3/_logs/history
-rw-r--r--   2 hac supergroup      14271 2011-12-04 11:18 /user/hac/output/2-3/_logs/history/job_201112
-rw-r--r--   2 hac supergroup      28473 2011-12-04 11:18 /user/hac/output/2-3/_logs/history/job_201112
drwxr-xr-x   - hac supergroup          0 2011-12-04 11:20 /user/hac/output/2-3/n
-rw-r--r--   2 hac supergroup   98785845 2011-12-04 11:19 /user/hac/output/2-3/n/925090727389790995
```

During the MapReduce job execution, if you open the HBase admin page from your browser, you will find that no request comes to HBase. This indicates that data is not written into the HBase table directly.

HBase Master: ip–10–160–22–148.us–west–1.compute.internal:60000

http://master1:60010/master.jsp

Q▾ Google

Region Servers

Address	Start Code	Load
ip-10-160-230-25.us-west-1.compute.internal:60030	1323026141301	requests=0, regions=3, usedHeap=32, maxHeap=998
ip-10-168-5-65.us-west-1.compute.internal:60030	1323026141527	requests=0, regions=1, usedHeap=31, maxHeap=998
ip-10-176-150-188.us-west-1.compute.internal:60030	1323026141682	requests=0, regions=0, usedHeap=27, maxHeap=998

Total: servers: 3   requests=0, regions=4

Load is requests per second and count of regions loaded

Important configurations affecting data migration

If you write data directly into the HBase table using `TableOutputFormat` from your MapReduce job, it could be a very write-heavy job on HBase. Although HBase is designed to be able to handle writes quickly, there are some important configurations you might want to tune, such as the following:

- ▸ JVM heap and GC setting
- ▸ Region server handler count
- ▸ Maximum region file size
- ▸ MemStore size
- ▸ Update block setting

You will need basic knowledge of HBase architecture to understand how these configurations affect the write performance of HBase. We will cover these in more detail in *Chapter 8, Basic Performance Tuning*, and *Chapter 9, Advanced Configurations and Tuning*.

There are several types of logs generated by the Hadoop and HBase clusters. Checking the logs gives you hints to find out the bottleneck of your cluster during the MapReduce data loading job. Important logs include the following:

- ▸ GC logs for the Hadoop/HBase/ZooKeeper daemon
- ▸ The HMaster daemon log

We will describe the details in *Chapter 8, Basic Performance Tuning*.

See also

> ▸ *Chapter 8, Basic Performance Tuning*

> ▸ *Chapter 9, Advanced Configurations and Tuning*

Precreating regions before moving data into HBase

Each HBase row belongs to a particular region. A region holds a range of sorted HBase rows. Regions are deployed and managed by a region server.

When we create a table in HBase, the table starts with a single region. All data inserted into the table goes to the single region, first. Data keeps being inserted, and when it reaches a threshold, the region will be split into two halves. This is called region splitting. Split regions will be distributed to other region servers, so that the load can be balanced among the clusters.

As you can imagine, if we can initialize the table with precreated regions, using an appropriate algorithm, the load of the data migration will be balanced over the entire cluster, which increases data load speed significantly.

We will describe how to create a table with precreated regions in this recipe.

Getting ready

Log in to your HBase client node.

How to do it...

Execute the following command on the client node:

```
$ $HBASE_HOME/bin/hbase org.apache.hadoop.hbase.util.RegionSplitter -c 10
-f n hly_temp2

12/04/06 23:16:32 DEBUG util.RegionSplitter: Creating table hly_temp2
with 1 column families.  Presplitting to 10 regions

...


12/04/06 23:16:44 DEBUG util.RegionSplitter: Table created!  Waiting for
regions to show online in META...

12/04/06 23:16:44 DEBUG util.RegionSplitter: Finished creating table with
10 regions
```

How it works...

This command calls the `RegionSplitter` class with the following parameters:

- ▸ `-c 10`—creates the table with 10 presplit regions
- ▸ `-f n`—creates a single column family named `n`
- ▸ `hly_temp2`— the name of the table

Open the HBase admin page from your browser, and click **hly_temp2** in the **User Tables** section. You will that find 10 regions were precreated:

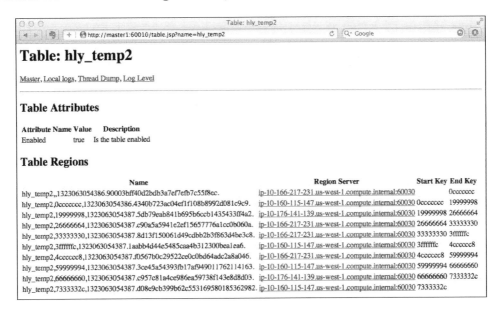

`RegionSplitter` is a utility class provided by HBase. By using `RegionSplitter` you can:

- ▸ Create a table with a specified number of precreated regions
- ▸ Execute a rolling split of all regions on an existing table
- ▸ Split regions using your custom algorithm

If you run the data load job discussed in the *Writing your own MapReduce job to import data* recipe, you may expect data writes to be distributed to all region servers in the cluster, but the result is different. From the admin page, you will find that all requests go to the same server during the MapReduce job execution time.

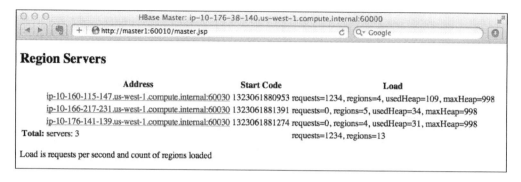

This is because the default splitting algorithm (MD5StringSplit) does not fit our case. All of our rows drop into the same region, thus all the API requests go to the region server that holds the region. We need to provide our custom algorithm to split regions properly.

Presplitting regions also changes the behaviour of the MapReduce job that generates the internal HFile format files. Run the job in the *Writing your own MapReduce job to import data* recipe, with the option for generating HFile files turned on in the hly_temp2 table. As shown in the following image, you will find that the **reduce** count of the MapReduce job jumped from the original of 1 to 10, which is the number of precreated regions:

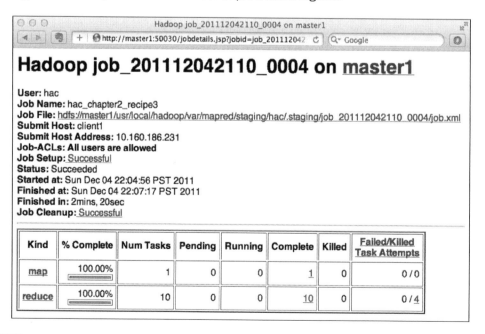

This is because the reducer count of the job is based on the region count of the target table. If the reducer count increases, it normally means that the load was distributed to multiple servers, and thus the job will be much faster.

See also

▶ The *Precreating regions using your own algorithm* recipe, in this *Chapter 9*

3
Using Administration Tools

In this chapter, we will focus on:

- ▶ HBase Master Web UI
- ▶ Using HBase Shell to manage tables
- ▶ Using HBase Shell to access data in HBase
- ▶ Using HBase Shell to manage the cluster
- ▶ Executing Java methods from HBase Shell
- ▶ Row counter
- ▶ WAL tool—manually splitting and dumping WALs
- ▶ HFile tool—viewing textualized HFile content
- ▶ HBase `hbck`—checking the health of an HBase cluster
- ▶ Hive on HBase—querying HBase using a SQL-like language

Introduction

Everyone expects their HBase administrator to keep the cluster running smoothly, storing a huge amount of data in it, handling maybe millions of requests simultaneously, quickly, and reliably. Keeping a large amount of data in HBase accessible, manageable, and easy to query, is a critical task for an administrator.

Besides a solid knowledge of the cluster you are operating, just as important are the tools you use. HBase ships with several administration tools to make life easier. There is a web-based administration page; on this page you can view the status of the cluster and execute simple administration tasks such as region splitting. However, more powerful than HBase web UI is the HBase Shell tool. This command-line tool has features to create and manage HBase tables, to insert and view data in the tables, and also has methods to manage the cluster itself.

HBase also provides a bunch of Java utilities with its installation. You can import and use these utilities directly from your HBase Shell prompt, which makes administration tasks much more efficient.

We have HBase tools to deal with its internal **Write Ahead Log** (**WAL**) and HFile files, too. These tools are useful for advanced users, who need to dig deeper into how data is stored in HBase.

HBase hbck is the tool that can be used to check the health of the cluster. In production, you might want to run hbck frequently, so that you can find out problems quickly.

Hive is a data warehouse software built for Hadoop. Hive has a **Hive Query Language** (**HQL**) to manage data in Hadoop. HQL is a powerful, easy-to-use, SQL-like query language. Although HBase has its own commands to access its data, the functionality is very limited. We can map HBase tables and columns to a Hive table so that it is possible to perform complex queries over HBase data using HQL.

In this chapter, we will describe the usage of these tools. We will explain what the tools are for, and how to use them to resolve a particular task.

HBase Master web UI

The HBase Master web UI is a simple but useful tool, to get an overview of the current status of the cluster. From its page, you can get the version of the running HBase, its basic configuration, including the root HDFS path and ZooKeeper quorum, load average of the cluster, and a table, region, and region server list.

Furthermore, you can manually split a region using a particular boundary row key. This is useful when you turn off the automatic region splitting of your cluster.

Getting ready

Make sure the port for your master page, which has a default value of 60010, is opened to your client computer from your network firewall. If you are running your cluster on Amazon EC2, you can open the port from **AWS Management Console | Amazon EC2 | NETWORK & SECURITY | Security Groups | Inbound**.

How to do it...

Access the following URL from your web browser:

```
http://hbase_master_server:60010/master.jsp
```

 You need to change `hbase_master_server` to the hostname of your HBase master server.

How it works...

The HBase Master web UI looks as follows:

Local logs, Thread Dump, Log Level, Debug dump

Attributes

Attribute Name	Value	Description
HBase Version	0.92.1, r1298924	HBase version and revision
HBase Compiled	Fri Mar 9 16:58:34 UTC 2012, jenkins	When HBase version was compiled and by whom
Hadoop Version	1.0.2, r1304954	Hadoop version and revision
Hadoop Compiled	Sat Mar 24 23:58:21 UTC 2012, hortonfo	When Hadoop version was compiled and by whom
HBase Root Directory	hdfs://master1:8020/hbase	Location of HBase home directory
HBase Cluster ID	46ebd683-09cd-428d-8a56-20b81f611d61	Unique identifier generated for each HBase cluster
Load average	3	Average number of regions per regionserver. Naive computation.
Zookeeper Quorum	master1:2181	Addresses of all registered ZK servers. For more, see zk dump.
Coprocessors	[]	Coprocessors currently loaded loaded by the master
HMaster Start Time	Mon Apr 30 19:31:40 JST 2012	Date stamp of when this HMaster was started
HMaster Active Time	Mon Apr 30 19:31:40 JST 2012	Date stamp of when this HMaster became active

Tasks

Show All Monitored Tasks Show non-RPC Tasks Show All RPC Handler Tasks Show Active RPC Calls Show Client Operations View as JSON

No tasks currently running on this node.

Tables

Catalog Table	Description
-ROOT-	The -ROOT- table holds references to all .META. regions.
.META.	The .META. table holds references to all User Table regions

4 table(s) in set. [Details]

User Table	Description
hly_temp	{NAME => 'hly_temp', FAMILIES => [{NAME => 'n', COMPRESSION => 'LZO', VERSIONS => '1'}, {NAME => 'q', COMPRESSION => 'LZO', VERSIONS => '1'}, {NAME => 't', VERSIONS => '1', COMPRESSION => 'LZO'}]}

As you can see, the **Attributes** section shows information about the HBase and Hadoop version, the HBase root directory on HDFS, load average of the cluster, and the ZooKeeper quorum. The HBase root directory and ZooKeeper quorum data are the values set in your HBase configuration file `hbase-site.xml`. The load average is the average number of regions per region server. A single region server's load is shown in the **Region Server** section.

There are two tables shown in the **Catalog Table** section, **-ROOT-** and **.META.**. These are the system tables of HBase. The **-ROOT-** table holds references of the region servers, where all the **.META.** tables are deployed, while the **.META.** table holds references of all user-table regions.

The **User Table** section displays a list of all user tables and their column families' properties. Clicking the link of the table name from the list will bring you to the table's details page. You will see a list of regions of that table, displayed on this page. You can also compact or split regions manually on the table's details page. The region key is optional for the compaction and splitting of regions. If specified, HBase will only take action on the region where the key drops in. If it is not specified, all the regions are targeted by this action.

Table: hly_temp

Master, Local logs, Thread Dump, Log Level

Table Attributes

Attribute Name	Value	Description
Enabled	true	Is the table enabled

Table Regions

Name	Region Server	Start Key	End Key	Requests
hly_temp,,1331433640093.a271eb0d09bb92b72bdda0fbfc09e30c.	ip-10-161-47-176.us-west-1.compute.internal:60030		USW000128350819	0
hly_temp,USW000128350819,1331433640093.46dcb87a2055a6963866f77be6868840.	ip-10-160-50-224.us-west-1.compute.internal:60030	USW000128350819	USW000138830523	0
hly_temp,USW000138830523,1327118470453.5740a39d9eaa59o4175487c14e0a272a.	ip-10-161-47-176.us-west-1.compute.internal:60030	USW000138830523	USW000149221223	0
hly_temp,USW000149221223,1326090127204.0b593d9dc044f1fe011ec0c902f68fc5.	ip-10-161-115-214.us-west-1.compute.internal:60030	USW000149221223		0

Regions by Region Server

Region Server	Region Count
http://ip-10-160-50-224.us-west-1.compute.internal:60030/	1
http://ip-10-161-115-214.us-west-1.compute.internal:60030/	1
http://ip-10-161-47-176.us-west-1.compute.internal:60030/	2

Actions:

Compact	Region Key (optional):	This action will force a compaction of all regions of the table, or, if a key is supplied, only the region containing the given key.
Split	Region Key (optional):	This action will force a split of all eligible regions of the table, or, if a key is supplied, only the region containing the given key. An eligible region is one that does not contain any references to other regions. Split requests for noneligible regions will be ignored.

The **Region Server** section shows all online region servers and their load. If you are sending lots of requests to the cluster, you can see which server the requests went to, from this section. Clicking the link of the region server address will show the details page of the clicked server. On the details page, you can see the metrics data of the server and all the regions deployed on that server, in detail.

The region server's details page is a simple, but very important interface for knowing the insight information of a region server.

Metrics	requestsPerSecond=0, numberOfOnlineRegions=20, numberOfStores=24, numberOfStorefiles=7, storefileIndexSizeMB=0, rootIndexSizeKB=3, totalStaticIndexSizeKB=0, totalStaticBloomSizeKB=0, memstoreSizeMB=0, readRequestsCount=190, writeRequestsCount=19, compactionQueueSize=0, flushQueueSize=0, usedHeapMB=42, maxHeapMB=991, blockCacheSizeMB=2.07, blockCacheFreeMB=245.85, blockCacheCount=7, blockCacheHitCount=96, blockCacheMissCount=7, blockCacheEvictedCount=0, blockCacheHitRatio=93%, blockCacheHitCachingRatio=93%, hdfsBlocksLocalityIndex=0

As shown in the previous screenshot, it displays very important metrics of the region server. For example, the Compaction Queue size (**compactionQueueSize**), the Block Cache hit ratio (**blockCacheHitRatio**), and so on.

Using HBase Shell to manage tables

HBase Shell is a command-line tool shipped with HBase. It provides basic functions to manage tables, access data in HBase, and manage the cluster. HBase Shell has several groups of commands. The group for managing tables is called **Data Definition Language** (**DDL**). Using DDL group commands, you can create, drop, and change HBase tables. You can also disable/enable tables from HBase Shell.

Getting ready

Start your HBase cluster.

How to do it...

The following steps will show you how to use DDL commands to manage HBase tables:

1. Execute the following command from the client node, to start an HBase Shell prompt:

   ```
   hac@client1$ $HBASE_HOME/bin/hbase shell
   ```

2. Create a table(t1) with a single column family(f1) from HBase Shell, using the create command:

   ```
   hbase> create 't1', 'f1'
   ```

3. Show the table list by using the `list` command:

```
hbase> list
TABLE
hly_temp
t1
```

4. Show the table properties using the `describe` command:

```
hbase> describe 't1'
DESCRIPTION            ENABLED
 {NAME => 't1', FAMILIES => [{NAME => 'f1', BLOOMFILTER => 'NONE',
REPLICATION_SCOPE => '0', COMPRESSION => 'NONE' true, VERSIONS
=> '3', TTL => '2147483647', BLOCKSIZE => '65536', IN_MEMORY =>
'false', BLOCKCACHE => 'true'}]}
```

5. Disable the table by using the `disable` command:

```
hbase> disable 't1'
hbase> is_enabled 't1'
false
```

6. Change the table's properties by using the `alter` command. In the following code snippet, we change `f1` to have only one version, and we also add a new column family, `f2`:

```
hbase> alter 't1', {NAME => 'f1', VERSIONS => '1'}, {NAME => 'f2'}
```

7. Enable the table by using the `enable` command:

```
hbase> enable 't1'
hbase> is_enabled 't1'
true
```

8. Enter the following commands to disable the table again and drop it:

```
hbase> disable 't1'
hbase> drop 't1'
```

How it works...

HBase Shell is started by using the `hbase shell` command. This command uses the HBase configuration file (`hbase-site.xml`) for the client to find the cluster to connect to. After connecting to the cluster, it starts a prompt, waiting for commands. As shown in the following code, you can also use the `--config` option, which allows you to pass a different configuration for HBase Shell to use:

```
$ hbase --config <configuration_directory> shell
```

From steps 2 to 8, we created a table, showed its properties, disabled it, changed some of the table's properties, enabled it again, and finally dropped it.

By using the `create` command, we created a table `t1` with a single column family `f1` and all the default table properties. The `list` command is used to show all tables in the cluster. After the table is created, we can show its properties by using the `describe` command. The `describe` command also displays whether the table is enabled.

In order to disable a table, use the `disable` command. We can only change a table's properties after it is disabled. In step 5, we changed the `f1` column family to save only one version of its data. We also added a new column family, `f2`. All properties shown by the `describe` command can be changed using the `alter` command. We can use the `enable` command to enable a table in HBase. To drop a table in HBase, first disable it and then use the `drop` command to drop the disabled table.

There's more...

The most useful command might be the `help` command:

```
hbase> help
HBase Shell, version 0.92.1, r1298924, Fri Mar  9 16:58:34 UTC 2012
Type 'help "COMMAND"', (e.g. 'help "get"' -- the quotes are necessary)
for help on a specific command.
Commands are grouped. Type 'help "COMMAND_GROUP"', (e.g. 'help
"general"') for help on a command group.


COMMAND GROUPS:
  Group name: general
  Commands: status, version
```

A single `help` command prints all the available commands and general usage of HBase Shell. To show the detailed description of a command, pass its name to the `help` command. For example, `help 'create'` displays the detailed use of the `create` command:

```
hbase> help 'create'
Create table; pass table name, a dictionary of specifications per
column family, and optionally a dictionary of table configuration.
Dictionaries are described below in the GENERAL NOTES section.
Examples:

  hbase> create 't1', {NAME => 'f1', VERSIONS => 5}
  hbase> create 't1', {NAME => 'f1'}, {NAME => 'f2'}, {NAME => 'f3'}
```

```
hbase> # The above in shorthand would be the following:
hbase> create 't1', 'f1', 'f2', 'f3'
hbase> create 't1', {NAME => 'f1', VERSIONS => 1, TTL => 2592000,
BLOCKCACHE => true}
hbase> create 't1', 'f1', {SPLITS => ['10', '20', '30', '40']}
hbase> create 't1', 'f1', {SPLITS_FILE => 'splits.txt'}
```

Using HBase Shell to access data in HBase

HBase Shell provides **Data Manipulation Language** (**DML**) group commands to manipulate data in HBase. The DML group includes the commands count, delete, deleteall, get, get_counter, incr, put, scan, and truncate. Just as their names express, these commands provide basic access and update operations on data in HBase.

> HBase has a feature called counter, which is useful to build a metrics gathering system on HBase. Get_counter and incr are commands for counter operations.
>
> The count, scan, and truncate commands may take time to finish when running them on a huge amount of data in HBase.
>
> To count a big table, you should use the rowcounter MapReduce job, which is shipped with HBase. We will describe it in the *Row counter* recipe, later in this chapter.

Getting ready

Start your HBase cluster, connect to the cluster from your client, and create a table called t1, if it does not exist.

How to do it...

The following steps are demonstrations of how to use DML commands for accessing data in HBase:

1. Insert the following data into the table by using the put command:
    ```
    hbase> put 't1', 'row1', 'f1:c1', 'value1'
    hbase> put 't1', 'row1', 'f1:c2', 'value2'
    hbase> put 't1', 'row2', 'f1:c1', 'value3'
    ```

2. Get a row count of the table by running the count command:
    ```
    hbase> count 't1'
    2 row(s) in 0.0160 seconds
    ```

3. Scan the data using the `scan` command. Don't forget to specify the `LIMIT` property when invoking `scan` on a table with a huge amount of rows:

```
hbase> scan 't1', {LIMIT => 10}
ROW          COLUMN+CELL
 row1         column=f1:c1, timestamp=1324100932695, value=value1
 row1         column=f1:c2, timestamp=1324101005928, value=value2
 row2         column=f1:c1, timestamp=1324101012054, value=value3
2 row(s) in 0.0800 seconds
```

4. Get a specified row by using the `get` command:

```
hbase> get 't1', 'row1'
COLUMN               CELL
 f1:c1                 timestamp=1324100932695, value=value1
 f1:c2                 timestamp=1324101005928, value=value2
2 row(s) in 0.0100 seconds
```

5. Delete a specified cell by using the `delete` command:

```
hbase> delete 't1', 'row1', 'f1:c1'
```

6. Execute the `get` command again; you will see that the `f1:c1` cell has been deleted from the row:

```
hbase> get 't1', 'row1'
COLUMN               CELL
 f1:c2                 timestamp=1324101005928, value=value2
1 row(s) in 0.0150 seconds
```

7. Delete all the cells in a given row using the `deleteall` command:

```
hbase> deleteall 't1', 'row1'
```

8. Execute the `get` command again; you will see that the entire `row1` row has been deleted from the table:

```
hbase> get 't1', 'row1'
COLUMN               CELL
0 row(s) in 0.0090 seconds
```

9. Increase a counter's (`row1:f1:c1`) value by 1 using the `incr` command:

```
hbase> incr 't1', 'row1', 'f1:c1', 1
COUNTER VALUE = 1
```

10. Increase the counter again, by 10:

```
hbase> incr 't1', 'row1', 'f1:c1', 10
COUNTER VALUE = 11
```

11. Get the new counter value by using the `get_counter` command:

```
hbase> get_counter 't1', 'row1', 'f1:c1'
COUNTER VALUE = 11
```

12. Truncate the table by running the `truncate` command:

```
hbase> truncate 't1'
Truncating 't1' table (it may take a while):
 - Disabling table...
 - Dropping table...
 - Creating table...
0 row(s) in 4.5700 seconds
```

How it works...

The `put` command takes the table name (`t1`), row key (`row1`), column family and qualifier (`f1:c1`), value to put (`value1`), and optionally, the timestamp as its arguments. The `:` in `f1:c1` works as a delimiter between column family (`f1`) and qualifier (`c1`). Use single quotes around the value if you want HBase Shell to treat it as a string value; otherwise, HBase Shell will try to guess the data type of the value you put. For example, if you type the following command:

```
hbase> put 't1', 'r1', 'f1:c1', 0000
```

You will have a numeric value of `0` put in the table:

```
hbase> get 't1', 'r1'
COLUMN                    CELL
 f1:c1                        timestamp=1324103322181, value=0
```

But when you enter the following command:

```
hbase> put 't1', 'r1', 'f1:c1', '0000'
```

You will get a string of `0000` in the table:

```
hbase> get 't1', 'r1'
COLUMN                    CELL
 f1:c1                        timestamp=1324103492444, value=0000
```

The `count` command counts the number of rows in a table. It counts an HBase table on row basis and shows the row number on its output. That's why it returned two rows in step 2, even though we put three cells into the table in step 1. This command may take a while to finish, when counting a large amount of data in HBase. In this case, a better option is to use the Row Counter utility provided by HBase, which will run a MapReduce job on HBase for counting it.

The `scan` command scans a table. You can specify the row range, columns to include, time range, and filter for the scanning. There is also an additional option—`CACHE_BLOCKS`—for advanced users, which specifies whether block caching of the scanner is on or off. The `help` command has a very detailed explanation of the usage of this command; type `help 'scan'` for more information. An alternative way of scanning an HBase table is to use Hive over HBase; it is the easier option, for scanning a table with complex conditions.

The `get` command is very straightforward; you must give the exact row key you want, to get to the command. While you can optionally specify the range of columns, timestamp, or versions you want to include in the result, you can also restrict the output length by specifying the `MAXLENGTH` parameter.

The `delete` command marks a cell as deleted, while the `deleteall` command deletes all the cells in a given row.

HBase counters are distributed, atomic counters, which are stored as the value of a specified cell. At specified table/row/column coordinates, use the `incr` command to increase a counter, and use the `get_counter` command to get the counter value.

The `truncate` command acts as a sequence for disabling, dropping, and recreating a table.

See also

In this chapter:

- *Row counter*
- *Hive on HBase—querying HBase using a SQL-like language*

Using HBase Shell to manage the cluster

There are a bunch of HBase Shell commands for managing the cluster. These commands belong to the tool's group.

Warning

Many of these commands are for advanced users only, as their misuse can cause unexpected damages to an HBase installation.

The tool's group commands provide an interface to manage HBase regions manually. Their features include:

- ▶ Region deployment
- ▶ Region splitting
- ▶ Cluster balancing
- ▶ Region flushing and compaction

Although HBase does all these operations automatically, by default, there are situations wherein you may want to balance your region server's load manually. This is especially true when the default, balancing algorithm does not work well for your data access pattern.

In this recipe, we will describe how to manually flush, compact, split, balance, and move HBase regions.

Getting ready

Start your HBase cluster, create a table, and put some data into it. We will use the `hly_temp` table we created in *Chapter 2, Data Migration*, for demonstration purposes. We assume that the table you are using already has several regions in it. As shown in the following screenshot, you can view the table's region list by clicking the table's link shown on your HBase web UI:

Table Regions

Name	Region Server
hly_temp,,1324174482248.e3d9b9952973964f3d8e61e191924698.	ip-10-166-211-64.us-west-1.comput
hly_temp,USW000138830523,1324174482248.a91ee5cc7c67881fa54a38b61eae6075.	ip-10-168-75-28.us-west-1.compute
hly_temp,USW000149221223,1324096201466.fff98c00bff7ac68be9e795716e46880.	ip-10-168-75-28.us-west-1.compute

How to do it...

We will start by manually flushing and compacting regions, and then split the regions manually. Finally, we will rebalance these regions to make them well-balanced within the cluster.

1. Flush all regions in the table using the `flush` command:

```
hbase> flush 'hly_temp'
```

2. You can also flush an individual region by passing the region name to the `flush` command:

```
hbase> flush 'hly_temp,,1324174482248.
e3d9b9952973964f3d8e61e191924698.'
```

You can find the region's name under the **Table Regions** section of the table's administration page:

Table Regions

Name	Region Server
hly_temp,,1324174482248.e3d9b9952973964f3d8e61e191924698.	ip-10-166-211-64.us-west-1.comput
hly_temp,USW000138830523,1324174482248.a91ee5cc7c67881fa54a38b61eae6075.	ip-10-168-75-28.us-west-1.compute
hly_temp,USW000149221223,1324096201466.fff98c00bff7ac68be9e795716e46880.	ip-10-168-75-28.us-west-1.compute

3. Compact all the regions in a table by running the `compact` command:

```
hbase> compact 'hly_temp'
```

4. Run a major compaction on a table by running the `major_compact` command:

```
hbase> major_compact 'hly_temp'
```

5. Split a region in a table by running the `split` command:

```
hbase> split 'hly_temp,,1324174482248.
e3d9b9952973964f3d8e61e191924698.'
```

In the table's administration page, you will find that the region has been split into two regions, so the total region count becomes four:

Table Regions

Name	Region Server	Start Key	End Key
hly_temp,1324196693253.9e6dd810550443bb488c871728d5dee0.	ip-10-166-211-64.us-west-1.compute.internal:60030		USW000128350706
hly_temp,USW000128350706,1324196693253.0d1604971684462a2860d43e2715558d.	ip-10-166-211-64.us-west-1.compute.internal:60030	USW000128350706	USW000138830523
hly_temp,USW000138830523,1324174482248.a91ee5cc7c67881fa54a38b61eae6075.	ip-10-168-75-28.us-west-1.compute.internal:60030	USW000138830523	USW000149221223
hly_temp,USW000149221223,1324096201466.fff98c00bff7ac68be9e795716e46880.	ip-10-168-75-28.us-west-1.compute.internal:60030	USW000149221223	

6. Use the `balance_switch` command to enable the balancer:

```
hbase> balance_switch true
false
```

The output (`false`) is the previous balancer state.

7. Balance the load of the cluster by using the `balancer` command:

   hbase> balancer

   true

   The output `true` indicates that a balancing call has been triggered successfully. It will run in the background on the master server.

8. Move a region to a specific region server by using the `move` command:

   hbase> move 'e3d9b9952973964f3d8e61e191924698', 'ip-10-168-75-28.
   us-west-1.compute.internal:60030:1324190304563'

How it works...

An HBase data edit will first be written to the Write Ahead Log (WAL) and then to the `MemStore` of a region server. The edits will not be flushed to disk until the size of `MemStore` has reached a threshold. The threshold, by default, is 128 MB, which is configured by the `hbase.hregion.memstore.flush.size` property in `hbase-site.xml`. The `flush` command flushes these pending records to disk synchronously. It takes either a table name, or a region name as its parameter. A region name consists of its table name, region start row key, region server start code, and a hash-encoded value of itself. You can find region names under the **Table Regions** section of the table's administration page.

Just like the `flush` command, if instead of a table name, a region name is passed to both `compact` and `major_compact` commands, the compaction will be performed on the specified region only. The `compact` and `major_compact` commands are asynchronous. Executing these commands queues the tables or regions for compaction, which will be executed in the background by the server hosting the specified region, or all regions of the table. You might want to execute major compaction manually, only at a low load time. This is because lots of disk IO and network traffic might happen during the compaction, and it might take a long time to complete.

The `split` command allows you to split a specific region or all regions in a table, if the table name is given to the command. When running HBase with very high write load, we recommend you turn off HBase's automatic region split feature, precreate regions using your own algorithm, and use the `split` command to split a specific region if it becomes too large. We will cover how to presplit tables in *Chapter 9, Advanced Configurations and Tuning*.

Our cluster might become unbalanced if data keeps growing. In order to balance the cluster, HBase runs its balancing functionality periodically in the background. On the other hand, you can also explicitly enable the balancer by running the `balance_switch` command, and then trigger a balancing operation by using the `balancer` command. It is also useful to stop the balancer when you need to stop a region server for maintenance.

The following screenshot shows the administration page of our cluster, before balancing was run in step 7. As you can see, the second region server holds almost all the regions (five of all the six regions) in the cluster, which means most of the cluster load will go to that server:

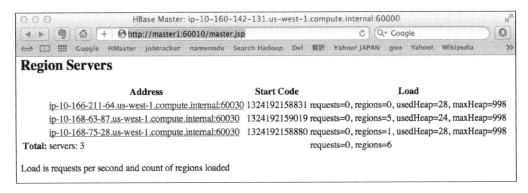

After the balancing operation was executed, our cluster became much more balanced as regions were distributed to all the region servers in the cluster:

The default, load-balancing algorithm just simply causes each region server to take a large number of regions deployed on it. If this algorithm does not fit your data access pattern, you can manually move a region to a specific server by using the `move` command. The `move` command takes an encoded region name and the target server name as its parameters. An encoded region name is the hash code suffix of a region name. The format of a target server name is `hostname:port:start-code`. A `move` call will close the region from its originally deployed server, open it on the target server, and then finally update the record of the region in the `.META.` system table.

See also

▸ *Precreating regions using your own algorithm* recipe, in *Chapter 9, Advanced Configurations and Tuning*

Executing Java methods from HBase Shell

HBase Shell is written in JRuby. As JRuby runs within **Java Virtual Machine** (**JVM**), it is very easy to execute Java methods from HBase Shell. HBase ships with many Java utility classes; the ability to execute Java methods from HBase Shell makes it possible to import and use these utilities directly from HBase Shell.

We will demonstrate two examples of how to call Java method from HBase Shell, in this recipe. The first one converts the timestamp of the HBase Shell output into a readable date format. The second one imports an HBase filter class, and performs the filtering on the scanner of the scan command.

Getting ready

Start your HBase cluster, create a table, and put some data into it. We will use the hly_temp table we created in *Chapter 2*, for demonstration purposes.

Connect to your cluster via HBase Shell, before you start.

How to do it...

To convert the timestamp of an HBase Shell output into a readable date format:

1. Enter the following command to get a row from HBase:

```
hbase> get 'hly_temp', 'AQW000617050101', 'n:'
COLUMN                    CELL          n:v01
timestamp=1323026325955, value=808C      n:v02
timestamp=1323026325955, value=806C      n:v03
timestamp=1323026325955, value=803C
...
```

2. Import the Java Date class to convert the output of timestamp, and then create an instance of the Date class using the timestamp of the get command:

```
hbase> import java.util.Date
=> Java::JavaUtil::Date
hbase> Date.new(1323026325955).toString()
=> "Mon Dec 05 04:18:45 JST 2011"
```

3. To use the HBase filter on a scan, import the following classes into HBase Shell:

```
hbase> import org.apache.hadoop.hbase.util.Bytes
=> Java::OrgApacheHadoopHbaseUtil::Bytes
hbase> import org.apache.hadoop.hbase.filter.PrefixFilter
=> Java::OrgApacheHadoopHbaseFilter::PrefixFilter
```

4. Execute the `scan` command with the imported `PrefixFilter` class:

```
hbase> scan 'hly_temp', {FILTER => PrefixFilter.new
    (Bytes.toBytes('AQW00061705010')), COLUMN => 'n:'}
ROW                         COLUMN+CELLAQW000617050101
column=n:v01,
  timestamp=1323026325955, value=808CAQW000617050101
column=n:v02,
  timestamp=1323026325955, value=806CAQW000617050101
column=n:v03,
  timestamp=1323026325955, value=803C


...


AQW000617050109              column=n:v24,
  timestamp=1323026325955, value=811C

9 row(s) in 0.1570 seconds
```

How it works...

As you can see from the output of step 1, the displayed timestamp is not human-friendly to read. We want to convert it to a normal date format.

The conversion can be easily done by using the `java.util.Date` class. In step 2, we import it into our shell session by using the `import` command. The `import` command is a basic JRuby feature, and it is not HBase-specific. After the `Date` class is imported, we create an instance of the class using the timestamp we want to convert. Finally, we call its `toString()` method to convert and print the timestamp to a normal date format.

Steps 3 and 4 show us how to import and use HBase utilities in HBase Shell. First, we import the `org.apache.hadoop.hbase.util.Bytes` class, which is a utility class, to convert other data types from/into byte array. This class is very useful, because all data in HBase is stored as byte arrays. We also imported the `org.apache.hadoop.hbase.filter.PrefixFilter` class in step 3. This class is a filtering class. Using this class with the `scan` command makes it only pass the data that has a specific row key prefix to the client. The prefix is specified by passing its byte array representation to the constructor of the `PrefixFilter` class. That's exactly what we did in step 4. We specified the prefix `AQW00061705010`, converted it to a byte array using the `Bytes` class, created an instance of the `PrefixFilter` class using the converted byte array, and then set it as the filter of the `scan` command. As you can see from the output, the filter works well for the `scan` command, as just nine rows (`AQW000617050101` to `AQW000617050109`) were returned to the client.

There's more...

There are many other useful Java classes shipped with HBase. The following link lists the Java APIs of HBase:

```
http://hbase.apache.org/apidocs/index.html
```

Have a glance at the following packages of HBase API:

- `org.apache.hadoop.hbase.util`
- `org.apache.hadoop.hbase.client`
- `org.apache.hadoop.hbase.filter`
- `org.apache.hadoop.hbase.mapreduce`

Row counter

The `count` command in HBase Shell is a straightforward way to count the row numbers on an HBase table. However, running the `count` command on a table with a huge amount of data might take a long time to complete. A better approach for this case is to use the `RowCounter` class. This class will kick a MapReduce job to count the row number on a table, which is much more efficient than the `count` command.

We will describe the usage of `RowCounter` in this recipe.

Getting ready

Make sure your Hadoop and HBase clusters are running. MapReduce is also required; if it is not running, start it by using the following command on your JobTracker server:

hadoop@master1$ $HADOOP_HOME/bin/start-mapred.sh

Log in to your HBase client node.

How to do it...

To run a row counter MapReduce job on the `hly_temp` table, follow these steps:

1. Add a ZooKeeper JAR file to the Hadoop class path on your client node:

    hadoop@client1$ vi $HADOOP_HOME/conf/hadoop-env.sh

    ```
    HBASE_HOME=/usr/local/hbase/current
    export HADOOP_CLASSPATH=$HADOOP_CLASSPATH:
      $HBASE_HOME/lib/zookeeper-3.4.3.jar:
      $HBASE_HOME/lib/guava-r09.jar
    ```

2. Execute the `rowcounter` command from your client:

   ```
   hac@client1$ $HADOOP_HOME/bin/hadoop jar
     $HBASE_HOME/hbase-0.92.1.jar rowcounter hly_temp
   ```

   You will get the following output:

```
● ○ ○                          ⬜ hbase — ssh — 114×35
11/12/22 07:00:15 INFO mapred.JobClient: Running job: job_201112220648_0002
11/12/22 07:00:16 INFO mapred.JobClient:  map 0% reduce 0%
11/12/22 07:00:54 INFO mapred.JobClient:  map 25% reduce 0%
11/12/22 07:01:03 INFO mapred.JobClient:  map 50% reduce 0%
11/12/22 07:01:15 INFO mapred.JobClient:  map 75% reduce 0%
11/12/22 07:01:27 INFO mapred.JobClient:  map 100% reduce 0%
11/12/22 07:01:35 INFO mapred.JobClient: Job complete: job_201112220648_0002
11/12/22 07:01:35 INFO mapred.JobClient: Counters: 20
11/12/22 07:01:35 INFO mapred.JobClient:   Job Counters
11/12/22 07:01:35 INFO mapred.JobClient:     SLOTS_MILLIS_MAPS=151225
11/12/22 07:01:35 INFO mapred.JobClient:     Total time spent by all reduces waiting after reserving slots (ms)=0
11/12/22 07:01:35 INFO mapred.JobClient:     Total time spent by all maps waiting after reserving slots (ms)=0
11/12/22 07:01:35 INFO mapred.JobClient:     Rack-local map tasks=2
11/12/22 07:01:35 INFO mapred.JobClient:     Launched map tasks=5
11/12/22 07:01:35 INFO mapred.JobClient:     Data-local map tasks=3
11/12/22 07:01:35 INFO mapred.JobClient:     SLOTS_MILLIS_REDUCES=0
11/12/22 07:01:35 INFO mapred.JobClient:   File Output Format Counters
11/12/22 07:01:35 INFO mapred.JobClient:     Bytes Written=0
11/12/22 07:01:35 INFO mapred.JobClient:   org.apache.hadoop.hbase.mapreduce.RowCounter$RowCounterMapper$Counters
11/12/22 07:01:35 INFO mapred.JobClient:     ROWS=95630
11/12/22 07:01:35 INFO mapred.JobClient:   FileSystemCounters
11/12/22 07:01:35 INFO mapred.JobClient:     HDFS_BYTES_READ=487
11/12/22 07:01:35 INFO mapred.JobClient:     FILE_BYTES_WRITTEN=118132
11/12/22 07:01:35 INFO mapred.JobClient:   File Input Format Counters
11/12/22 07:01:35 INFO mapred.JobClient:     Bytes Read=0
11/12/22 07:01:35 INFO mapred.JobClient:   Map-Reduce Framework
11/12/22 07:01:35 INFO mapred.JobClient:     Map input records=95630
11/12/22 07:01:35 INFO mapred.JobClient:     Physical memory (bytes) snapshot=152829952
11/12/22 07:01:35 INFO mapred.JobClient:     Spilled Records=0
11/12/22 07:01:35 INFO mapred.JobClient:     CPU time spent (ms)=23730
11/12/22 07:01:35 INFO mapred.JobClient:     Total committed heap usage (bytes)=65011712
11/12/22 07:01:35 INFO mapred.JobClient:     Virtual memory (bytes) snapshot=1501253632
11/12/22 07:01:35 INFO mapred.JobClient:     Map output records=0
11/12/22 07:01:35 INFO mapred.JobClient:     SPLIT_RAW_BYTES=487
hac@client1 ~$
```

3. As you can see from one of the counters of the output, we have 95,630 rows in the `hly_temp` table:

   ```
   11/12/22 07:14:30 INFO mapred.JobClient:
     org.apache.hadoop.hbase.mapreduce.RowCounter
   $RowCounterMapper$Counters
   ```

   ```
   11/12/22 07:14:30 INFO mapred.JobClient:      ROWS=95630
   ```

How it works...

When we run a JAR file by using the `hadoop jar` command, the dependencies of the JAR file must be included in Hadoop's class path. That's exactly what we did in step 1.

In step 2, we run `hbase-0.92.1.jar` using the `hadoop jar` command. Parameters after the name of the JAR file are passed to the main class of the JAR file. To run a row counter on the `hly_temp` table, we pass a fix string of `rowcounter` and the table name to the command. Specifying `rowcounter` will make Hadoop execute the `RowCounter` class from `hbase-0.92.1.jar`. The `RowCounter` class will take `hly_temp` as its parameter and finally kick the MapReduce job for us. You can also specify which column or column family to count, by passing the space separated column (family) names after the table name.

Besides row counter, there are other MapReduce jobs you can execute from the command line. Type the following for details:

```
$HADOOP_HOME/bin/hadoop jar $HBASE_HOME/hbase-0.92.1.jar
An example program must be given as the first argument.
Valid program names are:
  CellCounter: Count cells in HBase table
  completebulkload: Complete a bulk data load.
  copytable: Export a table from local cluster to peer cluster
  export: Write table data to HDFS.
  import: Import data written by Export.
  importtsv: Import data in TSV format.
  rowcounter: Count rows in HBase table
  verifyrep: Compare the data from tables in two different clusters.
WARNING: It doesn't work for incrementColumnValues'd cells since the
timestamp is changed after being appended to the log.
```

There's more...

When running `RowCounter` against large datasets, we recommend you to tune the scanner's caching setting on your client, as shown in the following snippet:

```
hac@client1$ vi $HBASE_HOME/conf/hbase-site.xml
    <property>
      <name>hbase.client.scanner.caching</name>
      <value>1000</value>
    </property>
```

This makes HBase fetch `1000` rows for each next call on the scanner. By default, HBase fetches `1` row per next call. Setting it to a higher value increases the scanner's speed, but consumes more memory.

WAL tool—manually splitting and dumping WALs

An HBase edit will first be written to a region server's Write Ahead Log (WAL). After the log is written successfully, `MemStore` of the region server will be updated. As WAL is a sequence file on HDFS, it will be automatically replicated to the two other DataNode servers by default, so that a single region server crash will not cause a loss of the data stored on it.

As WAL is shared by all regions deployed on the region server, the WAL needs to first be split so that it can be replayed on each relative region, in order to recover from a region server crash. HBase handles region server failover automatically by using this algorithm.

HBase has a WAL tool providing manual WAL splitting and dumping facilities. We will describe how to use this tool in this recipe.

Getting ready

We will need to put some data into an HBase table to have HBase generate WAL files for our demonstration. Again, we will use the `hly_temp` table in this recipe. We will put the following data into the `hly_temp` table using the HBase Shell `Put` command:

```
hbase> put 'hly_temp', 'AQW000617050101', 't:v25', 'wal tool demo'
hbase> put 'hly_temp', 'AQW000617050101', 't:v26', 'wal tool demo2'
hbase> put 'hly_temp', 'AQW000617050101', 't:v27', 'wal tool demo3'
hbase> delete 'hly_temp', 'AQW000617050101', 't:v27'
```

These commands will have HBase add four entries to its WAL on HDFS. Also, you will need to find out which region holds the row we put in the previous commands, and which region server holds that region. To do it, open your table's administration page. In the **Table Regions** section, you will find a **Start Key** and an **End Key** for each region. As the data in HBase is sorted by row key, in lexicographical order, a row belongs to the region that has the closest start/end key of the row key.

The following table is transferred from the **Table Regions** section of our HBase web UI. As you can see, the row key we put in the previous code (`AQW000617050101`) is smaller than the end key (`USW000128350706`) of the first region in the lexicographical order; the first region is the one which holds the row we put in the previous command:

Region Name	Region Server	Start Key	End Key
hly_temp,,1324196693.	slave1:60030		USW000128350706
hly_temp,USW000128.	slave2:60030	USW000128350706	USW000138830523
hly_temp,USW000138.	slave1:60030	USW000138830523	USW000149221223
hly_temp,USW000149.	slave1:60030	USW000149221223	

How to do it...

Follow these instructions to manually dump and split WAL logs:

1. Use either `hadoop fs` or the HDFS administration page to locate the full path of the WAL file. The WAL file of our previous `put` operations will be generated under the following directory on HDFS:

   `${hbase.rootdir}/.logs/target_region_server,port,start_code`

2. Execute the WAL tool with the dump option to dump the WAL file:

   ```
   $ $HBASE_HOME/bin/hbase org.apache.hadoop.hbase.regionserver.wal.
   HLog
     --dump /hbase/.logs/
     ip-10-168-151-193.us-west-1.compute.
     internal,60020,1324689025404/
     ip-10-168-151-193.us-west-1.compute.
     internal%3A60020.1324689026748
     -p -w 'AQW000617050101'
   ```

Sequence 96649 from region 9e6dd810550443bb488c871728d5dee0 in table hly_temp

   Action:

     row: AQW000617050101

     column: t:v25

     at time: Sat Dec 24 10:21:59 JST 2011

     value: wal tool demo

Sequence 96650 from region 9e6dd810550443bb488c871728d5dee0 in table hly_temp

   Action:

     row: AQW000617050101

     column: t:v26

     at time: Sat Dec 24 10:22:09 JST 2011

     value: wal tool demo2

Sequence 96651 from region 9e6dd810550443bb488c871728d5dee0 in table hly_temp

   Action:

     row: AQW000617050101

     column: t:v27

     at time: Sat Dec 24 10:22:18 JST 2011

     value: wal tool demo3

Sequence 96652 from region 9e6dd810550443bb488c871728d5dee0 in table hly_temp

```
Action:
    row: AQW000617050101
    column: t:v27
    at time: Sat Dec 24 10:22:27 JST 2011
    value:
```

3. To manually split the WAL files, switch to the user who started Hadoop and HBase; in our case it is the `hadoop` user:

   `hac@client1$ sudo su hadoop`

4. Execute the WAL tool with the split option to split the WAL files:

   ```
   hadoop@client1$ $HBASE_HOME/bin/hbase org.apache.hadoop.hbase.
   regionserver.wal.HLog
       --split hdfs://master1:8020/hbase/.logs/ip-10-160-51-22.us-
       west-1.compute.internal,60020,1324601160791

   ...

   11/12/24 10:35:43 INFO wal.HLogSplitter: hlog file splitting
   completed in 1700 ms for hdfs://master1:8020/hbase/.logs/ip-10-
   168-151-193.us-west-1.compute.internal,60020,1324689025404
   ```

 Do *not* manually split WAL if the hosting region server is online, as splitting WAL is only for closing a region server, or for recovery from a region server crash.

How it works...

HBase edits are represented by the `org.apache.hadoop.hbase.KeyValue` class internally. When a region server receives an edit, it will append it (a `KeyValue` instance) to its WAL files before actually updating its `MemStore` data. If the size of `MemStore` reaches the threshold (128MB by default), edits will be persisted onto HDFS by flushing them to the HFile files.

The WAL files are stored under the `${hbase.rootdir}/.logs/region_server,` `port,start_code` directory on HDFS. After locating the full path of the WAL file in step 1, we execute the `org.apache.hadoop.hbase.regionserver.wal.HLog` class from the `hbase` command in step 2. This class provides two functions—manually dumping and splitting WAL files. To dump a WAL file, pass the `--dump` option along with the full path of the file to be dumped to `HLog`. The third parameter `-p`, tells `HLog` to also print the value of the edit. The last parameter, `-w 'AQW000617050101'`, is a filter to only output the associate entries of row AQW000617050101.

You can also dump the JSON format WAL file by passing `-j` to the command. Here is a sample JSON output of a WAL dump:

```
[{"region":"9e6dd810550443bb488c871728d5dee0",
  "sequence":96649,"table":"hly_temp",
  "actions":[{"timestamp":1324689719111,"family":"t",
  "qualifier":"v25","row":"AQW000617050101"}]},
  {"region":"9e6dd810550443bb488c871728d5dee0",
  "sequence":96650,"table":"hly_temp",
  "actions":[{"timestamp":1324689729381,"family":"t","
  qualifier":"v26","row":"AQW000617050101"}]},
...]
```

When passing the `--dump` option to the `HLog` class, it internally invokes the `HLogPrettyPrinter` class to dump the WAL file. There are also options to filter by region or sequence number. Pass `-h` to the `HLogPrettyPrinter` class for help:

```
$hbase org.apache.hadoop.hbase.regionserver.wal.HLogPrettyPrinter
  -h
usage: HLog <filename...> [-h] [-j]
  [-p] [-r <arg>] [-s <arg>] [-w <arg>]
  -h,--help              Output help message
  -j,--json              Output JSON
  -p,--printvals         Print values
  -r,--region <arg>      Region to filter by. Pass region name;
  e.g. '.META.,,1'
  -s,--sequence <arg>    Sequence to filter by. Pass sequence number.
  -w,--row <arg>         Row to filter by. Pass row name.
```

The dump output has information about the table name, region, row, column, timestamp, and value of the edit. A delete operation has a value of `Null`. There's also a sequence number for each entry of WAL, which is used to keep a sequential order of edits. The highest sequence number of edits, which have been persisted, are written to a meta field of each HBase storage file (HFile).

As write permission under the HBase installation directory is required to manually split WAL files, we switched to the user who started HBase in step 3. Passing `--split` to `HLog` makes it kick a splitting task over a specific WAL directory. We must pass the directory of WAL files to the split command, as all WAL files have to be split and replayed, to recovery from a region server crash. Different from the `dump` command, you need to specify the HDFS name (`hdfs://master1:8020` in our case) for the target WAL directory too.

All the edits that have been recorded in the WAL files but not yet been persisted, will be replayed during the splitting. HFile files containing the edits will be generated at proper directories after the splitting. The following is the HFile file generated by our WAL splitting:

Contents of directory /hbase/hly_temp/9e6dd810550443bb488c871728d5dee0/t

Goto : /hbase/hly_temp/9e6 [go]

Go to parent directory

Name	Type	Size	Replication	Block Size	Modification Time	Permission	Owner	Group
5229337595615563418	file	0.47 KB	2	64 MB	2011-12-24 10:36	rw-r--r--	hadoop	supergroup
7455377084692262380	file	2.05 MB	2	64 MB	2011-12-24 10:16	rw-r--r--	hadoop	supergroup

You can use the HFile tool to view the content of the generated file:

```
$ $HBASE_HOME/bin/hbase org.apache.hadoop.hbase.io.hfile.HFile -p -f /
hbase/hly_temp/9e6dd810550443bb488c871728d5dee0/t/5229337595615563418
K: AQW000617050101/t:v25/1324689719111/Put/vlen=13 V: wal tool demo
K: AQW000617050101/t:v26/1324689729381/Put/vlen=14 V: wal tool demo2
K: AQW000617050101/t:v27/1324689747967/DeleteColumn/vlen=0 V:
K: AQW000617050101/t:v27/1324689738230/Put/vlen=14 V: wal tool demo3
Scanned kv count -> 4
```

The content is exactly the same as what was put in the _Getting ready_ section of this recipe. All edits are replayed successfully; no data is lost during the splitting.

WAL splitting is used when shutting down a region server, or to recover log edits after a region server goes down uncleanly. For almost all situations, you won't need to split WAL manually, as the master server will automatically start the splitting if a region server crashes. For a case where you have many nodes going down uncleanly, you could use this manually splitting option in parallel on many machines, to speed up the recovery. As of HBase 0.92, there is a new feature called Distributed Log Splitting, with which this WAL splitting is automatically distributed.

See also

▶ The _HFile tool—viewing textualized HFile content_ recipe, in this chapter.

HFile tool—viewing textualized HFile content

HFile is the internal file format for HBase to store its data. These are the first two lines of the description of HFile from its source code:

> File format for hbase.

> A file of sorted key/value pairs. Both keys and values are byte arrays.

We don't need to know the details of HFile for our administration tasks. However, by using the HFile tool, we can get some useful information from HFile.

The HFile tool provides the facility to view a textualized version of HFile content.

We can also get the metadata of an HFile file by using this tool. Some metadata, such as entry count and average Key/Value size, are important indicators of performance tuning.

We will describe how to use an HFile tool to show textualized content and metadata of HFile files.

Getting ready

Log in to your HBase client node.

Pick a region name or HFile file path to be viewed. A region name can be found in the **Table Regions** section of your HBase web UI. HFile files are stored under the ${hbase.rootdir}/table_name/region_name/column_family directory on HDFS.

We will use the hly_temp table in this recipe, for demonstration purposes.

How to do it...

Follow these instructions to view textualized content or metadata of HFile files:

1. Type the following to show the textualized Key/Value content of an HFile file:

```
$ $HBASE_HOME/bin/hbase org.apache.hadoop.hbase.io.hfile.
HFile -p -f /hbase/hly_temp/0d1604971684462a2860d43e2715558d
/n/1742023046455748097
K: USW000128350706/n:v01/1323026325955/Put/vlen=4 V: 773S
K: USW000128350706/n:v02/1323026325955/Put/vlen=4 V: 769S
K: USW000128350706/n:v03/1323026325955/Put/vlen=4 V: 764S
...
```

2. To show the metadata of an HFile file, use the `-m` option in the HFile tool:

```
$ $HBASE_HOME/bin/hbase org.apache.hadoop.hbase.io.hfile.
HFile -m -f /hbase/hly_temp/0d1604971684462a2860d43e2715558d
/n/1742023046455748097

Block index size as per heapsize: 12240

reader=/hbase/hly_temp/0d1604971684462a2860d43e2715558d
/n/1742023046455748097, compression=lzo, inMemory=false,
firstKey=USW000128350706/n:v01/1323026325955/Put,
lastKey=USW000138830522/n:v24/1323026325955/Put, avgKeyLen=31,
avgValueLen=4, entries=288024, length=2379789

fileinfoOffset=2371102, dataIndexOffset=2371361,
dataIndexCount=190, metaIndexOffset=0, metaIndexCount=0,
totalBytes=12387203, entryCount=288024, version=1

Fileinfo:

MAJOR_COMPACTION_KEY = \x00

MAX_SEQ_ID_KEY = 96573

TIMERANGE = 1323026325955....1323026325955

hfile.AVG_KEY_LEN = 31

hfile.AVG_VALUE_LEN = 4

hfile.COMPARATOR = org.apache.hadoop.hbase.KeyValue$KeyComparator

hfile.LASTKEY = \x00\x0FUSW000138830522\x01nv24\x00\x00\x014\x0A\
x83\xA1\xC3\x04

Could not get bloom data from meta block
```

3. Get the total entry count of a specific region, with the following command:

```
hbase org.apache.hadoop.hbase.io.hfile.HFile -m -r hly_temp,,13241
96693253.9e6dd810550443bb488c871728d5dee0. | grep entries
```

You will get the following output:

```
reader=hdfs://master1:8020/hbase/hly_temp/9e6dd810550443bb488c871728d5dee0/n/7691199011786369573, compression=
lzo, inMemory=false, firstKey=AQW000617050101/n:v01/1323026325955/Put, lastKey=USW000128350705/n:v24/1323026632
5955/Put, avgKeyLen=31, avgValueLen=4, entries=284790, length=2340317
reader=hdfs://master1:8020/hbase/hly_temp/9e6dd810550443bb488c871728d5dee0/q/6736124625288498468, compression=
lzo, inMemory=false, firstKey=AQW000617050101/q:v01/1322976927553/Put, lastKey=USW000128350705/q:v24/132297692
7553/Put, avgKeyLen=31, avgValueLen=4, entries=284784, length=2130165
reader=hdfs://master1:8020/hbase/hly_temp/9e6dd810550443bb488c871728d5dee0/t/2527659765575729938, compression=
lzo, inMemory=false, firstKey=AQW000617050101/t:25/1324601918502/Put, lastKey=USW000128350705/t:v24/1322960737
598/Put, avgKeyLen=30, avgValueLen=4, entries=284790, length=2145548
```

The total entry count of the region is the sum of entries from the output.

How it works...

The HFile format is implemented with `org.apache.hadoop.hbase.io.hfile.HFile`. We can also use this class as a tool for the HFile files.

In step 1, we simply show the textualized content of an HFile file. The file path is specified by the `-f` option. The `-p` flag tells the command to include the content of the Key/Value pair to its output as well. The HFile tool simply scans all the blocks of the specific HFile file, and prints all Key/Value entries to its output.

 Note that the deleted cell also has an entry in the HFile file until a major compaction is executed on that region.

In step 2, we pass the `-m` flag to the HFile tool to display the metadata of a specified HFile file. As you can see from the output, metadata has very useful information about the HFile file. This information includes the block index size, average Key/Value length, entry count, and so on.

A typical use case is to get the total entry count of each region in a table, so that we are able to know whether our data is well-balanced among all regions in the table. Step 3 shows how to achieve this purpose. Passing a region name with the `-r` option to the HFile tool makes it perform tasks on each HFile file belonging to the region. Collaborated with the `-m` flag, it displays the metadata for each HFile file in the region. Having displayed the metadata for each HFile file, we can simply sum the output entry count to get a total Key/Value entry count for that region.

There's more...

There are other useful options of the HFile tool. Type the following command to see its usage:

```
$ ${HBASE_HOME}/bin/hbase org.apache.hadoop.hbase.io.hfile.HFile
```

HBase hbck—checking the consistency of an HBase cluster

HBase provides the `hbck` command to check for various inconsistencies. The name `hbck` comes from the HDFS `fsck` command, which is the tool to check HDFS for inconsistencies. The following is a very easy-to-understand description from the source of `hbck`:

> *Check consistency among the in-memory states of the master and the region server(s) and the state of data in HDFS.*

HBase `hbck` not only has the facility to check inconsistencies, but also the functionality to fix an inconsistency.

In production, we recommend you run `hbck` frequently so that inconsistencies can be found earlier and fixed easily.

In this recipe, we will describe how to use `hbck` to check inconsistencies. We will also make some inconsistencies to the cluster and then demonstrate how to use `hbck` to fix it.

Getting ready

Start up your HBase cluster, and log in to your HBase client node.

How to do it...

The instructions to check and fix the inconsistencies of an HBase cluster using `hbck` are as follows:

1. Check the health of the cluster with the default `hbck` command option:

   ```
   $ $HBASE_HOME/bin/hbase hbck
   ```

   You will get the following output:

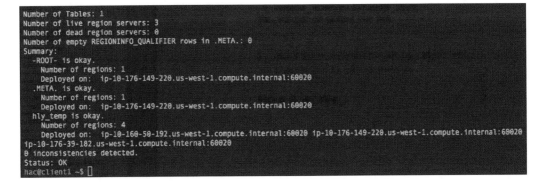

```
Number of Tables: 1
Number of live region servers: 3
Number of dead region servers: 0
Number of empty REGIONINFO_QUALIFIER rows in .META.: 0
Summary:
  -ROOT- is okay.
    Number of regions: 1
    Deployed on:  ip-10-176-149-220.us-west-1.compute.internal:60020
  .META. is okay.
    Number of regions: 1
    Deployed on:  ip-10-176-149-220.us-west-1.compute.internal:60020
  hly_temp is okay.
    Number of regions: 4
    Deployed on:  ip-10-160-50-192.us-west-1.compute.internal:60020 ip-10-176-149-220.us-west-1.compute.internal:60020
ip-10-176-39-182.us-west-1.compute.internal:60020
0 inconsistencies detected.
Status: OK
hac@client1 ~$ []
```

   At the end of the command's output it prints **Status: OK**, which indicates the cluster is in consistent status.

To demonstrate the fixing feature of `hbck`, make some inconsistencies by typing the following in HBase Shell:

1. Enter HBase Shell by typing the following command:

    ```
    $ $HBASE_HOME/bin/hbase shell
    ```

2. Manually close a region using the `close_region` command:

    ```
    hbase> close_region 'hly_temp,,1324196693253.9e6dd810550443bb488c8
    71728d5dee0.'
    ```

    Replace the last parameter with your region name, which can be found on the HBase web UI.

3. Run `hbck` again; you will find that, at the end of its output it reports the status of the cluster as inconsistent:

    ```
    $ $HBASE_HOME/bin/hbase hbck

    ERROR: Region hly_temp,,1324196693253.9e6dd810550443bb488c871728d5
    dee0. not deployed on any region server.

    ERROR: (region hly_temp,USW000128350706,1324196693253.0d16049716
    84462a2860d43e2715558d.) First region should start with an empty
    key.

    ERROR: Found inconsistency in table hly_temp

    ...


    2 inconsistencies detected.

    Status: INCONSISTENT
    ```

4. Use `hbck` with the `-fix` option, to fix the inconsistencies:

    ```
    $ $HBASE_HOME/bin/hbase hbck -fix

    ERROR: Region hly_temp,,1324196693253.9e6dd810550443bb488c871728d5
    dee0. not deployed on any region server.

    Trying to fix unassigned region...

    ...


    11/12/25 08:26:31 INFO util.HBaseFsck: Sleeping 10000ms before re-
    checking after fix...

    Version: 0.90.4

    ...


    0 inconsistencies detected.

    Status: OK
    ```

In this code, we skipped some output of the command to make it easy to understand.

How it works...

In step 1, we run the `hbck` command without any parameter. This will simply have `hbck` check the inconsistencies of the cluster. If no inconsistency is found, it will report `Status: OK` at the end of its output; otherwise, inconsistencies will be reported.

To demonstrate the fixing feature of `hbck`, we close a region from HBase Shell in step 2. The `close_region` command logs in via SSH into the region server that holds the specific region, and closes it directly. The master server will not be notified in this case. That's why, our cluster became inconsistent by the execution of the `close_region` command.

When we run `hbck` again in step 3, the command will find the inconsistent status of our cluster. As you can see from the output of the command, the region we closed in step 2 was reported as not being deployed on any region server—this is the result we expected. If you run a `get` command to get a row in that region, HBase will report an error to you, as the region is offline.

In step 4, we execute `hbck` with the `-fix` option. As you can see from the output of step 4, specifying the `-fix` option caused `hbck` to first check the inconsistencies of the cluster; if inconsistencies are found, it will try to fix it automatically. After that, a check is performed again to ensure the fixing works properly. Now, you can get data from the fixed region again.

There are other options of the `hbck` command, such as displaying a full report of all regions, checking `ROOT` and `META` tables only, and so on. Type the following command for help:

```
$ $HBASE_HOME/bin/hbase hbck -h
```

See also

▶ *Simple scripts to report status of the cluster* recipe, in *Chapter 5, Monitoring and Diagnosis*

Hive on HBase—querying HBase using a SQL-like language

HBase supports several interfaces to access data in its tables, such as the following:

▶ HBase Shell

▶ Java Client API

▶ REST, Thrift, and Avro

HBase Shell is straightforward, but a little too simple to perform complex queries on. Other interfaces need programming, which is not suitable for ad hoc queries.

As data keeps growing, people might want an easy way to analyze the large amount of data stored in HBase. The analysis should be efficient, ad hoc, and it should not require programming. Hive is currently the best approach for this purpose.

Hive is a data warehouse infrastructure built for Hadoop. Hive is used for ad hoc querying, and analyzing a large data set without having to write a MapReduce program. Hive supports a SQL-like query language called **HiveQL** (**HQL**) to access data in its table.

We can integrate HBase and Hive, so that we can use HQL statements to access HBase tables, both to read and write.

In this recipe, we will describe how to install and run Hive over HBase tables. We will show simple demonstrations of reading/writing data from/into HBase tables using Hive.

Getting ready

Hive stores its metadata in RDBMS such as MySQL or PostgreSQL. We will use MySQL in this recipe, so a running MySQL installation is required. Here is the online *MySQL 5.5 Reference Manual* to help you install MySQL:

```
http://dev.mysql.com/doc/refman/5.5/en/index.html.
```

Hive only needs to be installed on your client node. We assume you have installed Hive on the same node of an HBase client (`client1` in our case).

We will use the user `hadoop` as the owner of all Hive files. All Hive files and data will be stored under `/usr/local/hive`. Create a `/usr/local/hive` directory on your client node in advance; change the owner of the directory to the `hadoop` user.

HQL is translated into a MapReduce job by Hive, internally. Besides a running HBase installation, you will need to start MapReduce to use Hive to query the HBase data. You can start MapReduce by using the following command:

```
hadoop@master1$ $HADOOP_HOME/bin/start-mapred.sh
```

We will load data from a TSV file into Hive, and then write the data from Hive to the HBase table. Just as a demonstration, our TSV file (`hly_temp.tsv`) will only contain the following data:

```
AQW000617050101    808C    806C    803C
AQW000617050102    808C    805C    803C
AQW000617050103    807C    805C    802C
```

Put the `hly_temp.tsv` file under `/home/hac`; we will load it into Hive later.

How to do it...

To install Hive and run it over HBase, follow these instructions:

1. Download the latest version of Hive from `http://www.apache.org/dyn/closer.cgi/hive/`.

   While this book was being written, the latest release was 0.8.0.

2. Download the tarball and decompress it to our root directory for Hive. Add a symbolic link and environment variable:

   ```
   hadoop@client1$ ln -s hive-0.8.0 current
   hadoop@client1$ export HIVE_HOME=/usr/local/hive/current
   ```

3. Create the following directories on HDFS:

   ```
   hadoop@client1$ $HADOOP_HOME/bin/hadoop fs -mkdir /tmp
   hadoop@client1$ $HADOOP_HOME/bin/hadoop fs -mkdir /user/hive/warehouse
   ```

4. Change the owner and permission of the created directories:

   ```
   hadoop@client1$ $HADOOP_HOME/bin/hadoop fs -chmod 777 /tmp
   hadoop@client1$ $HADOOP_HOME/bin/hadoop fs -chown -R hac:hac /user/hive/warehouse
   ```

   i. Add dependencies to the Hive library: Download the JDBC driver for MySQL from `http://www.mysql.com/downloads/connector/j/`.

   ii. Move the downloaded JAR file to `$HIVE_HOME/lib`:

   ```
   hadoop@client1$ mv mysql-connector-java-5.1.18.jar $HIVE_HOME/lib/
   ```

   iv. Replace the HBase and ZooKeeper JAR files with the versions we are using:

   ```
   hadoop@client1$ rm $HIVE_HOME/lib/hbase-0.89.0-SNAPSHOT*.jar
   hadoop@client1$ rm $HIVE_HOME/lib/zookeeper-3.3.1.jar
   hadoop@client1$ cp $HBASE_HOME/hbase-0.92.1.jar $HIVE_HOME/lib
   hadoop@client1$ cp $HBASE_HOME/lib/zookeeper-3.4.3.jar $HIVE_HOME/lib
   ```

5. Add dependencies to Hive for running the MapReduce job:

   ```
   hadoop@client1$ mkdir $HIVE_HOME/auxlib
   hadoop@client1$ cp $HBASE_HOME/hbase-0.92.1.jar $HIVE_HOME/auxlib
   hadoop@client1$ cp $HBASE_HOME/lib/zookeeper-3.4.3.jar $HIVE_HOME/auxlib
   hadoop@client1$ cp $HIVE_HOME/lib/hive-hbase-handler-0.8.0.jar $HIVE_HOME/auxlib
   ```

6. Connect to your MySQL server:

```
$ mysql -h<mysql_server_host> -uroot -p
```

    i. Create a database and tables for Hive in MySQL:

```
mysql> create database metastore;
mysql> use metastore;
mysql> source /usr/local/hive/current/scripts/metastore/
upgrade/mysql/hive-schema-0.8.0.mysql.sql
```

7. Create a MySQL user for Hive:

```
mysql> create user 'hive'@'%' identified by 'your_password';
mysql> grant select,insert,update,delete on metastore.* to
'hive'@'%';
mysql> revoke alter,create on metastore.* from 'hive'@'%';
```

8. Set HADOOP_HOME in Hive's environment setting file (hive-env.sh):

```
hadoop@client1$ cp $HIVE_HOME/conf/hive-env.sh.template $HIVE_
HOME/conf/hive-env.sh
hadoop@client1$ vi $HIVE_HOME/conf/hive-env.sh
HADOOP_HOME=/usr/local/hadoop/current
```

9. Add the following to Hive's configuration file (hive-site.xml). You will need to adjust the MySQL server, password, and the ZooKeeper quorum setting to your environment:

```
hadoop@client1$ vi $HIVE_HOME/conf/hive-site.xml
<?xml version="1.0"?>
<?xml-stylesheet type="text/xsl" href="configuration.xsl"?>
<configuration>
  <property>
    <name>javax.jdo.option.ConnectionURL</name>
    <value>jdbc:mysql://mysql_server_host/metastore</value>
  </property>
  <property>
    <name>javax.jdo.option.ConnectionDriverName</name>
    <value>com.mysql.jdbc.Driver</value>
  </property>
  <property>
    <name>javax.jdo.option.ConnectionUserName</name>
    <value>hive</value>
  </property>
  <property>
    <name>javax.jdo.option.ConnectionPassword</name>
    <value>your_password</value>
```

```
        </property>
        <property>
          <name>datanucleus.autoCreateSchema</name>
          <value>false</value>
        </property>
        <property>
          <name>datanucleus.fixedDatastore</name>
          <value>true</value>
        </property>
        <property>
          <name>hbase.zookeeper.quorum</name>
          <value>zoo1,zoo2,zoo3</value>
        </property>
      </configuration>
```

10. We will use the `hac` user to run the Hive job in this recipe. Switch to the user and test the Hive installation from the Hive **Command Line Interface** (**CLI**). Here we just create, show, and drop a Hive table to confirm our Hive installation:

```
hac@client1$ $HIVE_HOME/bin/hive

hive> create table pokes (foo int, bar string);

hive> show tables;

OK

pokes

hive> drop table pokes;
```

11. Map an existing HBase table (`hly_temp`) to a Hive table (`hbase_hly_temp`) by using the following command:

```
hive> create external table hbase_hly_temp
    (key string, v01 string, v02 string, v03 string)
    stored by 'org.apache.hadoop.hive.hbase.HBaseStorageHandler'
    with serdeproperties ("hbase.columns.mapping" =
    ":key,n:v01,n:v02,n:v03")
    tblproperties("hbase.table.name" = "hly_temp");
```

12. Query HBase data from the table we mapped in Hive:

```
hive> select * from hbase_hly_temp where v01='808C';

Total MapReduce jobs = 1

Launching Job 1 out of 1

...

2011-12-25 15:25:58,134 Stage-1 map = 100%,  reduce = 100%,
Cumulative CPU 27.51 sec

MapReduce Total cumulative CPU time: 27 seconds 510 msec

Ended Job = job_201112251140_0001
```

```
MapReduce Jobs Launched:

Job 0: Map: 4    Accumulative CPU: 27.51 sec    HDFS Read: 1204 HDFS
Write: 2345 SUCESS

Total MapReduce CPU Time Spent: 27 seconds 510 msec

OK

AQW000617050101        808C    806C    803C

AQW000617050102        808C    805C    803C

AQW000617050104        808C    805S    803C

...
```

13. Create a Hive table (`hive_hly_temp2`) to store data from the TSV file:

```
hive> create table hive_hly_temp2
(key string, v01 string, v02 string, v03 string)
  row format delimited fields
  terminated by '\t' lines terminated by '\n';
```

14. Load the TSV file into the Hive table:

```
hive> load data local inpath '/home/hac/hly_temp.tsv' overwrite
into table hive_hly_temp2;

Copying data from file:/home/hac/hly_temp.tsv

Copying file: file:/home/hac/hly_temp.tsv

Loading data to table default.hive_hly_temp2

Deleted hdfs://master1/user/hive/warehouse/hive_hly_temp2

OK
```

15. Create a Hive-managed HBase table and map it with a Hive table:

```
hive> create table hbase_hly_temp2
(key string, v01 string, v02 string, v03 string)
  stored by 'org.apache.hadoop.hive.hbase.HBaseStorageHandler'
  with serdeproperties ("hbase.columns.mapping" =
  ":key,n:v01,n:v02,n:v03")
    tblproperties ("hbase.table.name" = "hly_temp2");
```

Here, we created one table in HBase called `hly_temp2`; this table is managed by Hive, with the table name `hbase_hly_temp2`.

16. Write data from the Hive table (`hive_hly_temp2`) into the HBase table (`hbase_hly_temp2`) via HQL:

```
hive> insert overwrite table hbase_hly_temp2 select * from hive_hly_temp2;
```

17. Confirm the data in HBase, which we inserted via HQL in the previous step:

    ```
    hac@client1$ $HBASE_HOME/bin/hbase shell
    hbase> scan 'hly_temp2'
    ```

    You will get the following output:

```
hbase(main):006:0> scan 'hly_temp2'
ROW                                    COLUMN+CELL
 AQW000617050101                       column=n:v01, timestamp=1324795944193, value=808C
 AQW000617050101                       column=n:v02, timestamp=1324795944193, value=806C
 AQW000617050101                       column=n:v03, timestamp=1324795944193, value=803C
 AQW000617050102                       column=n:v01, timestamp=1324795944193, value=808C
 AQW000617050102                       column=n:v02, timestamp=1324795944193, value=805C
 AQW000617050102                       column=n:v03, timestamp=1324795944193, value=803C
 AQW000617050103                       column=n:v01, timestamp=1324795944193, value=807C
 AQW000617050103                       column=n:v02, timestamp=1324795944193, value=805C
 AQW000617050103                       column=n:v03, timestamp=1324795944193, value=802C
3 row(s) in 0.1740 seconds
```

How it works...

Hive's table data is stored on HDFS; the default path is /user/hive/warehouse. That's why we create this directory and change its owner to the hac user in steps 3 and 4. We also need to create a /tmp directory on HDFS, so that Hive can save its temporary files under it.

In step 5, we add the JDBC driver for MySQL to the Hive library folder. We need to do this because we will configure Hive to store its metadata in MySQL. The JDBC driver is required to access MySQL from Hive. As HBase and ZooKeeper JAR files, shipped with Hive, are out of date, we replace them with the files from our HBase installation.

In step 6, we create a directory called auxlib under $HIVE_HOME. This is a special directory. When Hive starts a MapReduce job, all JAR files under this directory will be shipped to TaskTrackers via Hadoop Distributed Cache, and added to the job task's class path. The JAR files we put under $HIVE_HOME/auxlib are dependencies of all Hive MapReduce jobs.

We create the database and tables for Hive in MySQL in step 7. As all Hive schemas are defined in $HIVE_HOME/scripts/metastore/upgrade/mysql/hive-schema-0.8.0.mysql.sql, we can simply execute this SQL script to create Hive tables in MySQL. The MySQL user for Hive is created in step 8. We recommend you to limit this user's privileges to prevent it from creating or altering tables in the metastore database schema.

We need to set up HADOOP_HOME in Hive's environment setting file (hive-env.sh) to notify to Hive the location where Hadoop is installed. Metastore database and ZooKeeper quorum settings are set in Hive's configuration file (hive-site.xml). Hive will use these settings to connect to the Metastore database and HBase cluster. If everything is set up properly, you should be able to connect to Hive using its Command Line Interface (CLI).

In step 12, we create an external Hive table to map an existing HBase table. An external Hive table is defined by the `create external table` statement. When dropping an external table, the data is not deleted from HBase. To create a Hive table over HBase, use `org.apache.hadoop.hive.hbase.HBaseStorageHandler` as its storage handler. For each Hive column, it must be mapped to a corresponding HBase column or column family in the comma-delimited `hbase.columns.mapping` string. Be careful *not* to include whitespace between entries. There must be exactly one `:key` entry for mapping HBase row keys. It is not necessary to map every HBase column, but only mapped columns are accessible from Hive. The `hbase.table.name` property is optional. If not specified, then the table will have the same name in Hive and in HBase.

For most of the cases, a Hive query will be translated into a MapReduce job. If you open your MapReduce Administration Page, you will find the MapReduce job translated from the query we executed in step 12.

master1 Hadoop Map/Reduce Administration

http://master1:50030/jobtracker.jsp

Quick Links

Running Jobs

Jobid	Priority	User	Name	Map % Complete	Map Total	Maps Completed	Reduce % Complete	Reduce Total	R C
job_201112251140_0001	NORMAL	hac	select * from hbase_hly_temp wh...v01='808C'(Stage-1)	100.00%	4	4	0.00%	0	0

Steps 14 to 18 show how to insert data from Hive into an HBase table. In step 14, we create a regular Hive table as the data source, then we load our TSV file into this table in step 15.

The target HBase table was created in step 16. Note that this table is not an external table as we have not specified the `external` keyword in the creator. Dropping this table from Hive will drop the table from HBase, too. After executing the command in step 15, you should be able to see the new (empty) table in HBase Shell.

As the table was created, we can insert data into it using the `insert overwrite` HQL statement. Data inserted into `hbase_hly_temp2` was actually stored in the `hly_temp2` HBase table by `HbaseStorageHandler`. That's exactly the result we saw in step 18.

As you can see, integrating Hive with HBase provides a powerful data access interface on top of HBase. While the drawback is that some HBase features, such as timestamp/version support, composite row key mapping, and updating on a single HBase row from Hive, are not supported.

Although it is not meant for latency-sensitive systems, as it is still a MapReduce job each time, Hive integrating is a good add-on to HBase, for ad hoc querying capabilities.

4
Backing Up and Restoring HBase Data

In this chapter, we will cover:

- ▶ Full shutdown backup using `distcp`
- ▶ Using `CopyTable` to copy data from one table to another
- ▶ Exporting an HBase table to dump files on HDFS
- ▶ Restoring HBase data by importing dump files from HDFS
- ▶ Backing up NameNode metadata
- ▶ Backing up region starting keys
- ▶ Cluster replication

Introduction

If you are thinking about using HBase in production, you will probably want to understand the backup options and practices of HBase. The challenge is that the dataset you need to back up might be huge, so the backup solution must be efficient. It is expected to be able to scale to hundreds of terabytes of storage, and finish restoring the data in a reasonable time frame.

There are two strategies for backing up HBase:

- ▶ Backing it up with a full cluster shutdown
- ▶ Backing it up on a live cluster

A full shutdown backup has to stop HBase (or disable all tables) at first, then use Hadoop's `distcp` command to copy the contents of an HBase directory to either another directory on the same HDFS, or to a different HDFS. To restore from a full shutdown backup, just copy the backed up files, back to the HBase directory using `distcp`.

There are several approaches for a live cluster backup:

▸ Using the `CopyTable` utility to copy data from one table to another

▸ Exporting an HBase table to HDFS files, and importing the files back to HBase

▸ HBase cluster replication

The `CopyTable` utility could be used to copy data from one table to either another one on the same cluster, or to a different cluster. The `Export` utility dumps the data of a table to HDFS, which is on the same cluster. As a set of `Export`, the `Import` utility is used to restore the data of the dump files.

Each aforementioned approach has its pros and cons. The benefit of a full shutdown backup is that there is no chance of writing data into the cluster during the backup process, so it is possible to ensure a consistent status of the backup. The downside is obvious—the cluster is down. As for the live cluster backup approach, since the cluster is up, there is a risk that edits could be missed during the backup process. Furthermore, as HBase edits are atomic only at the row level, if your tables depend on each other, your backup might end up with inconsistencies if the tables are being modified while `Export` or `CopyTable` is being performed. Making a snapshot of HBase tables is not supported in the current Apache Release.

HBase supports cluster replication. It is a way to copy data between the different HBase deployments. Cluster replication can be considered as a disaster recovery solution at the HBase level.

Besides the tables, what you will likely want to back up are your HDFS metadata and HBase region starting keys. HDFS metadata contains the filesystem image and commit logs of HDFS. A metadata corruption might damage the entire HDFS metadata; it is suggested to back up the metadata frequently. Region starting keys represent the data distribution in HBase. Backing up the region starting keys makes it possible to restore not only the data, but also the data distribution. If we split the tables in advance, using well-distributed region starting keys, the speed of restoring data by using the `CopyTable`/`Import` utility could be increased dramatically.

In this chapter, we will describe how to back up HBase data using the aforementioned approaches, their pros and cons, and which approach to choose, depending on your dataset size, resources, and requirements.

Full shutdown backup using distcp

`distcp` (**distributed copy**) is a tool provided by Hadoop for copying a large dataset on the same, or different HDFS cluster. It uses MapReduce to copy files in parallel, handle error and recovery, and report the job status.

As HBase stores all its files, including system files on HDFS, we can simply use `distcp` to copy the HBase directory to either another directory on the same HDFS, or to a different HDFS, for backing up the source HBase cluster.

Note that this is a full shutdown backup solution. The `distcp` tool works because the HBase cluster is shut down (or all tables are disabled) and there are no edits to files during the process. Do *not* use `distcp` on a live HBase cluster. Therefore, this solution is for the environment that can tolerate a periodic full shutdown of their HBase cluster. For example, a cluster that is used for backend batch processing and not serving frontend requests.

We will describe how to use `distcp` to back up a fully shut down HBase cluster to a different HDFS cluster. Backing up on a different cluster can serve as a disaster recovery solution and can contribute to higher availability of data. In production, it is recommended to back up a fully shut down HBase cluster to a different HDFS cluster.

We will also demonstrate how to restore data from the backup, later in this chapter.

Getting ready

You will need a secondary cluster if you are going to use `distcp` to back up your HBase data to a different cluster. You could also back up HBase data to the same cluster as your source HBase cluster. For this situation, another cluster is not required.

In this recipe we will use a different cluster for backup. The backup cluster runs on different EC2 instances. We will assume that the HDFS running on the backup cluster is `hdfs://l-master1:8020`; `l-master1` indicates that this cluster runs on EC2 large instances. This is because we will use this cluster for our performance tuning recipes later, while small instance specification is too low for that usage.

Start HDFS on the source and backup clusters, respectively.

The `distcp` tool uses MapReduce to copy files in parallel, so you will need to start MapReduce on the source cluster as well. MapReduce can be started from the JobTracker node, using the following command:

```
hadoop@master1$ $HADOOP_HOME/bin/start-mapred.sh
```

We will back up the HBase directory under the /backup directory, on the backup cluster. Create this directory in advance, from the Hadoop client (1-client1) of the backup cluster, using the following command:

```
hadoop@1-client1$ $HADOOP_HOME/bin/hadoop fs -mkdir /backup
```

How to do it...

Follow these instructions to back up/restore HBase data using distcp:

1. Shut down the source and backup HBase clusters, if they are running:

   ```
   hadoop@master1$ $HBASE_HOME/bin/stop-hbase.sh
   ```

2. Make sure HBase has shut down on the source cluster by checking if the HMaster daemon has started:

   ```
   hadoop@master1$ $JAVA_HOME/bin/jps
   1567 JobTracker
   1416 NameNode
   1705 Jps
   1690 QuorumPeerMain
   ```

   Make sure the HMaster daemon is not listed in the output.

3. Also, make sure mapred.map.tasks.speculative.execution is not set to final and true on the client of the source cluster.

   This property is set in the MapReduce configuration file (mapred-site.xml) under the $HADOOP_HOME/conf directory. If it is set to final and true, remove the setting. This is a client-side change; it will only affect the MapReduce jobs submitted from that client.

4. Use distcp to copy the HBase root directory from the source cluster to the backup cluster. The HBase root directory is set by the hbase.rootdir property in the HBase configuration file (hbase-site.xml). We will assume it is hdfs://master1:8020/hbase, in this recipe:

   ```
   hadoop@client1$ $HADOOP_HOME/bin/hadoop distcp hdfs://
   master1:8020/hbase hdfs://1-master1:8020/backup

   12/01/03 12:27:53 INFO tools.DistCp: srcPaths=[hdfs://
   master1:8020/hbase]

   12/01/03 12:27:53 INFO tools.DistCp: destPath=hdfs://1-
   master1:8020/backup

   12/01/03 12:27:54 INFO tools.DistCp: sourcePathsCount=76

   12/01/03 12:27:54 INFO tools.DistCp: filesToCopyCount=34

   12/01/03 12:27:54 INFO tools.DistCp: bytesToCopyCount=102.0m
   ```

```
12/01/03 12:27:55 INFO mapred.JobClient: Running job:
job_201201031153_0002
12/01/03 12:27:56 INFO mapred.JobClient:  map 0% reduce 0%
...
```

You will find a running MapReduce job of the source cluster from the admin page of your JobTracker:

After the `distcp` job is completed, you should be able to find the copied HBase directory under the /backup directory on the backup cluster:

```
hadoop@l-client1$ $HADOOP_HOME/bin/hadoop fs -lsr /backup/hbase

drwxr-xr-x   - hadoop hadoop          0 2012-01-03 12:28 /backup/hbase/-
ROOT-

...
```

The steps for restoring data from the previous backup are as follows:

1. Start MapReduce on the backup cluster by using the following command:

    ```
    hadoop@l-master1$ $HADOOP_HOME/bin/start-mapred.sh
    ```

2. Make sure `mapred.map.tasks.speculative.execution` is not set to `final` and `true` on your client of the backup cluster.

3. Make sure HBase is not running on the source and backup clusters. If HBase is running, stop it first:

    ```
    hadoop@l-master1$ $HBASE_HOME/bin/stop-hbase.sh
    ```

4. Make sure there are no files under the `hbase.rootdir` directory on the source cluster. If files are present, move them to another path:

    ```
    hadoop@client1$ $HADOOP_HOME/bin/hadoop fs -mv /hbase /tmp
    ```

    You may remove the files if you are sure they are not required.

5. Copy the HBase directory from the backup cluster to the source cluster:

```
hadoop@l-client1$ $HADOOP_HOME/bin/hadoop distcp hdfs:
  //l-master1:8020/backup/hbase hdfs://master1:8020/
```

6. Start HBase on the source cluster; you should be able to access the restored data via HBase Shell:

```
hadoop@master1$ $HBASE_HOME/bin/start-hbase.sh
```

How it works...

As we mentioned, `distcp` is a full shutdown backup option; therefore, we stop HBase in step 1 and confirm the stopping in step 2. `jps` is a convenient command shipped with Java SDK. It shows all the Java processes owned by the executed user. As all HBase-related daemons are started by the `hadoop` user in our case, we can use the `jps` command to see whether HBase's master daemon (HMaster) is running.

`distcp` uses MapReduce to copy files in parallel. If the property `mapred.map.tasks.speculative.execution` is set to `true`, multiple instances of some map tasks may be executed in parallel, performing the same tasks. This is a client-side property for each job. `distcp` will set this property to `false` for its MapReduce job, as HDFS does not handle multiple writers to the same file. But a final property cannot be changed in a single MapReduce job. If `mapred.map.tasks.speculative.execution` is set to `final` and `true`, the result of the copy is undefined. In step 3, we remove the final setting to enable `distcp` to configure this property in its MapReduce job.

All we need to copy is the `hbase.rootdir` directory. We execute `distcp` to copy it from the source cluster to our backup cluster in step 4. The parameters include the full path of the source directory, including its HDFS schema, and the HDFS schema and path of the destination directory on the backup cluster. As you can see from its output, `distcp` starts a MapReduce job to copy data in parallel.

The MapReduce job started by `distcp` copies data only in its Map phase. The maximum number of maps is specified by the `-m` option. Note that this is just a hint to the MapReduce job; more maps may not always increase the number of simultaneous copies or the overall throughput.

In order to restore from the backup, we copy the data back from the backup cluster to the source cluster and then start HBase on the source cluster.

For a full list of the `distcp` options, type the following command:

```
$HADOOP_HOME/bin/hadoop distcp
```

Using CopyTable to copy data from one table to another

CopyTable is a utility to copy the data of one table to another table, either on the same cluster, or on a different HBase cluster. You can copy to a table that is on the same cluster; however, if you have another cluster that you want to treat as a backup, you might want to use CopyTable as a live backup option to copy the data of a table to the backup cluster.

CopyTable is configurable with a start and an end timestamp. If specified, only the data with a timestamp in the specific time frame will be copied. This feature makes it possible for incremental backup of an HBase table in some situations.

 "Incremental backup" is a method to only back up the data that has been changed during the last backup.

 Note: Since the cluster keeps running, there is a risk that edits could be missed during the copy process.

In this recipe, we will describe how to use CopyTable to copy the data of a table to another one, on a different HBase cluster. We will demonstrate copying data from the hly_temp table into the hly_temp2 table; we will only copy data in column family n.

Getting ready

On the client node, you will need to add the HBase configuration file (hbase-site.xml) to Hadoop's class path, so that a MapReduce job can access the HBase cluster. You can do it by linking hbase-site.xml under the Hadoop configuration directory, as follows:

```
hadoop@client1$ ln -s $HBASE_HOME/conf/hbase-site.xml $HADOOP_HOME/conf/
hbase-site.xml
```

Also, add HBase dependency JARs to Hadoop's class path, by editing hadoop-env.sh:

```
hadoop@client1$ vi $HADOOP_HOME/conf/hadoop-env.sh
    export HADOOP_CLASSPATH=
        /usr/local/zookeeper/current/zookeeper-3.4.3.jar
```

 The aforementioned steps are the minimum requirements to run MapReduce over HBase. And since this is a common process, we will skip its details henceforth, in this book.

Start HBase on both the source and backup clusters. If you do not have another cluster, you could also copy a table to another table on the local cluster. However, it is not recommended for backup purposes in production. We will assume that the ZooKeeper quorum of the backup cluster is `l-master1:2181`, and the HBase root directory is `/hbase`.

`CopyTable` uses MapReduce to copy data in parallel; you will need to start MapReduce on the source cluster, using the following command:

```
hadoop@master1$ $HADOOP_HOME/bin/start-mapred.sh
```

How to do it...

The following are instructions to copy data in column family `n`, from the `hly_temp` table into the `hly_temp2` table on the backup cluster:

1. Connect to the backup HBase cluster via HBase Shell and create the destination table if it does not exist:

   ```
   hbase> create 'hly_temp2', {NAME => 'n'}
   ```

2. Run the following command from your client node of the source cluster to copy data from the `hly_temp` table to `hly_temp2` on the backup cluster:

   ```
   hac@client1$ $HADOOP_HOME/bin/hadoop jar $HBASE_HOME/hbase-
   0.92.1.jar copytable --families=n --peer.adr=l-master1:2181:/hbase
   --new.name=hly_temp2 hly_temp

   2/01/09 15:24:34 INFO zookeeper.ZooKeeper: Initiating client
   connection, connectString=l-master1:2181 sessionTimeout=10000
   watcher=hconnection

   12/01/09 15:24:34 INFO zookeeper.ClientCnxn: Opening socket
   connection to server l-master1/10.170.114.96:2181

   12/01/09 15:24:34 INFO zookeeper.ClientCnxn: Socket connection
   established to l-master1/10.170.114.96:2181, initiating session

   12/01/09 15:24:34 INFO zookeeper.ClientCnxn: Session establishment
   complete on server l-master1/10.170.114.96:2181, sessionid =
   0x134c11bb47c000a, negotiated timeout = 10000

   12/01/09 15:24:34 INFO mapreduce.TableOutputFormat: Created table
   instance for hly_temp2

   12/01/09 15:24:34 INFO zookeeper.ZooKeeper: Initiating client
   connection, connectString=master1:2181 sessionTimeout=10000
   watcher=hconnection

   12/01/09 15:24:34 INFO zookeeper.ClientCnxn: Opening socket
   connection to server master1/10.166.105.212:2181

   12/01/09 15:24:34 INFO zookeeper.ClientCnxn: Socket connection
   established to master1/10.166.105.212:2181, initiating session
   ```

```
12/01/09 15:24:34 INFO zookeeper.ClientCnxn: Session establishment
complete on server master1/10.166.105.212:2181, sessionid =
0x134c11d62a20019, negotiated timeout = 10000

12/01/09 15:24:34 INFO mapred.JobClient: Running job:
job_201201091517_0001

12/01/09 15:24:35 INFO mapred.JobClient:  map 0% reduce 0%

12/01/09 15:24:49 INFO mapred.JobClient:  map 50% reduce 0%

...
```

You will find a running MapReduce job of the source cluster from the admin page of your JobTracker:

Jobid	Priority	User	Name	Map % Complete	Map Total	Maps Completed	Reduce % Complete	Reduce Total	Reduces Completed
job_201201091517_0001	NORMAL	hac	copytable_hly_temp	50.00%	2	1	0.00%	0	0

master1 Hadoop Map/Reduce Administration

`http://master1:50030/jobtracker.jsp`

Running Jobs   Quick Links

3. You should be able to access the data in `hly_temp2` on the backup cluster via HBase Shell:

```
hbase> scan 'hly_temp2', { LIMIT => 1 }
ROW                     COLUMN+CELL
 AQW000617050101         column=n:v01, timestamp=1323026325955, valu
e=808C
 AQW000617050101         column=n:v02, timestamp=1323026325955, valu
e=806C
 AQW000617050101         column=n:v03, timestamp=1323026325955,
value=803C
hbase> count 'hly_temp2'
95630 row(s) in 22.4740 seconds
```

4. Type the following command to only copy the data that has a specific timestamp range:

```
hac@client1$ $HADOOP_HOME/bin/hadoop jar $HBASE_HOME/hbase-
0.92.1.jar copytable --families=n --peer.adr=1-master1:2181:/
hbase --new.name=hly_temp2 --starttime=1324173586754
--endtime=1324189940000 hly_temp
```

How it works...

In step 1, we create the destination table (`hly_temp2`) on the backup cluster with the column family (`n`) we want to copy.

In step 2, we copy data in the column family `n` from the `hly_temp` table to the `hly_temp2` table on the backup cluster. The backup cluster is specified by the `--peer.adr` option, by specifying the ZooKeeper quorum address, whose format is `hbase.zookeeper.quorum:hbase.zookeeper.client.port:zookeeper.znode.parent`, such as `server,server2,server3:2181:/hbase`.

The `--families` option is used to specify a comma-separated list of families to be copied. The destination table is specified by the `--new.name` option; skip this option if the two tables have the same names.

As you can see from the output, data is copied in a MapReduce job. The `hadoop jar` command is used to run a JAR file in MapReduce. The MapReduce job scans the source table, reads data entries belonging to the target families, and then writes them into the destination table on the backup cluster using its normal client API.

From the output of step 3, you will find that the `hly_temp` table's data in the column family `n`, including the timestamp of each entry, has been copied into the `hly_temp2` table on the backup cluster. HBase uses timestamps to order edits; edits with a bigger timestamp have the newer version for the cell. By default, timestamp is set automatically by HBase using a long value, representing the difference in milliseconds between the current time and midnight—January 1, 1970 UTC.

We add timestamp range parameters to the `CopyTable` command in step 4. Data out of the specific time frame will be skipped in the scanning phase of the copy job. The minimum timestamp value, which is specified by the `--starttime` option, is inclusive. The maximum timestamp value, which is specified by the `--endtime` option, is exclusive.

Step 2 can be used for a full backup, while step 3 can be used for an incremental backup in some situations. Using `CopyTable` with a specific timestamp range is not identical to an incremental backup. This is because, when putting data into HBase, the timestamp can be specified explicitly by the client, and there is no insurance that the newly inserted data has a larger timestamp. Another reason is that `CopyTable` will not handle deletes. There is no way to know if data was deleted. We recommend you to implement your own incremental backup solution at the application level.

For a full description of `CopyTable` usage, type the following command:

```
$HADOOP_HOME/bin/hadoop jar $HBASE_HOME/hbase-0.92.1.jar copytable
```

Exporting an HBase table to dump files on HDFS

The HBase `export` utility dumps the contents of a table to the same HDFS cluster. The dump file is in a Hadoop sequence file format. Exporting data to Hadoop sequence files has merits for data backup, because the Hadoop sequence file format supports several compression types and algorithms. With it we can choose the best compression options to fit our environment.

Like the `copytable` utility we mentioned in the previous recipe, `export` is configurable with a start and an end timestamp, so that only the data within a specific time frame will be dumped. This feature enables `export` to incrementally export an HBase table to HDFS.

HBase `export` is also a live backup option. As the cluster is running, there is a risk that edits could be missed during the export process. In this recipe, we will describe how to use the `export` utility to export a table to HDFS on the same cluster. We will introduce the `import` utility in the next recipe, which is used to restore the data from an `export` dump.

Getting ready

First, start your HDFS and HBase cluster.

We will export our `hly_temp` table to `/backup/hly_temp` on our HDFS cluster. You will need to create a `/backup` directory in advance.

The `export` utility uses MapReduce to export data. Add HBase's configurable file (`hbase-site.xml`) and dependency JAR files to Hadoop's class path on your client node.

How to do it...

Follow these instructions to export an HBase table to HDFS using the `export` utility:

1. Run the following command from your client node to export all the data in the `hly_temp` table:

   ```
   hadoop@client1$ $HADOOP_HOME/bin/hadoop jar $HBASE_HOME/hbase-
   0.92.1.jar export -D mapred.output.compress=true -D mapred.output.
   compression.codec=org.apache.hadoop.io.compress.BZip2Codec -D
   mapred.output.compression.type=BLOCK hly_temp /backup/hly_temp
   2147483647

   12/01/08 07:39:35 INFO mapreduce.Export: verisons=2147483647,
   starttime=0, endtime=9223372036854775807

   ...
   ```

```
12/01/08 07:39:37 INFO zookeeper.ClientCnxn: Session establishment
complete on server master1/10.160.229.77:2181, sessionid =
0x134ba4a09070013, negotiated timeout = 10000

12/01/08 07:39:38 INFO mapred.JobClient: Running job:
job_201201080737_0001

12/01/08 07:39:39 INFO mapred.JobClient:  map 0% reduce 0%

12/01/08 07:42:56 INFO mapred.JobClient:  map 25% reduce 0%
```

You will find the export MapReduce job from the admin page of your JobTracker:

After the MapReduce job has finished, you will find the dump files (part-m-000x) generated under the /backup/hly_temp directory on HDFS:

2. Execute the following command to only export the data that has a specific timestamp range:

```
hadoop@client1$ $HADOOP_HOME/bin/hadoop jar $HBASE_HOME/hbase-
0.92.1.jar export -D mapred.output.compress=true -D mapred.output.
compression.codec=org.apache.hadoop.io.compress.BZip2Codec -D
mapred.output.compression.type=BLOCK hly_temp /backup/hly_temp_2
2147483647 1324601918502 1324693970000
```

How it works...

Running an HBase JAR file with the `export` argument will execute the `export` utility to dump the contents of an HBase table. In step 1, we dumped the `hly_temp` table to the `/backup/hly_temp` directory on HDFS. The last parameter specifies the maximum version of the data to export. HBase supports storing multiple versions of data within a cell. The maximum version a cell can store is determined by its column family's `VERSIONS` property, which is specified at the time of creating a table. To dump a table with multi-version column families, we must pass the maximum version we want to export to the `export` command, otherwise only the latest version will be exported. In our case, we just specify `Integer.MAX_VALUE` (`2147483647`) to export all versions of the data.

Many `-D` properties have been passed to the `export` command. These are set to the export MapReduce job controlling its runtime properties. The `mapred.output.compress` property is set to `true` to cause MapReduce to compress its output (the sequence files). The `mapred.output.compression.codec` property controls which compression algorithm to use for the export. We have set it to use the BZip2 codec, which has the highest compression ratio.

When this book was being written, these were the widely used codecs for Hadoop. Which codec to choose, depends on your requirement; all of them have a space/time trade-off:

Compression format	Hadoop CompressionCodec	Compression ratio	(De-) Compression speed
gzip	`org.apache.hadoop.io.compress.GzipCodec`	Medium	Medium
BZip2	`org.apache.hadoop.io.compress.BZip2Codec`	High	Slow
LZO	`com.hadoop.compression.lzo.LzoCodec`	Low	Fast

LZO is not contained in the Hadoop package because of license issues; refer to the *Using compression* recipe for the installation of LZO, in *Chapter 8, Basic Performance Tuning*.

The `mapred.output.compression.type` property is used to specify the compression type for a Hadoop sequence file. The available values are `NONE`, `RECORD`, and `BLOCK`. For most cases, you should choose `BLOCK` as it compresses sequences of records together in blocks, which is the most efficient way for compression.

As you can see from the output, data is exported via MapReduce. This is done by the `hadoop jar` command, which runs a JAR file in MapReduce. The MapReduce job scans the table, reads all the data entries, and then writes them to the Hadoop sequence files under the output path on the same HDFS cluster.

We have added the timestamp range parameters to the `export` command in step 2. Data out of the specific time frame will be skipped in the scanning phase of the export job. The minimum timestamp value (`1324601918502`) is inclusive, whereas the maximum timestamp value (`1324693970000`) is exclusive.

Just like the `CopyTable` utility we have mentioned in the previous recipe, step 1 (without a specific start/end time) can be used for a full backup, while step 2 (with a specific start/end time) is for incremental backups in some situations.

There's more...

As data is exported to HDFS on the same cluster, there is a risk that backups will not be available if the HDFS crashes. We recommend you to copy the exported files to a different HDFS cluster, using the Hadoop `distcp` tool. If your data size is not very large, an even better option is to copy the dumped files to tapes, for offline backup.

See also

- ▸ *Restoring HBase data by importing dump files from HDFS* recipe, in this chapter
- ▸ *Using compression* recipe, in *Chapter 8, Basic Performance Tuning*

Restoring HBase data by importing dump files from HDFS

The HBase `Import` utility is used to load data that has been exported by the `Export` utility into an existing HBase table. It is the process to restore data from the `Export` utility backup solution.

We will look at the usage of the `Import` utility in this recipe.

Getting ready

First, start your HDFS and HBase cluster.

We will import the files that we exported in the previous recipe into our `hly_temp` table. If you do not have those dump files, refer to the *Exporting HBase table to dump files on HDFS* recipe, to generate the dump files in advance. We assume the dump files are saved in the `/backup/hly_temp` directory.

The `Import` utility uses MapReduce to import data. Add the HBase configurable file (`hbase-site.xml`) and dependency JAR files to Hadoop class path on your client node.

How to do it...

To import dump files into the `hly_temp` table:

1. Connect to your HBase cluster via HBase Shell and create the target table if it does not exist:

   ```
   hbase> create 'hly_temp', {NAME => 'n'}
   ```

2. Run the following command from your client node to import data into the `hly_temp` table:

   ```
   hadoop@client1$ $HADOOP_HOME/bin/hadoop jar $HBASE_HOME/hbase-
   0.92.1.jar import hly_temp /backup/hly_temp

   12/01/08 08:52:42 INFO mapreduce.TableOutputFormat: Created table
   instance for hly_temp

   12/01/08 08:52:42 INFO input.FileInputFormat: Total input paths to
   process : 4

   12/01/08 08:52:42 INFO mapred.JobClient: Running job:
   job_201201080737_0004

   12/01/08 08:52:43 INFO mapred.JobClient:  map 0% reduce 0%

   12/01/08 08:53:09 INFO mapred.JobClient:  map 1% reduce 0%

   ...
   ```

   You will find the import MapReduce job from the admin page of your JobTracker:

master1 Hadoop Map/Reduce Administration
http://master1:50030/jobtracker.jsp

Quick Links

Running Jobs

Jobid	Priority	User	Name	Map % Complete	Map Total	Maps Completed	Reduce % Complete	Reduce Total	Reduces Completed
job_201201080737_0004	NORMAL	hadoop	import_hly_temp	18.95%	4	0	0.00%	0	0

3. You should be able to access data in the `hly_temp` table via HBase Shell after the MapReduce job has finished:

```
hbase> scan 'hly_temp', {LIMIT => 1}
ROW                     COLUMN+CELL
 AQW000617050101         column=n:v01, timestamp=1323026325955, valu
e=808C
 AQW000617050101         column=n:v02, timestamp=1323026325955, valu
e=806C
 AQW000617050101         column=n:v03, timestamp=1323026325955,
value=803C
...
```

How it works...

We create the target table in step 1. The table must have all the column families that exist in the dump files; without that, the import job will fail with a `NoSuchColumnFamilyException` error message.

As you can see from the output of step 2, data is imported via MapReduce. This was done with the `hadoop jar` command, which executes the MapReduce code that is packaged in a JAR file. The import MapReduce job reads data entries from dump files under the input directory (`/backup/hly_temp`), and then writes them into the target table (`hly_temp`) using HBase's client API.

Data in the dump files, including the timestamp of each entry, will be restored by the `Import` utility. After that, we recommend you to run a major compaction on the table and perform cluster balancing manually, to cause the cluster to run in the best status. This can be done via HBase Shell by using the following command:

```
hbase> major_compact 'hly_temp'
hbase> balancer
```

There's more...

If you are importing data into a newly created table, you may find that the importing speed is not as fast as you had expected. This is because the table starts with only one region, and all the edits will go to that region. This makes the hosting region server busy to handle those requests. At the same time, other region servers are free of load. The cluster keeps running on this unbalanced status until the data in the first region reaches a threshold and the region is split into two regions. It will take a long time before a new table becomes well balanced by this automatic region splitting.

The solution is to precreate enough regions at the time of creating the table. The regions need to be created with proper boundaries so that edits can be distributed well to all these precreated regions. In order to determine proper boundaries, you might also want to back up your region starting keys, which can also be used to restore the region distribution of an HBase table.

Since HBase 0.94, the `Import` utility can generate the HBase internal files (HFiles) for bulk load. With this feature, we are able to restore the dump files in a shorter time frame. Refer to *HBASE-5440* for more details (`https://issues.apache.org/jira/browse/HBASE-5440`).

See also

In this chapter:

- *Exporting HBase table to dump files on HDFS*
- *Backing up region starting keys*

In *Chapter 9, Advanced Configurations and Tuning*:

- *Precreating regions using your own algorithm*

In *Chapter 3, Using Administration Tools*:

- *Using HBase Shell to manage the cluster*

Backing up NameNode metadata

As HBase runs within HDFS, in addition to taking care of the HBase cluster, it is also important to keep your HDFS running on a healthy status. NameNode is the most important component in an HDFS cluster. A NameNode crash makes the entire HDFS cluster inaccessible. The metadata of an HDFS cluster, including the filesystem image and edit log, is managed by NameNode.

We need to protect our NameNode metadata for two situations:

- Metadata lost in the event of a crash
- Metadata corruption by any reason

For the first situation, we can set up NameNode to write its metadata to its local disk, along with an NFS mount. As described in the *Setting up multiple, highly available (HA) masters* recipe, in *Chapter 1, Setting Up HBase Cluster*, we can even set up multiple NameNode nodes to achieve high availability.

Our solution for the second situation, is to back up the metadata frequently so that we can restore the NameNode state in case of metadata corruption.

We will describe how to back up and restore NameNode metadata in this recipe.

Getting ready

Start your HDFS and log in to your client node. We assume that NameNode is running on the `master1` server using the default web UI port `50070`. Make sure the port is opened for your client node.

The `dfs.name.dir` property specifies where the NameNode metadata has been saved. Grep the HDFS configuration file (`hdfs-site.xml`) to find out the value of this property, which is required to perform the restoration task. We assume the value is `/usr/local/hadoop/var/dfs/name`, in the demonstration.

We will save the backup under `/backup/namenode` on the client node and use `/restore/namenode` on the NameNode server as a working directory for the restoring. Create these directories and make sure that the user running the backup task has write permission on them.

How to do it...

In order to back up the NameNode metadata:

1. Set an environment variable:

    ```
    hadoop@client1$ export BACKUP_DIR=/backup/namenode
    ```

2. Get HDFS's filesystem image from the NameNode web UI:

    ```
    hadoop@client1$ curl http://master1:50070/getimage?getimage=1 >
    $BACKUP_DIR/fsimage
    ```

3. Get HDFS's edit log from the NameNode web UI:

    ```
    hadoop@client1$ curl http://master1:50070/getimage?getedit=1 >
    $BACKUP_DIR/edits
    ```

4. Make a tarball for the fetched metadata by using the following command:

    ```
    hadoop@client1$ tar cfvj $BACKUP_DIR/metadata.`date +%Y%m%d`.tar.
    bz2 -C $BACKUP_DIR fsimage edits
    ```

In order to restore the NameNode state from a metadata backup:

1. Stop the NameNode daemon if it is running from your NameNode server:

    ```
    hadoop@master1$ $HADOOP_HOME/bin/hadoop-daemon.sh stop namenode
    ```

    If the previous command does not work for any reason, just kill the Java process of NameNode.

2. Copy metadata from the backup to the `dfs.name.dir` directory on the NameNode server:

```
hadoop@master1$ cd /usr/local/hadoop/var/dfs/name/current

hadoop@master1$ tar cfvj /restore/namenode/metadata-org.tar.bz2
fsimage edits

hadoop@master1$ scp client1:/backup/namenode/metadata.`date
+%Y%m%d`.tar.bz2 ./

hadoop@master1$ tar xfvj metadata.`date +%Y%m%d`.tar.bz2

hadoop@master1$ rm metadata.`date +%Y%m%d`.tar.bz2
```

3. Start the NameNode daemon again:

```
hadoop@master1$ $HADOOP_HOME/bin/hadoop-daemon.sh start namenode
```

4. Run `hadoop fsck` to check inconsistencies after the NameNode server has been restarted:

```
hadoop@master1$ $HADOOP_HOME/bin/hadoop fsck / -files | grep
CORRUPT
```

If many files have been corrupted, as you can see from the web UI, NameNode might continue in safe mode until you explicitly turn it off:

5. Turn off safe mode by explicitly using the following command:

```
hadoop@master1$ $HADOOP_HOME/bin/hadoop dfsadmin -safemode leave
Safe mode is OFF
```

The web UI will not state that safe mode is turned off; instead, it may show a warning message on the page:

Hadoop NameNode ip-10-160-46-22.us-west-1.compute.internal:8020

http://master1:50070/dfshealth.jsp   Google

NameNode 'ip-10-160-46-22.us-west-1.compute.internal:8020'

Started: Sun Jan 08 22:02:59 JST 2012
Version: 0.20.205.0, r1179940
Compiled: Fri Oct 7 06:26:14 UTC 2011 by hortonfo
Upgrades: There are no upgrades in progress.

Browse the filesystem
Namenode Logs

Cluster Summary

318 files and directories, 158 blocks = 476 total. Heap Size is 31.57 MB / 966.69 MB (3%)

WARNING : There are about 1 missing blocks. Please check the log or run fsck.

Configured Capacity	:	14.79 GB
DFS Used	:	1.82 GB
Non DFS Used	:	6.97 GB

6. Run `hadoop fsck -move` to move the corrupt files, if any, to `/lost+found`:

```
hadoop@master1$ $HADOOP_HOME/bin/hadoop fsck / -move
The filesystem under path '/' is CORRUPT
```

7. Run `hadoop fsck` again, after the delete, to confirm that no inconsistency exists:

```
hadoop@master1$ $HADOOP_HOME/bin/hadoop fsck /
The filesystem under path '/' is HEALTHY
```

How it works...

NameNode supports getting its filesystem image and edit log from its web UI. From step 1 to 4, we use this feature to fetch the NameNode metadata to the local disk on the client node, and then make a tarball of the fetched metadata as a backup.

In order to restore the metadata from a backup, we first stop the NameNode daemon in step 5, and then in step 6, move the original metadata to our working directory, just in case you want to cancel the restoration for any reason. After that, we copy the backup to the `$dfs.name.dir/current` directory, where the NameNode metadata is stored, and then start the NameNode daemon again.

If there are edits that happened after our latest backup, the metadata we restored will not match the actual data on DataNodes, in which case our HDFS becomes inconsistent. We run the `hadoop fsck` command to check the HDFS inconsistencies in step 8. If the path and the `-files` option are provided, `fsck` will check the inconsistencies under the specified path and print the file it is checking.

If corrupt files are detected, we need to delete them to make HDFS consistent. If many files have been corrupted, NameNode will not be able to reach the threshold of the reported blocks ratio that it will keep in safe mode. Before we can delete the corrupt files, we need to turn off the NameNode safe mode explicitly. This is done by the `hadoop dfsadmin` command in step 9. `Dfsadmin` is an HDFS command for administration tasks. Running it with the `-safemode leave` option turns off the NameNode safe mode explicitly.

As the safe mode is turned off, we can use the `fsck` command with the `-move` option to move the corrupt files to `/lost+found`. After that, `fsck` should report the filesystem as healthy, and you should be able to access the HDFS.

There's more...

Restoring the NameNode state from a metadata backup can take a long time to complete. This is because the restart of a NameNode daemon will at first load the filesystem image from disk, and then replay the edit log to reconstruct the final system state. The edit log can be huge and the replaying can take a long time.

HDFS has a SecondaryNameNode component for this issue. Note that SecondaryNameNode is not a backup daemon for the NameNode. It periodically (default 1 hour) compacts the edit log into a checkpoint, so that a restart of NameNode then loads the latest checkpoint, and a much smaller edit log that contains only the edits since the checkpoint. With this compaction capability, SecondaryNameNode makes the backup and restoring of NameNode metadata much more efficient.

SecondaryNameNode, by default, runs on the same node as NameNode. We recommend you to run it on a separate server from the NameNode server, for scalability and durability. It is configured in the `masters` file under Hadoop's configuration directory:

hadoop@master1$ vi $HADOOP_HOME/conf/masters

```
secondary_namenode_host
```

In order to start SecondaryNameNode in this file, add the hostname you want, and restart HDFS to apply the change.

Backing up region starting keys

Besides the tables in HBase, we should back up the region starting keys for each table. Region starting keys determine the data distribution in a table, as regions are split by region starting keys. A region is the basic unit for load balancing and metrics gathering in HBase.

There is no need to back up the region starting keys if you are performing full shutdown backups using `distcp`, because `distcp` also copies region boundaries to the backup cluster.

But for the live backup options, backing up region starting keys is as important as the table data, which is especially true if your data distribution is difficult to calculate in advance or your regions are manually split. It is important because live backup options, including the `CopyTable` and `Export` utilities use the normal HBase client API to restore data in a MapReduce job. The restoring speed can be improved dramatically if we precreate well-split regions before running the restore MapReduce job.

We will describe how to back up an HBase table's region starting keys in this recipe. We will create a script to get the region starting keys from an HBase table.

Getting ready

Start your HBase cluster, create a table, and put some data in it. The table needs to have several regions in it so that we can verify whether our script works well or not. If your table has only one region, manually split it into several regions from the table page of the HBase web UI. We will use the `hly_temp` table in this recipe; its web UI page looks like the web page shown in the following screenshot:

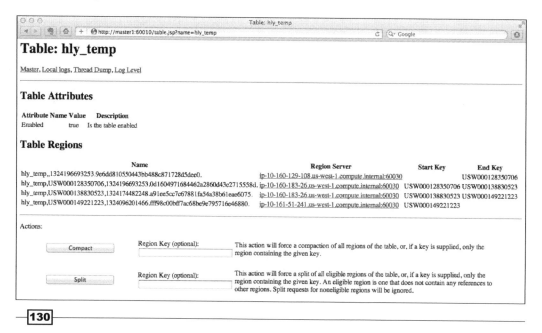

We will back up the `hly_temp` table's region starting keys under the `/backup/hly_temp` directory on our client node. Create this directory and grant write privilege to the user who will run the backup script.

How to do it...

Follow these instructions to back up the `hly_temp` table's region starting keys:

1. Create a `region-start-keys.rb` script file:

```
include Java
import org.apache.hadoop.hbase.util.Bytes
import org.apache.hadoop.hbase.client.HTable

table_name = ARGV[0]
output_file = ARGV[1]

table = HTable.new(table_name)
starting_keys = table.getStartKeys()
f = File.open(output_file, 'w')
for starting_key in starting_keys
    str_starting_key = Bytes.toString(starting_key)
    f.puts str_starting_key
end

f.close()
table.close()
```

2. Run the script on the client node:

```
hac@client1 $HBASE_HOME/bin/hbase org.jruby.Main region-starting-keys.rb hly_temp /backup/hly_temp/regions
```

3. A file (`/backup/hly_temp/regions`) containing the region starting keys will be created by the script. The file looks like as follows:

```
hac@client1$ cat /backup/hly_temp/regions


USW000128350706
USW000138830523
USW000149221223
```

How it works...

To get the region starting keys of an HBase table, we need to access the HBase Java client API from the script. There are several JVM-based scripting languages, such as Jython, Scala, and JRuby. Our script created in step 1 was written in JRuby. We chose JRuby because, as HBase Shell is written in JRuby, there is no need to introduce another language and its dependencies.

In the script, we create an `HTable` instance to access our `hly_temp` table. The `HTable` class is used to communicate with a single HBase table. We only pass the table name (`hly_temp`) to the constructor of the `HTable` class. The ZooKeeper quorum connection string for the HBase cluster is set to the default value, which is achieved from HBase's configuration file (`hbase-site.xml`) on the client, by using the `hbase` command. If the `HTable` instance was created successfully, a connection session to the ZooKeeper quorum will be established. After that, we can communicate to our `hly_temp` table via the `HTable` instance.

Next, we call the `getStartKeys()` method of the `HTable` instance, which returns an array of region starting keys for the table. A region starting key is a row key represented by a byte array in HBase.

In the next step of the script, we convert the keys to strings using the `Bytes` class. The `Bytes` class is a utility class converting other objects from/to a byte array. This class is useful because all Key/Values are stored as byte array in HBase, regardless of their original data type.

In the last step of the script, we write the converted strings to the output file, and finally close the connection to the cluster.

In step 2, we execute the script by running the `hbase` command. The `hbase` command is used to run a Java class in the current HBase context. To run a JRuby script, we pass `org.jruby.Main`—the main class of JRuby, to the `hbase` command. Our script is passed to the `org.jruby.Main` class and run in the HBase context. The table name and output file's path are also passed to the script via the command line.

As you can see from the output of step 3, the region starting keys we wrote to the output file are the same as what we have seen on the table's administration web page.

See also

> ▶ *Precreating regions using your own algorithm* recipe, in *Chapter 9, Advanced Configurations and Tuning*

Cluster replication

HBase supports cluster replication, which is a way to copy data between the HBase clusters. For example, it can be used as a way to easily ship edits from a real-time frontend cluster to a batch purpose cluster on the backend.

The basic architecture of an HBase replication is very practical. The master cluster captures write ahead log (WAL), and puts replicable Key/Values (edits of the column family with replication support) from the log into the replication queue. The replication message is then sent to the peer cluster, and then replayed on that cluster using its normal HBase client API. The master cluster also keeps the current position of the WAL being replicated in ZooKeeper for failure recovery.

Because the HBase replication is done asynchronously, the clusters participating in the replication can be geographically distant. It is not a problem if the connections between them are offline for some time, as the master cluster will track the replication, and recover it after connections are online again. This means that the HBase replication can serve as a disaster recovery solution at the HBase layer.

We will look at how to enable the replication of a table between two clusters, in this recipe.

Getting ready

You will need two HBase clusters—one is the master, and the other is the replication peer (slave) cluster. Here, let's say the master is `master1:2181/hbase`, and the peer is `l-master1:2181/hbase`; the two clusters do not need to be of the same size.

ZooKeeper should be handled independently, and not by HBase. Check the `HBASE_MANAGES_ZK` setting in your `hbase-env.sh` file, and make sure it is set to `false`.

All machines, including the ZooKeeper clusters and HBase clusters, need to be able to reach other machines. Make sure both clusters have the same HBase and Hadoop major version. For example, having 0.92.1 on the master and 0.92.0 on the peer is correct, but 0.90 is not.

How to do it...

Follow these instructions to replicate data between HBase clusters:

1. Add the following code to HBase's configuration file (`hbase-site.xml`) to enable replication on the master cluster:

   hadoop@master1$ vi $HBASE_HOME/conf/hbase-site.xml

   ```
   <property>
       <name>hbase.replication</name>
       <value>true</value>
   </property>
   ```

2. Sync the change to all the servers, including the client nodes in the cluster, and restart HBase.

3. Connect to HBase Shell on the master cluster and enable replication on the table you want to replicate:

```
hac@client1$ $HBASE_HOME/bin/hbase shell
hbase> create 'reptable1', { NAME => 'cf1', REPLICATION_SCOPE =>
1}
```

If you are using an existing table, alter it to support replication:

```
hbase> disable 'reptable1'
hbase> alter 'reptable1', NAME => 'cf1',  REPLICATION_SCOPE => '1'
hbase> enable 'reptable1'
```

4. Execute steps 1 to 3 on the peer (slave) cluster as well. This includes enabling replication, restarting HBase, and creating an identical copy of the table.

5. Add a peer replication cluster via HBase Shell from the master cluster:

```
hbase> add_peer '1', '1-master1:2181:/hbase'
```

6. Start replication on the master cluster by running the following command:

```
hbase> start_replication
```

7. Add some data into the master cluster:

```
hbase> put 'reptable1', 'row1', 'cf1:v1', 'foo'
hbase> put 'reptable1', 'row1', 'cf1:v2', 'bar'
hbase> put 'reptable1', 'row2', 'cf1:v1', 'foobar'
```

You should be able to see the data appear in the peer cluster table in a short while.

8. Connect to HBase Shell on the peer cluster and do a scan on the table to see if the data has been replicated:

```
hac@1-client1$ $HBASE_HOME/bin/hbase shell
hbase> scan ' reptable1'
ROW          COLUMN+CELL
 row1        column=cf1:v1, timestamp=1326095294209, value=foo
 row1        column=cf1:v2, timestamp=1326095300633, value=bar
 row2        column=cf1:v1, timestamp=1326095307619, value=foobar
2 row(s) in 0.0280 seconds
```

9. Verify the replicated data on the two clusters by invoking the `verifyrep` command on the master cluster:

```
hac@client1$ $HADOOP_HOME/bin/hadoop jar $HBASE_HOME/hbase-
0.92.1.jar verifyrep 1 reptable1

12/01/09 16:50:22 INFO replication.ReplicationZookeeper:
Replication is now started
```

...

```
12/01/09 16:50:24 INFO mapred.JobClient: Running job:
job_201201091517_0005

12/01/09 16:50:25 INFO mapred.JobClient:  map 0% reduce 0%

12/01/09 16:50:46 INFO mapred.JobClient:  map 100% reduce 0%

12/01/09 16:50:51 INFO mapred.JobClient: Job complete:
job_201201091517_0005

12/01/09 16:50:51 INFO mapred.JobClient: Counters: 19

...

12/01/09 16:50:51 INFO mapred.JobClient:    File Output Format
Counters

12/01/09 16:50:51 INFO mapred.JobClient:       Bytes Written=0

12/01/09 16:50:51 INFO mapred.JobClient:    org.apache.hadoop.
hbase.mapreduce.replication.VerifyReplication$Verifier$Counters

12/01/09 16:50:51 INFO mapred.JobClient:       GOODROWS=2

...
```

We skipped some output of the `verifyrep` command to make it clearer.

10. Stop the replication on the master cluster by running the following command:

    ```
    hbase> stop_replication
    ```

11. Remove the replication peer from the master cluster by using the following command:

    ```
    hbase> remove_peer '1'
    ```

How it works...

Replication is still considered an experimental feature, and it is disabled by default. In order to enable it, we added the `hbase.replication` property into HBase's configuration file (`hbase-site.xml`) and set it to `true`. In order to apply the change, we sync it to all nodes, including the client node in the cluster, and then restart HBase in step 2. Data replication is configured at column family level. Setting a column family with the `REPLICATION_SCOPE =>` `'1'` property enables that column family to support replication. We did this in step 3, by either altering an existing table, or creating a new one with the replication scope set to `1`.

For the peer cluster, we did the same procedure in step 4—enabling replication support and creating an identical table with the exact same name— for those replicated families.

With the preparation done between steps 1 and 4, we add the replication peer cluster to the master cluster in step 5, so that edits can be shipped to it subsequently. A replication peer is identified by an ID (1 in our case) and a full description of the cluster's ZooKeeper quorum, whose format is `hbase.zookeeper.quorum:hbase.zookeeper.client.port:zookeeper.znode.parent`, such as `server,server2,server3:2181:/hbase`. After that, we start the actual shipping of edit records to the peer cluster.

To test our replication setting, we put some data into the table, and after a while, as you can see from the output of the `scan` command on the peer cluster, data has been shipped to the peer cluster correctly. While this is easy to do when looking at only a few rows, the better way is to use the `verifyrep` command to do a comparison between the two tables. The following is the help description of the `verifyrep` command:

```
hac@client1$ $HADOOP_HOME/bin/hadoop jar $HBASE_HOME/hbase-0.92.1.jar
verifyrep

Usage: verifyrep [--starttime=X] [--stoptime=Y] [--families=A] <peerid>
<tablename>


Options:
  starttime    beginning of the time range

               without endtime means from starttime to forever
  stoptime     end of the time range
  families     comma-separated list of families to copy


Args:
 peerid        Id of the peer used for verification, must match the one
given for replication
  tablename    Name of the table to verify


Examples:
 To verify the data replicated from TestTable for a 1 hour window with
peer #5

 $ bin/hbase org.apache.hadoop.hbase.mapreduce.replication.
VerifyReplication --starttime=1265875194289 --stoptime=1265878794289 5
TestTable
```

Running `verifyrep` from the `hadoop jar` command, with parameters of the peer ID (the one used to establish a replication stream in step 5) and the table name, will start a MapReduce job to compare each cell in the original and replicated tables. Two counters are provided by using the `verifyrep` command—`Verifier.Counters.GOODROWS` and `Verifier.Counters.BADROWS`. Good rows means that the rows between the two tables were an exact match, while the bad rows are the rows that did not match. As our data was replicated successfully, we got the following output:

```
12/01/09 16:50:51 INFO mapred.JobClient:     GOODROWS=2
```

If you got some bad rows, check the MapReduce job's map log to see the reason.

Finally, we stop the replication and remove the peer from the master cluster. Stopping the replication will still complete shipping all the queued edits to the peer, but not accept further processing.

There's more...

In order to dig deeper into the architecture used for HBase cluster replication, refer to the following document—`http://hbase.apache.org/replication.html`.

5

Monitoring and Diagnosis

In this chapter, we will focus on:

- ▶ Showing the disk utilization of HBase tables
- ▶ Setting up Ganglia to monitor an HBase cluster
- ▶ OpenTSDB—using HBase to monitor an HBase cluster
- ▶ Setting up Nagios to monitor HBase processes
- ▶ Using Nagios to check Hadoop/HBase logs
- ▶ Simple scripts to report the status of the cluster
- ▶ Hot region—write diagnosis

Introduction

It is vital to monitor the status of an HBase cluster to ensure that it is operating as expected. The challenge of monitoring a distributed system, besides taking the case of each server separately, is that you will also need to look at the overall status of the cluster.

HBase inherits its monitoring APIs from Hadoop's metrics framework. It exposes a large amount of metrics, giving the insight information of the cluster. These metrics are subsequently configured to expose other monitoring systems, such as Ganglia or OpenTSDB, to gather and make them visible through graphs. Ganglia/OpenTSDB graphs help us understand the insight of the cluster, both for a single server and the entire cluster.

Graphs are good for getting an overview of the historical status, but we also need a mechanism to check the current state of the cluster, and send us notifications or take some automatic actions if the cluster has some problem. A good solution for this kind of monitoring task is Nagios. Nagios sits at the center of a monitoring system to watch cluster resources and alert users.

We will describe how to monitor and diagnose an HBase cluster with Ganglia, OpenTSDB, Nagios, and other tools. We will start with a simple task to show the disk utilization of HBase tables. We will install and configure Ganglia to monitor HBase metrics and show an example using Ganglia graphs. We will also set up OpenTSDB, which is similar to Ganglia but more scalable, as it is built on top of HBase.

We will set up Nagios to check everything we want to check, including HBase-related daemon health, Hadoop/HBase logs, HBase inconsistencies, HDFS health, and space utilization.

In the last recipe, we will describe an approach to diagnose and fix the frequently asked hot spot region issue.

Showing the disk utilization of HBase tables

In this recipe, we will show the answer to the following simple question:

How much space is HBase or a single HBase table using on HDFS?

It is a really simple task, but you might need to answer this question frequently. We will give you a tip to make it a bit easier.

Getting ready

Start your HBase cluster and log in to your HBase client node. We assume your HBase root directory on HDFS is /hbase.

How to do it...

The instructions to show the disk utilization of HBase tables are as follows:

1. Show the disk utilization for all HBase objects by executing the following command:

```
$ $HADOOP_HOME/bin/hadoop fs -dus /hbase
hdfs://master1:8020/hbase          1016842660
```

2. Show the disk utilization of a particular HBase table (hly_temp) by executing the following command:

```
$ $HADOOP_HOME/bin/hadoop fs -dus /hbase/hly_temp
hdfs://master1:8020/hbase/hly_temp          54738763
```

3. Show a list of the regions of an HBase table and their disk utilization, by executing the following command:

```
$ $HADOOP_HOME/bin/hadoop fs -du /hbase/hly_temp
Found 3 items
27709729    hdfs://master1:8020/hbase/hly_temp/
0b593d9dc044f1fe011ec0c902f68fc5
13545245    hdfs://master1:8020/hbase/hly_temp/
5740a39d9eaa59c4175487c14e0a272a
13483789    hdfs://master1:8020/hbase/hly_temp/
5ef67f6d2a792fb0bd737863dc00b6a7
```

How it works...

All HBase objects are stored under the HBase root directory on HDFS. The HBase root directory is configured by the `hbase.rootdir` property in the HBase configuration file (`hbase-site.xml`). By default, the root directory is `/hbase`. Thus the disk utilization of all HBase objects equals the HDFS usage under the HBase root directory.

In step 1, to show the HDFS usage, we ran the `hadoop fs -dus` command passing our HBase root directory (`/hbase`) to it. The amount of space under the `/hbase` directory is shown in the output in bytes.

In step 2, to show the `hly_temp` table's disk utilization, we just passed `/hbase/hly_temp` to the `hadoop fs -dus` command. This is possible because a particular HBase table's objects are stored under the `${hbase.rootdir}/<table_name>` directory on HDFS.

Step 3 is a little different. We ran the `hadoop fs -du` command to show a list of the regions of the `hly_temp` table and their disk utilization. The `hadoop fs -du` command is similar to the `hadoop fs -dus` command, but displays the amount of space for each directory/file under a specific path.

There's more...

As you can see from the output, the disk utilization is displayed in bytes, which is not human-friendly, especially when it is a large number. The following is a simple JRuby script, used to convert the output to a humanly readable format:

1. Create a `dus.rb` file with the following content:

```
$ vi dus.rb
include Java
import org.apache.hadoop.util.StringUtils

path = ARGV[0]
```

```
dus = %x[$HADOOP_HOME/bin/hadoop fs -dus #{path}]
splited = dus.split
byteDesc = StringUtils.byteDesc(splited[1].to_i)
puts splited[0] + "\t" + byteDesc
```

2. Run `dus.rb` to show HBase's disk utilization with a humanly readable output:

   ```
   $ $HBASE_HOME/bin/hbase org.jruby.Main dus.rb /hbase
   hdfs://master1:8020/hbase          969.74 MB
   ```

In `dus.rb`, we simply execute the same `hadoop fs -dus` command to determine the amount of space HBase is using. After that, we use the `org.apache.hadoop.util.StringUtils` class to convert the value to a human-friendly format, and then display the converted value to output.

Setting up Ganglia to monitor an HBase cluster

One of the most important parts of HBase operation tasks is to monitor the cluster and make sure it is running as expected. HBase inherits its monitoring APIs from Hadoop. It exposes a lot of metrics, which gives the insight information of the cluster's current status, including region-based statistics, RPC details, and the **Java Virtual Machine** (**JVM**) memory and garbage collection data.

These metrics are then subsequently configured to expose to JMX and Ganglia, which makes the metrics visible through graphs. Ganglia is the recommended tool for monitoring large-scale clusters. Ganglia itself is a scalable, distributed system; it is said to be able to handle clusters with 2000 nodes.

We will describe how to use Ganglia to monitor an HBase cluster in this recipe. We will install **Ganglia Monitoring Daemon** (**Gmond**) on each node in the cluster, which will gather the server and HBase metrics of that node. These metrics are then subsequently polled to **Ganglia Meta Daemon** (**Gmetad**) servers, where the metrics are computed and saved in round-robin, time-series databases using **round-robin database tool** (**RRDtool**). We will set up only one Gmetad node here, but it is possible to scale out to multiple Gmetad nodes, where at each Gmetad node it aggregates its assigned Gmond nodes' results.

We will also install a PHP web frontend on the same Gmetad server, so that we can access Ganglia from web browsers. Finally, we will describe how to configure HBase to expose its metrics to Ganglia.

Getting ready

Besides the servers in the cluster, you will need a Gmetad server to run the Gmetad daemon on it. In our demonstration, we will use `master2` as the Gmetad server.

Add a `ganglia` user as the owner of the Ganglia daemons:

```
# adduser --disabled-login --no-create-home ganglia
```

On all nodes you want to monitor, download Ganglia-3.0.7 from: `http://downloads.sourceforge.net/project/ganglia/ganglia%20monitoring%20core/3.0.7%20%28Fossett%29/ganglia-3.0.7.tar.gz`.

Extract the downloaded tarball. You will need root privileges on all the servers to install Ganglia.

How to do it...

The instructions to set up Gmond are as follows; they need to be performed on all the nodes you want to monitor:

1. Install the dependencies:

   ```
   # apt-get install build-essential libapr1-dev libconfuse-dev
   libexpat1-dev python-dev
   ```

2. Build and install Ganglia:

   ```
   # cd ganglia-3.0.7
   ```
   ```
   # ./configure
   ```
   ```
   # make
   ```
   ```
   # make install
   ```

3. Generate a default configuration file:

   ```
   # gmond --default_config > /etc/gmond.conf
   ```

4. Make the following changes to the generated configuration file:

   ```
   # vi /etc/gmond.conf
   globals {
   user = ganglia
   }
   cluster {
   name = "hbase-cookbook"
   }
   udp_send_channel {
   #   mcast_join = 239.2.11.71
   host = master2
   ```

```
port = 8649
#   ttl = 1
}
udp_recv_channel {
#   mcast_join = 239.2.11.71
port = 8649
#   bind = 239.2.11.71
}
```

5. Start Gmond:

    # gmond

    Set up Gmetad by using the following instructions. Only execute them on the Gmetad nodes.

6. Install the dependencies:

    # apt-get install build-essential libapr1-dev libconfuse-dev libexpat1-dev python-dev librrd2-dev

7. Build and install Gmetad:

    # cd ganglia-3.0.7

    # ./configure --with-gmetad

    # make

    # make install

8. Copy the sample configuration file (`gmetad.conf`) to its default location:

    # cp ganglia-3.0.7/gmetad/gmetad.conf /etc/gmetad.conf

9. Find the following settings and change them, as shown in the next snippet:

    # vi /etc/gmetad.conf

    ```
    data_source "hbase-cookbook" master2
    gridname "hbase-cookbook"
    setuid_username "ganglia"
    ```

10. Create a directory for the round-robin databases, to store collected data:

    # mkdir -p /var/lib/ganglia/rrds

    # chown -R ganglia:ganglia /var/lib/ganglia

11. Start Gmetad:

    # gmetad

    The following are instructions to set up the Ganglia web frontend. Perform these steps on your web frontend node only. It is usually the same as the Gmetad node.

12. Install the dependencies:

```
# apt-get install rrdtool apache2 php5-mysql
libapache2-mod-php5 php5-gd
```

13. Copy the PHP files of the Ganglia web frontend to the location where Apache's web files are stored:

```
# cp -r ganglia-3.0.7/web /var/www/ganglia
```

14. Restart the Apache web server:

```
# /etc/init.d/apache2 restart
```

You should be able to access your Ganglia web frontend page at:
`http://master2/ganglia/.`

The Ganglia frontend page has all the graphs of metrics that Ganglia has collected, as shown in the following screenshot:

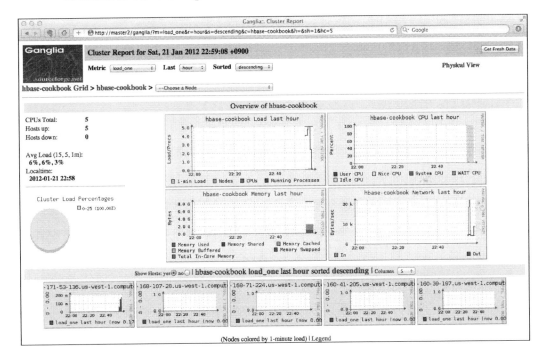

Lastly, the following instructions are for HBase to export its metrics to Ganglia:

15. Edit the HBase metrics configuration file (`hadoop-metrics.properties`) as follows:

```
hadoop@master1$ vi $HBASE_HOME/conf/hadoop-metrics.properties
hbase.extendedperiod = 3600

hbase.class=org.apache.hadoop.metrics.ganglia.GangliaContext
hbase.period=10
hbase.servers=master2:8649

jvm.class=org.apache.hadoop.metrics.ganglia.GangliaContext
jvm.period=10
jvm.servers=master2:8649

rpc.class=org.apache.hadoop.metrics.ganglia.GangliaContext
rpc.period=10
rpc.servers=master2:8649
```

16. Sync `hadoop-metrics.properties` to the slave nodes and restart HBase. You will find that HBase metrics are now collected by Ganglia automatically, as shown in the following screenshot:

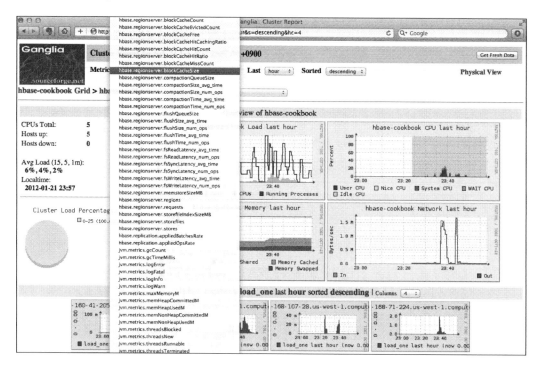

How it works...

When this book was being written, HBase only supported Ganglia 3.0.x versions. This is because the network protocol changed in the newer 3.1.x releases. That's why we have to install Ganglia from the source rather than using a package management system.

We generated a default configuration file by executing the `gmond --default_config` command in step 3. The file is created at `/etc/gmond.conf`, which is the default configuration file the Gmond daemon will read.

In step 4, we set the owner of the Gmond daemon as the `ganglia` user and the name of the cluster to `hbase-cookbook`. Instead of the default UDP multicast communication method we use between Gmonds, we have configured it to use unicast messages. This is done by commenting out the multicast address and **time to live** (**TTL**) settings, and adding a dedicated master Gmond node (`master2`) in the `gmond.conf` file. We chose unicast because multicast is not supported in the Amazon EC2 environment. Another reason is that using unicast is good for a large cluster, say a cluster with more than a hundred nodes.

Gmond needs to be installed and started on all the nodes you want to monitor. Gmond, by default, monitors some basic server metrics on that node, such as load averages and CPU/memory/disk usage.

To install Gmetad, we added the `--with-gmetad` option to compile Gmetad from the source. In steps 8 and 9, we copied the sample configuration file (`gmetad.conf`) to the default location `/etc/gmetad.conf`, and added some changes, including setting the data source, grid name, and owner user of the Gmetad daemon. Note that when using unicast, you need to set `data_source` to the dedicated Gmond server configured in the Gmond setup.

In step 10, we created the default directory (`/var/lib/ganglia/rrds`), where Gmetad stores the collected data in round-robin databases. After that, we started the Gmetad daemon on the Gmetad server (`master2`).

The last part of the Ganglia setup is the PHP web frontend. It is usually set up on the same Gmetad node, so that it can access the round-robin databases created by the Gmetad daemon. This was shown in steps 12 through 14 of the preceding instructions. You should now be able to access the Ganglia web page at `http://master2/ganglia/`, where `master2` is the host running Gmetad. You will only see the basic graphs of the Gmond nodes, because HBase is not yet configured to expose its metrics to Ganglia.

It is set up in the `hadoop-metrics.properties` configuration file to integrate HBase and Ganglia. Do not change the filename, as HBase inherits its monitoring APIs from Hadoop. In this file, we directed HBase to use the `org.apache.hadoop.metrics.ganglia.GangliaContext` class to send its metrics collected by the server process to the Gmond daemon running on `master2:8649`, which is the dedicated Gmond node we specified earlier.

Sync `hadoop-metrics.properties` to the slave nodes and then restart HBase; you will find HBase metric graphs on the Ganglia web page now.

There are some graphs you should pay more attention to, such as the following:

- CPU and memory usage
- JVM GC count and time
- HBase RegionServer compaction queue size
- HBase RegionServer flush queue size

For example, the compaction queue size indicates how many Stores have been queued for compaction in a region server. Usually this should be quite low (up to several tens of a RegionServer). When the server is overloaded, or has I/O issues, you will see a spike on the graph.

The following screenshot shows the CPU usage, JVM GC time, and HBase compaction queue size of a region server, after several rounds of heavy writes rush. As you can see, the CPU usage and long garbage collection time indicates that the server is overloaded. This significantly increased the compaction queue size.

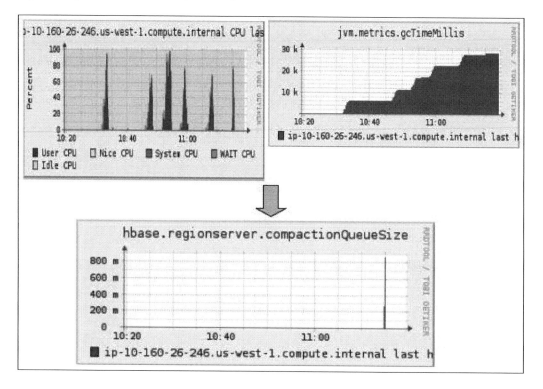

There's more...

Ganglia can be used to monitor Hadoop too. The setup is similar to what we described in this recipe. The following Hadoop metrics can be monitored by Ganglia:

- ▸ HDFS metrics
- ▸ MapReduce metrics
- ▸ JVM metrics
- ▸ Hadoop RPC metrics

See also

In this chapter:

- ▸ *OpenTSDB—using HBase to monitor an HBase cluster*

OpenTSDB—using HBase to monitor an HBase cluster

OpenTSDB is an extremely scalable **Time Series Database** (**TSDB**) built on top of HBase. Like Ganglia, OpenTSDB can be used to monitor various systems including HBase. As compared to Ganglia, which stores its data in RRDtool, OpenTSDB leverages HBase's scalability to monitor it at a larger scale. The following is an introduction from the OpenTSDB homepage (`http://opentsdb.net/`):

> *Thanks to HBase's scalability, OpenTSDB allows you to collect many thousands of metrics from thousands of hosts and applications, at a high rate (every few seconds). OpenTSDB will never delete or downsample data and can easily store billions of data points.*

To use OpenTSDB, we need to write little scripts to collect data from our systems, and push them into OpenTSDB every few seconds. **Tcollector** is a framework for collecting metrics from Linux, MySQL, Hadoop, HBase, and so on for OpenTSDB. It is interesting that OpenTSDB uses HBase (to store metrics) to monitor HBase itself.

In this recipe, we will describe how to set up OpenTSDB and Tcollector and use them to monitor our HBase cluster. We will only start one **Time Series Daemon** (**TSD**) in the demonstration. However, it is possible to run more TSDs on multiple servers as they are independent from each other.

Getting ready

You will need a server to run TSD on. In our demonstration, we will use `master2` as the TSD server.

On the TSD server (`master2`), add a `tsdb` user as the owner of the TSD daemon. We will have all OpenTSDB files and data stored under `/usr/local/opentsdb`:

```
root# adduser --disabled-login --no-create-home tsdb
root# mkdir /usr/local/opentsdb
root# chown tsdb:tsdb /usr/local/opentsdb
```

We will install Tcollector under the `/usr/local/tcollector` directory.

You need root privileges on the TSD server and on all the nodes you want to monitor, such as Hadoop DataNodes and HBase RegionServers.

Finally, make sure your HBase cluster is running. We assume your `HBASE_HOME` environment variable is `/usr/local/hbase/current` and your ZooKeeper quorum runs at `master1:2181`.

How to do it...

The instructions for setting up OpenTSDB and Tcollector are as follows:

▶ **Set up OpenTSDB on the TSD server**: First we will install and configure OpenTSDB on the TSD server (`master2`) as follows:

1. Install the dependencies:

```
hac@master2$ sudo apt-get install gnuplot
hac@master2$ sudo apt-get install autoconf
```

2. Download the latest version of OpenTSDB from `https://github.com/stumbleupon/opentsdb`. We assume the downloaded directory is `$TSDB_INSTALL`. To build and install OpenTSDB, execute the following commands:

```
hac@master2$ cd $TSDB_INSTALL
hac@master2$ PATH=$PATH:$JAVA_HOME/bin
hac@master2$ ./build.sh
hac@master2$ cd build
hac@master2$ sudo make install
```

3. Create OpenTSDB tables in HBase:

```
hac@master2$ export COMPRESSION=LZO
hac@master2$ export HBASE_HOME=/usr/local/hbase/current
hac@master2$ sh $TSDB_INSTALL/src/create_table.sh
```

This step requires the HBase cluster to support LZO compression. If your cluster does not support LZO, don't invoke the first command. Refer to the *Using compression* recipe in *Chapter 8*, *Basic Performance Tuning*, on how to add LZO support to HBase.

4. Create directories where OpenTSDB stores its files and then start the TSD daemon:

```
hac@master2$ sudo su tsdb
tsdb@master2$ cd /usr/local/opentsdb
tsdb@master2$ PATH=$PATH:$JAVA_HOME/bin
tsdb@master2$ tsdtmp=/usr/local/opentsdb/var
tsdb@master2$ mkdir -p "$tsdtmp"

tsdb@master2$ tsdstatic=/usr/local/share/opentsdb/static

tsdb@master2$ nohup tsdb tsd --port=4242
--staticroot="$tsdstatic"
--cachedir="$tsdtmp" --zkquorum=master1:2181 &
```

5. To verify our installation, create OpenTSDB's own metrics, by executing the following command:

```
tsdb@master2$ echo stats | nc -w 1 localhost 4242 \
  | awk '{ print $1 }' | sort -u \
  | xargs tsdb mkmetric
metrics tsd.compaction.count: [0, 0, 2]
metrics tsd.connectionmgr.connections: [0, 0, 3]
metrics tsd.connectionmgr.exceptions: [0, 0, 4]
metrics tsd.hbase.latency_50pct: [0, 0, 5]
metrics tsd.hbase.latency_75pct: [0, 0, 6]
metrics tsd.hbase.latency_90pct: [0, 0, 7]
metrics tsd.hbase.latency_95pct: [0, 0, 8]
metrics tsd.hbase.meta_lookups: [0, 0, 9]
metrics tsd.hbase.root_lookups: [0, 0, 10]
metrics tsd.http.graph.requests: [0, 0, 11]
```

```
metrics tsd.http.latency_50pct: [0, 0, 12]
metrics tsd.http.latency_75pct: [0, 0, 13]
metrics tsd.http.latency_90pct: [0, 0, 14]
metrics tsd.http.latency_95pct: [0, 0, 15]
metrics tsd.jvm.ramfree: [0, 0, 1]

metrics tsd.jvm.ramused: [0, 0, 16]

metrics tsd.rpc.errors: [0, 0, 17]

metrics tsd.rpc.exceptions: [0, 0, 18]
metrics tsd.rpc.received: [0, 0, 19]

metrics tsd.uid.cache-hit: [0, 0, 20]
metrics tsd.uid.cache-miss: [0, 0, 21]
metrics tsd.uid.cache-size: [0, 0, 22]
```

6. Create a simple script to collect stats, which OpenTSDB exposes, and use OpenTSDB to monitor itself:

    tsdb@master2$ vi tsdb-status.sh

```
#!/bin/bash

INTERVAL=15

while :; do

echo stats || exit

sleep $INTERVAL

done | nc -w 30 localhost 4242 \

| sed 's/^/put /' \

| nc -w 30 localhost 4242
```
    tsdb@master2$ chmod 755 tsdb-status.sh
    tsdb@master2$ nohup ./tsdb-status.sh &

7. By opening your browser and accessing `http://master2:4242/`, you will get the OpenTSDB web UI (make sure the 4242 port is open to your client). Enter a time period of the graph to show in the **From** and **To** fields, and metric name in the **Metric** (type `tsd.`, and metrics that start with `tsd.` will pop up) field, you should get a graph, as shown in the following screenshot:

▶ **Set up Tcollector**: For all nodes you want to monitor, for example Hadoop DataNodes and HBase RegionServers, we need to set up Tcollector on them. The following steps need to be executed on every node you want to monitor:

8. Download the latest version of Tcollector from `http://github.com/ stumbleupon/tcollector`, and execute the following commands:

```
$ sudo mv tcollector /usr/local
$ cd /urs/local/tcollector
```

9. There is a collector, which comes with Tcollector, to collect metrics from the HBase RegionServer. Grep the following lines in `hbase_regionserver_ jmx.py` and modify them to fit your environment:

```
$ sudo vi collectors/0/hbase_regionserver_jmx.py
#USER = "hadoop"
USER = "your_running_user"

CLASSPATH = [

#    "/usr/lib/jvm/java-6-sun/lib/tools.jar",
     "/your/java_home/lib/tools.jar",
]

jmx = subprocess.Popen(
#    ["java", "-enableassertions", …
     ["/your/java_home/bin/java", "-enableassertions", …
```

10. In Tcollector's startup script, add the DNS name of the server where the TSD daemon is running:

```
$ sudo vi startstop
TSD_HOST=master2
```

11. On your TSD server, restart the TSD daemon with the `--auto-metric` option:

```
tsdb@master2$ nohup tsdb tsd --port=4242
--staticroot="$tsdstatic" --cachedir="$tsdtmp"
--zkquorum=master1:2181 --auto-metric &
```

12. Start Tcollector to collect metrics and send them to TSD:

```
$ sudo /usr/local/tcollector/startstop start
```

After a while, you should be able to view the metrics collected by Tcollector on the OpenTSDB web UI. The following screenshot shows our HBase cluster's metrics collected by Tcollector:

How it works...

In steps 1 and 2 of the previous instructions, we installed OpenTSDB and its dependencies. As OpenTSDB is built on top of HBase, we need to create OpenTSDB's tables in HBase first. In step 3, we configured OpenTSDB to create its tables with LZO compression support. This requires the HBase cluster to support LZO. You can also use other HBase-supported compressions such as Snappy and Gzip, but just make sure that compression is available on your HBase cluster.

After that, we specify where HBase is installed by setting the `HBASE_HOME` environment variable. Then we invoke `create_table.sh` to actually create the tables in HBase. This script comes with OpenTSDB; it creates two tables—`tsdb` and `tsdb-uid`. You will find these tables on your HBase master UI.

In step 4, we created the necessary directories and started OpenTSDB with options to use those directories. We also passed the `--zkquorum=master1:2181` option to specify where our ZooKeeper quorum is placed.

To verify our installation, we set up OpenTSDB to collect its own metrics in steps 5 and 6. By default, we need to make a metric with the `tsdb mkmetric` command before we can store that metric in OpenTSDB. This is a design to prevent making too many metrics, which makes the metric namespace a mess. As we have shown in step 11, starting the TSD daemon with the `--auto-metric` option configures OpenTSDB to automatically make the metrics that it received.

The TSD daemon accepts the `stats` command to expose its own metrics. We used this to make metrics in step 5.

In step 6, we created a simple script to periodically get the TSD daemon's metrics with the `stats` command, and then put them into OpenTSDB by using the `put` command. As shown in step 7, the collected OpenTSDB's own metrics are displayed as graphs on its web UI.

In steps 8 to 12, we set up Tcollector on each server we want to monitor. Tcollector collects metrics from Hadoop, HBase, and so on and sends them to the TSD daemons. In Tcollector's startup script (`startstop`), we have set `TSD_HOST` to the DNS name of the TSD server to specify which server we should send the metrics to.

In step 11, we restarted our TSD daemon with the `--auto-metric` option, so that metrics received from Tcollector will automatically be created in OpenTSDB. As we mentioned earlier, the automatic creation of metrics is not considered a good practice. You should be aware of what metrics the system is collecting, and create those metrics manually to assure that the metric namespace is clean.

Finally, we started Tcollector to start collecting metrics and sending them to the TSD daemon. Metrics will be stored in HBase and shown as graphs on the OpenTSDB's web UI.

There's more...

TSDash is an alternative web UI/dashboard for OpenTSDB. TSDash provides the same features as the OpenTSDB web UI, but the user interface is a little different. The following screenshot shows TSDash's UI and an example graph:

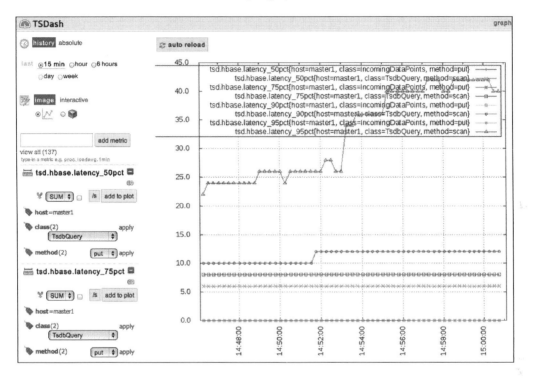

TSDash is available at `https://github.com/facebook/tsdash/`.

Setting up Nagios to monitor HBase processes

Monitoring HBase-related processes in the cluster is an important part of operating HBase. A basic monitoring is done by running health checks on the HBase processes and notifying the administrators if any process is down.

Nagios is a popular, open source monitoring software used to watch hosts, services, and resources, and alert users when something goes wrong and when it gets recovered again. Nagios can be easily extended by custom-modules, which are called **plugins**. The `check_tcp` plugin is shipped with the Nagios installation. We can use this plugin to send a ping to a Hadoop/HBase daemon's RPC port, to check whether the daemon is alive.

In this recipe, we will set up a monitor server running Nagios to watch all the HBase-related processes in the entire cluster. We will configure Nagios to send us e-mail notifications if any Hadoop/HBase/ZooKeeper process is down.

Getting ready

You will need a monitor server to run Nagios on. We assume that you are using a Debian machine with minimal setup. The monitor server needs to be able to communicate with all machines in the cluster via proper TCP ports. In our demonstration, we will use `master2` as the monitor server.

Start the HBase cluster you want to monitor, and then log in to the monitor server. Make sure you have root privileges on the monitor server.

How to do it...

The instructions to install and configure Nagios to monitor your HBase cluster are as follows:

1. Install Nagios on the monitor server using your Linux distribution's package management tool:

   root@master2# apt-get install nagios3 nagios-plugins

   During the installation process, you are asked for a `nagiosadmin` password and Samba workgroup settings; enter your password and let the Samba workgroup settings be set as default.

2. You should be able to access the Nagios admin page from your web browser using the URL `http://<monitor_host>/nagios3/`.

   You will be asked for an account and a password; use `nagiosadmin` and the password you set in the installation to log in to the Nagios admin page. The Nagios admin page looks like the following screenshot:

3. Add all hosts in the HBase cluster to the Nagios hosts configuration file:

```
root@master2# vi /etc/nagios3/conf.d/hosts_nagios2.cfg
#master1
define host{
        use                     generic-host
        host_name               master1
        alias                   master1
        address                 10.160.41.205
        hostgroups              masters
}

#slave1
define host{
        use                     generic-host
        host_name               slave1
        alias                   slave1
        address                 10.168.71.224
        hostgroups              slaves
}

#slave2
define host{
        use                     generic-host
        host_name               slave2
        alias                   slave2
        address                 10.168.107.28
        hostgroups              slaves
}

#slave3
define host{
        use                     generic-host
        host_name               slave3
        alias                   slave3
        address                 10.160.39.197
        hostgroups              slaves
}
```

4. Add the `masters` and `slaves` host groups to Nagios by executing the following command:

```
root@master2# vi /etc/nagios3/conf.d/hostgroups_nagios2.cfg
# A list of your master servers
define hostgroup {
```

```
                hostgroup_name   masters
                alias            Master servers
                members          master1
        }


        # A list of your slave servers
        define hostgroup {
                hostgroup_name   slaves
                alias            Slave servers
                members          slave1,slave2,slave3
        }
```

5. Configure Nagios to monitor master daemons on the master node. We assume that
   the NameNode, ZooKeeper, and HMaster daemons are running on the same master
   node (master1).

   root@master2# vi /etc/nagios3/conf.d/services_nagios2.cfg

```
# check that NameNode is running
define service{
        use                     generic-service
        host_name               master1
        normal_check_interval   1
        service_description     NameNode health
        check_command           check_tcp!8020!
}


# check that ZooKeeper is running
define service{
        use                     generic-service
        host_name               master1
        normal_check_interval   1
        service_description     Zookeeper health
        check_command           check_tcp!2181!
}


# check that HMaster is running
define service{
        use                     generic-service
        host_name               master1
        normal_check_interval   1
        service_description     HMaster health
        check_command           check_tcp!60000!
}
```

6. Configure Nagios to monitor slave daemons on all the slave nodes:

root@master2# vi /etc/nagios3/conf.d/services_nagios2.cfg

```
# check that DataNodes are running
define service{
        use                     generic-service
        hostgroup_name          slaves
        normal_check_interval   1
        service_description     DataNode health
        check_command           check_tcp!50010!
}

# check that HRegionServers are running
define service{
        use                     generic-service
        hostgroup_name          slaves
        normal_check_interval   1
        service_description     HRegionServer health
        check_command           check_tcp!60020!
}
```

7. Change the notification e-mail address; set it to your own:

root@master2# vi /etc/nagios3/conf.d/contacts_nagios2.cfg

```
define contact{
        contact_name                    root
        alias                           Root
        service_notification_period     24x7
        host_notification_period        24x7
        service_notification_options    w,u,c,r
        host_notification_options       d,r
        service_notification_commands   notify-service-by-email
        host_notification_commands      notify-host-by-email
        email                           address@example.com
}
```

8. Install the Postfix e-mail server to let Nagios send out e-mails:

root@master2# apt-get install postfix

During the installation, configure Postfix as **Internet Site** and set a domain from where the Nagios mails will be received.

9. Verify the configuration changes by executing the following command:

root@master2# /usr/sbin/nagios3 -v /etc/nagios3/nagios.cfg

```
Total Warnings: 0

Total Errors:   0
```

10. If everything is fine, restart Nagios to apply the configuration changes:

```
root@master2# /etc/init.d/nagios3 restart
```

As shown in the following screenshot of the Nagios admin page, Nagios starts checking the HBase-related processes we just configured. All the hosts, the Hadoop/HBase/ ZooKeeper daemons, and their statuses are now shown on the Nagios admin page:

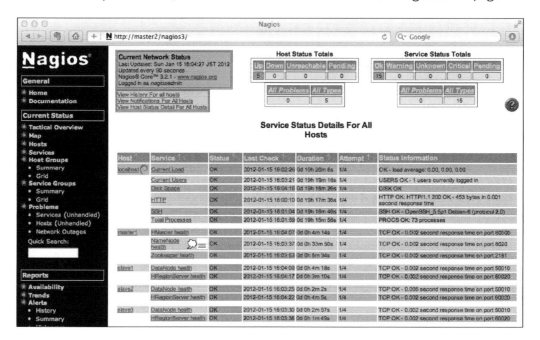

11. To test our Nagios settings, we stop the HRegionServer daemon from one of the slave nodes:

```
hadoop@slave1$ hbase-daemon.sh stop regionserver
```

After a while, the region server that is down will be detected by Nagios and a **CRITICAL** status will be shown on the Nagios admin page, as shown in the following screenshot:

You will also receive an alert e-mail from Nagios reporting that a region server is down, as shown in the following screenshot:

---

nagios@hbase-admin-cookbook.com
** PROBLEM Service Alert: slave1/HRegionServer health is CRITICAL **
January 15, 2012 4:25 PM

***** Nagios *****

Notification Type: PROBLEM

Service: HRegionServer health
Host: slave1
Address: 10.166.223.150
State: CRITICAL

Date/Time: Sun Jan 15 16:21:25 JST 2012

Additional Info:

Connection refused

---

12. Now restart the HRegionServer daemon again, to test Nagios' recovery notification:

```
hadoop@slave1$ hbase-daemon.sh start regionserver
```

You will find that the status has changed to **OK** again. You will also receive a recovery e-mail notification.

How it works...

Nagios is available for many Linux distributions. It is easy to install Nagios using your distribution's package management system.

Nagios has an admin web page, from where you will see the current status of the cluster you are monitoring. You can see the status as per host, host group, service, and service group basis. You can also generate very detailed availability and trend reports on the admin page. The admin page's URL is http://<monitor_host>/nagios3/, where monitor_host is the hostname of your monitor server.

In step 3, we added the host definitions of our cluster to the Nagios host configuration file (hosts_nagios2.cfg), so that Nagios can monitor these remote nodes. We also set up two host groups in step 4, the masters and slaves host groups. This setting allows us to monitor servers on a host group basis.

In step 5, we added several service definitions to the services_nagios2.cfg file, to configure Nagios to monitor the master daemons running on the master node (master1). A service is monitored by check_command, where we use the predefined check_tcp command, passing the RPC port of the NameNode/ZooKeeper/HMaster daemons to it.

In a similar way, we defined services to monitor the slave daemons running on the slave nodes. Note that we used the host group (`slaves`) we added previously in these service definitions.

In step 7, we configured Nagios to send notifications to a specific e-mail address by editing the `contacts_nagios2.cfg` file. After that, we installed the Postfix e-mail server to let Nagios send out e-mails. Finally, we restarted Nagios to apply our changes.

Nagios periodically sends a ping to the RPC port of the daemon, which it is monitoring to check if the daemon is alive. If Nagios cannot get a response from the daemon, it will mark the status of the daemon as **CRITICAL** on its admin page, and send an alert e-mail to the address we specified. This e-mail contains details about the hostname, state of the daemon, when it detected the **CRITICAL** status, and other additional information.

There's more...

Using proper ports, you can also configure Nagios to monitor other Hadoop/HBase/ZooKeeper daemons, such as MapReduce's JobTracker and TaskTracker daemon. The following table shows a quick reference of the Hadoop daemons you might want to monitor and their default RPC/HTTP ports:

Daemon	Default port	Configuration file	Configuration parameter
NameNode	8020	`core-site.xml`	`fs.default.name`
SecondaryNameNode	50090	`hdfs-site.xml`	`dfs.secondary.http.address`
JobTracker	50030	`mapred-site.xml`	`mapred.job.tracker.http.address`
HMaster	60000	`hbase-site.xml`	`hbase.master.port`
ZooKeeper Quorum	2181	`zoo.cfg`	`clientPort`
DataNode	50010	`hdfs-site.xml`	`dfs.datanode.address`
TaskTracker	50060	`mapred-site.xml`	`mapred.task.tracker.http.address`
HRegionServer	60020	`hbase-site.xml`	`hbase.regionserver.port`

Using Nagios to check Hadoop/HBase logs

Hadoop, ZooKeeper, and HBase, all produce logs. These logs include information about normal operations, as well as warning/error output, and internal diagnostic data. It is ideal to have a system gathering and processing all these logs to extract useful insight information of the cluster. A most basic task is to check these logs and get notified if anything abnormal is shown in them. The NRPE and `check_log` Nagios plugins can be used to achieve this simple goal, with a few simple steps.

The description from NRPE plugin's homepage (`http://exchange.nagios.org/directory/Addons/Monitoring-Agents/NRPE--2D-Nagios-Remote-Plugin-Executor/details`) is as follows:

> *NRPE allows you to remotely execute Nagios plugins on other Linux/Unix machines. This allows you to monitor remote machine metrics (disk usage, CPU load, etc.).*

Using NRPE, we can remotely execute the `check_log` Nagios plugin on a cluster node to check the Hadoop/HBase logs generated by that node.

The `check_log` plugin greps a particular query word incrementally in a specified logfile. If any line in the logfile matches the query word, `check_log` reports a critical status to the NRPE server running on the same node. NRPE then reports it to the Nagios server.

As the scope of the book is limited, we will only demonstrate setting up Nagios to check HBase's master daemon log in this recipe. You can easily copy it and make a few changes to set up Nagios to monitor other logs as well.

Getting ready

We assume that you have set up a Nagios monitor server properly, as described in the previous recipe.

The `check_log` plugin will save the previously checked logs so that it only needs to check the newly appended ones. Create a directory on the master node for the `check_log` plugin to save its previously checked logs:

```
root@master1# mkdir -p /var/nagios/oldlog
```

Check your HBase log4j configuration file (`log4j.properties`), and find out where your HBase generates its logfile. We assume that it is `/usr/local/hbase/logs/hbase-hadoop-master-master1.log` in this recipe.

How to do it...

To use Nagios to check Hadoop/HBase logs, perform the following steps:

1. Install the NRPE plugin on the monitor server (`master2`):

   ```
   root@master2# apt-get install nagios-nrpe-plugin
   ```

2. Install the NRPE server and plugin on the master node of the HBase cluster:

   ```
   root@master1# apt-get install nagios-nrpe-server nagios-plugins
   ```

3. Set NRPE on the master node to allow the monitor server to talk to the NRPE daemon running on it. Change the `allowed_hosts` setting for the monitor server in the `nrpe.cfg` file, and then restart the NRPE daemon. This step is implemented as follows:

   ```
   root@master1# vi /etc/nagios/nrpe.cfg
   #allowed_hosts=127.0.0.1
   allowed_hosts=master2
   root@master1# /etc/init.d/nagios-nrpe-server restart
   ```

4. Check the NRPE service before we continue to change the configuration. Do this from the monitor server.

   ```
   root@master2# /usr/lib/nagios/plugins/check_nrpe -H master1
   -c check_users
   ```

   The output should be something as follows:

   ```
   USERS OK - 2 users currently logged in |users=2;5;10;0
   ```

5. Configure the `check_log` command on the master node to check the HBase's master daemon log. Add the following command to the `nrpe.cfg` file on the master node. You will need to change the logfile path of the command definition to fit your environment.

   ```
   root@master1# vi /etc/nagios/nrpe.cfg
   command[check_log_hmaster]=/usr/lib/nagios/plugins/
   check_log       -F /usr/local/hbase/logs/hbase-hadoop-
   master-master1.log -O/var/nagios/oldlog/hbase-hadoop-
   master-master1.log -q "ERROR|FATAL"
   ```

6. Restart the NRPE daemon on the master node to apply our changes:

   ```
   root@master1# /etc/init.d/nagios-nrpe-server restart
   ```

7. Add the following service definitions on the monitor server to check the master logs:

   ```
   root@master2# vi /etc/nagios3/conf.d/services_nagios2.cfg
   # check HMaster log
   define service{
           use                     generic-service
   ```

```
host_name                master1
normal_check_interval    1
service_description      HMaster log check
max_check_attempts       1
notification_options     w,u,c
check_command            check_nrpe_1arg!check_log_hmaster
}
```

8. Restart Nagios on the monitor server to apply the service definitions:

   root@master2# /etc/init.d/nagios3 restart

   You will find that the added services are shown on your Nagios admin page. Nagios starts checking the HMaster daemon's log on the master node.

master1	HMaster health	OK	2012-01-21 15:32:11	0d 0h 22m 53s	1/4	TCP OK - 0.002 second response time on port 60000
	HMaster log check	OK	2012-01-21 15:32:49	0d 0h 1m 15s	1/1	Log check data initialized...
	NameNode health	OK	2012-01-21 15:32:06	0d 0h 23m 58s	1/4	TCP OK - 0.002 second response time on port 8020
	Zookeeper health	OK	2012-01-21 15:32:43	0d 0h 23m 21s	1/4	TCP OK - 0.002 second response time on port 2181

9. Test the setup by adding a `FATAL` entry to the master daemon log:

   hadoop@master1$ echo "FATAL ..." >> /usr/local/hbase/logs/hbase-
   hadoop-master-master1.log

   After a while, this will be detected by Nagios and a **CRITICAL** status will be shown on the Nagios admin page, as shown in the following screenshot:

master1	HMaster health	OK	2012-01-21 16:08:11	0d 0h 58m 51s	1/4	TCP OK - 0.002 second response time on port 60000
	HMaster log check	CRITICAL	2012-01-21 16:08:49	0d 0h 0m 13s	1/1	(1) < FATAL ...
	NameNode health	OK	2012-01-21 16:08:06	0d 0h 59m 56s	1/4	TCP OK - 0.002 second response time on port 8020
	Zookeeper health	OK	2012-01-21 16:08:43	0d 0h 59m 19s	1/4	TCP OK - 0.002 second response time on port 2181

You will also receive an alert e-mail from Nagios reporting that something is wrong in the HBase's master daemon log, as shown in the following screenshot:

nagios@hbase-admin-cookbook.com
** PROBLEM Service Alert: master1/HMaster log check is CRITICAL **
January 21, 2012 4:08 PM

***** Nagios *****

Notification Type: PROBLEM

Service: HMaster log check
Host: master1
Address: 10.160.181.38
State: CRITICAL

Date/Time: Sat Jan 21 16:08:50 JST 2012

Additional Info:

(1) FATAL ...

How it works...

First of all, we need to install the NRPE plugin on the monitor server, and the NRPE server and Nagios plugins on all nodes in the HBase cluster.

In step 3, in order to allow the monitor server to talk to the NRPE daemon on a remote node, we edited the `nrpe.cfg` file on that node, changed the `allowed_hosts` setting to the monitor server (`master2`), and then restarted the NRPE daemon.

After testing the NRPE setting in step 4, we added a `check_log_hmaster` command definition in step 5. This is added to the NRPE configuration file (`nrpe.cfg`) on the node we want to check (the HBase master node). The `check_log_hmaster` command executes the `check_log` plugin in order to check the HBase's master daemon log.

The following syntax shows the usage of the `check_log` plugin:

```
check_log <log_file> <old_log_file> <pattern>
```

We passed the full path of the HBase master logfile, a temporary old logfile name, and the regular expression for matching the abnormal status log. We only searched for ERROR or FATAL in the logfile, which are the keywords when log4j logs errors or fatal information.

In step 7, we defined a service in the `services_nagios2.cfg` file on the monitor server. Note that in the service definition:

▶ The `max_check_attempts` option should be 1

▶ Do not add the `r` option to `notification_options`

These are necessary because of the way the `check_log` plugin operates.

The `check_command` option of the service is `check_nrpe_1arg!check_log_hmaster`, which means it uses NRPE to execute the `check_log_hmaster` command on the remote server.

Restart the NRPE server on the HBase master node and the Nagios daemon on the monitor server. You will find that Nagios starts monitoring the HBase master log and sends notifications to us if ERROR or FATAL appears in the logfile.

There's more...

The following are some other logs that you might want monitored by Nagios:

▶ The NameNode log on the master node

▶ The SecondaryNameNode log on the master node

▶ The JobTracker log on the master node

▶ The ZooKeeper log on all of the ZooKeeper nodes

> ▸ The RegionServer log on all of the region servers

> ▸ The DataNode log on all of the slave nodes

> ▸ The TaskTracker log on all of the slave nodes

You can simply copy the settings we made in this recipe and change the logfile path to configure Nagios to monitor these logs. Your Nagios admin page should look like the following screenshot, if all these logs are monitored by Nagios:

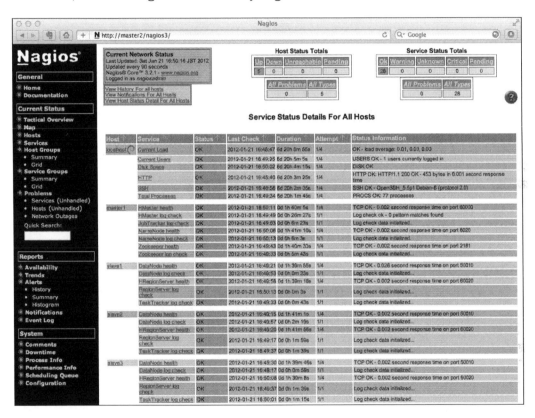

See also

In this chapter:

> ▸ *Setting up Nagios to monitor HBase processes*

Simple scripts to report the status of the cluster

Besides the health of the HBase-related daemons and their logs, what you might want to monitor is the overview of the current status of the cluster. This status basically includes:

▶ The HBase hbck result showing whether the HBase tables are consistent

▶ The Hadoop fsck result showing whether HDFS is healthy

▶ The remaining HDFS space

In this recipe, we will create a check_hbase Nagios plugin to perform the task of monitoring. We will install our check_hbase plugin on the master node of the cluster, and remotely execute it with Nagios from the monitor server using the NRPE Nagios plugin.

Getting ready

We assume that you have installed and configured the Nagios NRPE plugin on your monitor and master server. If you have not installed it yet, refer to the previous recipe for detailed installation instructions.

How to do it...

The following are instructions to get the status of the HBase cluster and monitor it by Nagios:

1. Create a check_hbase script shown as follows:

```
$ vi check_hbase
#/bin/bash
bin=`dirname $0`
bin=`cd $bin;pwd`
. $bin/utils.sh
HADOOP_HOME=/usr/local/hadoop/current
HBASE_HOME=/usr/local/hbase/current

DFS_REMAINING_WARNING=15
DFS_REMAINING_CRITICAL=5
ABNORMAL_QUERY="INCONSISTENT|CORRUPT|FAILED|Exception"

# hbck and fsck report
output=/tmp/cluster-status
$HBASE_HOME/bin/hbase hbck >> $output
$HADOOP_HOME/bin/hadoop fsck /hbase >> $output
```

```
# check report
count=`egrep -c "$ABNORMAL_QUERY" $output`
if [ $count -eq 0 ]; then
    echo "[OK] Cluster is healthy." >> $output
else
    echo "[ABNORMAL] Cluster is abnormal!" >> $output
    # Get the last matching entry in the report file
    last_entry=`egrep "$ABNORMAL_QUERY" $output | tail -1`
    echo "($count) $last_entry"
    exit $STATE_CRITICAL
fi


# HDFS usage
dfs_remaining=`curl -s http://master1:50070/dfshealth.jsp |egrep -
o "DFS Remaining%.*%" | egrep -o "[0-9]*\.[0-9]*"`
dfs_remaining_word="DFS Remaining%: ${dfs_remaining}%"
echo "$dfs_remaining_word" >> $output


# check HDFS usage
dfs_remaining=`echo $dfs_remaining | awk -F '.' '{print $1}'`
if [ $dfs_remaining -lt $DFS_REMAINING_CRITICAL ]; then
    echo "Low DFS space. $dfs_remaining_word"
    exit_status=$STATE_CRITICAL
elif [ $dfs_remaining -lt $DFS_REMAINING_WARNING ]; then
    echo "Low DFS space. $dfs_remaining_word"
    exit_status=$STATE_WARNING
else
    echo "HBase check OK - DFS and HBase healthy.
 $dfs_remaining_word"
    exit_status=$STATE_OK
fi
exit $exit_status
```

2. Copy the script to the Nagios plugin folder on your master node and change its execution permission:

   root@master1# cp check_hbase /usr/lib/nagios/plugins

   root@master1# chmod 755 /usr/lib/nagios/plugins/check_hbase

3. Add the check_hbase command to the NRPE configuration on the master node, by editing the nrpe.cfg file:

   root@master1# vi /etc/nagios/nrpe.cfg

   command[check_hbase]=/usr/lib/nagios/plugins/check_hbase

4. Restart the NRPE daemon on the master node to apply the changes:

```
root@master1# /etc/init.d/nagios-nrpe-server restart
```

5. Add the `check_hbase` service definition on the monitor server:

```
root@master2# vi /etc/nagios3/conf.d/services_nagios2.cfg
# check hbck, fsck, and HDFS usage
define service{
        use                     generic-service
        host_name               master1
        normal_check_interval   5
        service_description     hbck/fsck report and DFS usage
  check
        check_command           check_nrpe_1arg!check_hbase
}
```

6. Restart Nagios to apply the changes:

```
root@master2# /etc/init.d/nagios3 restart
```

   You will find that this service has been added to your Nagios admin page, as shown in the following screenshot:

master1	HMaster health	OK	2012-01-22 17:06:33	0d 1h 9m 5s	1/4	TCP OK - 0.048 second response time on port 60000
	HMaster log check	OK	2012-01-22 17:06:24	0d 1h 11m 14s	1/1	Log check ok - 0 pattern matches found
	JobTracker log check	OK	2012-01-22 17:05:43	0d 1h 10m 55s	1/1	Log check data initialized...
	NameNode health	OK	2012-01-22 17:05:52	0d 1h 10m 46s	1/4	TCP OK - 0.025 second response time on port 8020
	NameNode log check	OK	2012-01-22 17:06:21	0d 1h 11m 17s	1/1	Log check data initialized...
	Zookeeper health	OK	2012-01-22 17:05:40	0d 1h 10m 58s	1/4	TCP OK - 0.002 second response time on port 2181
	Zookeeper log check	OK	2012-01-22 17:06:11	0d 1h 10m 27s	1/1	Log check data initialized...
	hbck/fsck/dfsadmin report and DFS usage check	OK	2012-01-22 17:06:28	0d 0h 49m 10s	1/4	HBase check OK - DFS and HBase healthy. DFS Remaining%: 32.55%

7. Change the warning/critical threshold or abnormal query words to test the plugin. For example, if you change `DFS_REMAINING_CRITICAL` in the plugin to a very high value, you will get an alert notification from Nagios after a while. This is implemented as follows:

```
$ vi check_hbase

#DFS_REMAINING_CRITICAL=10
DFS_REMAINING_CRITICAL=40
```

   Nagios will detect this **CRITICAL** status if your remaining HDFS space is lower than 40 percent, as shown in the following screenshot:

master1	HMaster health	OK	2012-01-22 17:33:33	0d 1h 36m 17s	1/4	TCP OK - 0.029 second response time on port 60000
	HMaster log check	OK	2012-01-22 17:33:24	0d 1h 38m 26s	1/1	Log check ok - 0 pattern matches found
	JobTracker log check	OK	2012-01-22 17:33:43	0d 1h 38m 7s	1/1	Log check data initialized...
	NameNode health	OK	2012-01-22 17:32:52	0d 1h 37m 58s	1/4	TCP OK - 0.022 second response time on port 8020
	NameNode log check	OK	2012-01-22 17:33:21	0d 1h 38m 29s	1/1	Log check data initialized...
	Zookeeper health	OK	2012-01-22 17:33:40	0d 1h 38m 10s	1/4	TCP OK - 0.014 second response time on port 2181
	Zookeeper log check	OK	2012-01-22 17:33:11	0d 1h 37m 39s	1/1	Log check data initialized...
	hbck/fsck/dfsadmin report and DFS usage check	**CRITICAL**	2012-01-22 17:33:28	0d 0h 0m 22s	1/4	Low DFS space. DFS Remaining%: 32.55%

How it works...

In the `check_hbase` script, we firstly execute the `hbase hbck` command to get a report of the current status of the HBase deployment. We also run the `hadoop fsck /hbase` command to check the HDFS health under the `/hbase` directory, which is the default root directory for HBase. The output of these commands is redirected to a temporary file.

We subsequently grep the temporary file, if any `ABNORMAL_QUERY` was found, and show the matched count and last matched entry to standard out and then exit with the `STATE_CRITICAL` status.

The remaining HDFS space is obtained from the HDFS admin web URL. We access the URL and extract the remaining space value from the HTML output using regular expression. Lastly, we compare this value to the warning/critical threshold and generate the proper output and exit status of the script. The output and exit status will subsequently be used as the monitoring result of Nagios.

In step 2, we just copied the script to the Nagios plugin directory and made it executable enough to install as a Nagios plugin. Then in steps 3 and 4, we added the NRPE command definition and restarted our NRPE server on the master node.

On the monitor server, we defined a Nagios service in the `services_nagios2.cfg` file, and then restarted the Nagios daemon to apply the change.

As you can see, Nagios starts monitoring the cluster's status using our `check_hbase` plugin, sending out notifications if either the `hbck` result, `fsck` result, or the HDFS usage has anything abnormal.

There's more...

You might also want to monitor the following statuses of the cluster:

- Available free space in the directory where NameNode stores the filesystem image (`dfs.name.dir` in `hdfs-site.xml`)
- Available free space in the directory where NameNode stores the transaction (edit) file (`dfs.name.edits.dir` in `hdfs-site.xml`, same as `dfs.name.dir` by default)
- The number of regions hosted by a region server; the upper limit should be about 100

These can be done in a similar way to what we have just discussed.

See also

> ▸ *Setting up Nagios to monitor HBase processes* in this chapter
>
> ▸ *Using Nagios to check Hadoop/HBase logs* in this chapter
>
> ▸ *HBase hbck—checking the health of anHBase cluster* in *Chapter 3, Using Administration Tools*

Hot region—write diagnosis

As the data keeps growing, the HBase cluster may become unbalanced due to poorly designed table schema or row keys, or for some other reasons. Many requests may go to a small part of the regions of a table. This is usually called the **hot spot region issue**.

There are two types of hot spot region issues—hot write and hot read issues. Hot write is generally more important for us, because hot read would benefit greatly from the HBase internal cache mechanism. A solution for the hot write region issue is to find out the hot regions, split them manually, and then distribute the split regions to other region servers.

An HBase edit will firstly be written to the region server's **Write-ahead-Log** (**WAL**). The actual update to the table data occurs once the WAL is successfully appended. This architecture makes it possible to get an approximate write diagnosis easily.

We will create a `WriteDiagnosis.java` Java source to get write diagnostic information from WAL, in this recipe. This information can be used to find out the hot spot write regions in an HBase cluster for some situations.

Getting ready

Start your HBase cluster and log in to your HBase client node.

How to do it...

To diagnose your HBase hot region issues:

1. Create a `WriteDiagnosis.java` file, which has a `printWriteDiagnosis()` method shown as follows:

```
private static void printWriteDiagnosis(String logPath) throws
  IOException {
  Configuration conf = HBaseConfiguration.create();
  FileSystem fs = FileSystem.get(conf);
  FileStatus[] regionServers = fs.listStatus(new Path(logPath));
```

```
HLog.Reader reader = new SequenceFileLogReader();
Map<String, Long> result = new HashMap<String, Long>();

for (FileStatus regionServer : regionServers) {
  Path regionServerPath = regionServer.getPath();
  FileStatus[] logs = fs.listStatus(regionServerPath);
  Map<String, Long> parsed = new HashMap<String, Long>();

  for (FileStatus log : logs) {
    System.out.println("Processing: " +
     log.getPath().toString());

    reader.init(fs, log.getPath(), conf);
    try {
      HLog.Entry entry;
      while ((entry = reader.next()) != null) {
        String tableName =
         Bytes.toString(entry.getKey().getTablename());
        String encodedRegionName =
         Bytes.toString(entry.getKey().getEncodedRegionName());
        String mapkey = tableName + "/" + encodedRegionName;
        Long editNum = parsed.get(mapkey);
        if (editNum == null) {
          editNum = 0L;
        }
        editNum += entry.getEdit().size();
        parsed.put(mapkey, editNum);
      }
    } finally {
      reader.close();
    }
  }

  for (String key : parsed.keySet()) {
    result.put(key, parsed.get(key));
  }
}

System.out.println();
System.out.println("==== HBase Write Diagnosis ====");
for (String region : result.keySet()) {
  long editNum = result.get(region);
  System.out.println(String.format("Region: %s    Edits #: %d",
   region, editNum));
}
}
```

2. The `main()` method entry of the previous Java source is shown as follows:

```java
public static void main(String[] args) {

    try {
        if (args.length < 1) {
            usage();
            System.exit(-1);
        }
        String logPath = args[0];
        printWriteDiagnosis(logPath);

    } catch (Exception e) {
        e.printStackTrace();
        System.exit(-1);
    }
}

private static void usage() {
    System.err.println("Usage: WriteDiagnosis <HLOG_PATH>");
    System.err.println("HLOG_PATH:");
    System.err
        .println("  Path on HDFS where HLogs are stored. For example:
        /hbase/.logs");
}
```

3. Package it as a JAR file (`hac-chapter5.jar`) and run it using the `hadoop jar` command:

**$HADOOP_HOME/bin/hadoop jar hac-chapter5.jar
hac.chapter5.WriteDiagnosis /hbase/.logs**

4. You will get an output as shown in the following screenshot:

```
hac@client1 java$ ./run-write-diagnosis.sh /hbase/.logs
Processing: hdfs://master1:8020/hbase/.logs/ip-10-160-142-131.us-west-1.compute.internal,60020,13271
18312652/ip-10-160-142-131.us-west-1.compute.internal%3A60020.1327118313839
Processing: hdfs://master1:8020/hbase/.logs/ip-10-160-226-48.us-west-1.compute.internal,60020,132711
8312806/ip-10-160-226-48.us-west-1.compute.internal%3A60020.1327118313939
Processing: hdfs://master1:8020/hbase/.logs/ip-10-168-255-188.us-west-1.compute.internal,60020,13271
18312933/ip-10-168-255-188.us-west-1.compute.internal%3A60020.1327118314108

==== HBase Write Diagnosis ====
Region: hly_temp/5740a39d9eaa59c4175487c14e0a272a     Edits #: 574538
Region: hly_temp/0b593d9dc044f1fe011ec0c902f68fc5     Edits #: 1147778
Region: -ROOT-/70236052    Edits #: 2
Region: .META./1028785192    Edits #: 22
Region: hly_temp/5ef67f6d2a792fb0bd737863dc00b6a7     Edits #: 572809
```

How it works...

HBase WALs are stored under the `${hbase.rootdir}/.logs/<region_server>/` directories on HDFS. WALs are stored and rotated on a region server basis, which means a single WAL file only contains entries to the regions of the same hosting region server and to no other region server. A WAL entry has information about the table and region name of the edits, and the amount of edits.

Our `WriteDiagnosis.java` file simply goes through all the WALs under a specific path, extracts the table name, region name, and edits count from the WALs, and then prints the total edits count for each region.

The main logic is done in the `printWriteDiagnosis()` method. We first create an `HLog.Reader` instance. For each WAL file, we call the `init()` method of the instance to read data from the WAL file. An entry of the WAL file is represented by the `HLog.Entry` class. For each entry, we get the table name and region name the entry belongs to, from its key. We also get the number of edits from the entry using the `getEdit().size()` method of the `HLog.Entry` class. With all this information, we can aggregate the total number of edits on a region basis.

The `main()` method of `WriteDiagnosis.java` only checks the log path parameter from the command line, and passes it to the `printWriteDiagnosis()` method.

Package the Java source as a JAR file and run it with the `hadoop jar` command. As you can see from the output, there are many write requests for the `hly_temp` table, while one region in the table handles twice the requests of the other two regions. This is a typical case of non-uniform data distribution. You will want to take action on the hot spot region we just found, such as manually splitting it into two.

Note that the number of edits shown in the output is an approximate value. This is because WAL may get deleted by a background thread, if all the edits in WAL have been persisted; there is no way of knowing the number of edits in that deleted WAL.

However, an approximate write diagnosis is a good enough solution for many situations. You can use `WriteDiagnosis.java` to help find out the hot spot write regions. It's especially useful when you turn off the automatic region splitting of your cluster.

There's more...

A more convenient way to compile and execute our `WriteDiagnosis.java` is through the following commands:

```
$ $HBASE_HOME/bin/hbase com.sun.tools.javac.Main WriteDiagno
sis.java
$ $HBASE_HOME/bin/hbase WriteDiagnosis /hbase/.logs
```

See also

▸ *Using HBase Shell to manage the cluster* in *Chapter 3, Using Administration Tools*

6
Maintenance and Security

In this chapter, we will focus on:

- ▶ Enabling HBase RPC DEBUG-level logging
- ▶ Graceful node decommissioning
- ▶ Adding nodes to the cluster
- ▶ Rolling restart
- ▶ Simple script for managing HBase processes
- ▶ Simple script for making deployment easier
- ▶ Kerberos authentication for Hadoop and HBase
- ▶ Configuring HDFS security with Kerberos
- ▶ HBase security configuration

Introduction

After a cluster is delivered for operation, maintenance will be a necessary ongoing task while the cluster is in use. Typical maintenance tasks include finding out and correcting faults, changing cluster size, making configuration changes, and so on.

One of the most important HBase features is that it is extremely easy to scale in and out. As your service and data keeps growing, you might need to add nodes to the cluster.

Graceful node decommissioning and rolling restart will also become necessary. Minimizing the offline time during the decommission and restart is an important task. What is important is to keep the data distribution the same as what it was before the restart, to retain data locality.

Another maintenance task is to manage HBase deployment. There are many ways to deploy your HBase to the cluster. The simplest way is to use a script-based approach to sync HBase installations and configurations across the cluster.

We will cover these topics in the first six recipes of this chapter.

What we will also look at in this chapter is *security*. As HBase becomes more and more popular, different users and groups may store more data in a shared HBase cluster. You may not like all the users to have full permissions to every HBase table. This has risks to your data; for example, security risks or missing data operations. You might want to verify users' identities and have access control for the HBase tables based on their identities.

Before the release of Hadoop 0.20.203, there were no mechanisms to verify a user identity in Hadoop. Hadoop uses the user's current login as their Hadoop username (that is, the equivalent of whoami). HDFS itself does not verify whether this username is genuine and belongs to the actual operator.

Newer releases of Hadoop (0.20.203 and above) support the optional Kerberos authentication of clients. With this security support, it is allowed to store sensitive data such as financial data on a shared HDFS cluster.

HBase leverages HDFS security to provide its client with secure access. HBase added security support from its 0.92 release. Only authenticated users are allowed to access a secured HBase. It is also possible to add a table basis or column family basis access control in HBase.

In the last three recipes of this chapter, we will install Kerberos and then set up HDFS security with Kerberos, and finally set up secure HBase client access.

Enabling HBase RPC DEBUG-level logging

Hadoop and HBase use the log4j library to write their logs. Logging level is set in the log4j. properties file. In production, the logging level is usually set to the INFO level, which is good for many situations. However, there will be cases where you might want to see the debug information of a particular Hadoop/HBase daemon.

HBase inherits its online logging level change capability from Hadoop. It is possible to change an HBase daemon's logging level from its web UI without restarting the daemon.

This feature is useful when you need to know the debug information of an HBase daemon but cannot restart it. A typical situation is to troubleshoot a production HBase cluster.

We will describe how to enable HBase RPC DEBUG-level logging in this recipe.

Getting ready

Start the HBase cluster and open the HBase web UI from the following URL:

```
http://<master_host>:60010/master.jsp
```

How to do it...

The instructions to enable HBase RPC DEBUG-level logging without restarting an HBase daemon are as follows:

1. Show the region server web UI from the HBase web UI by clicking on the region server link.
2. Click on the **Log Level** link at the top left of the region server web UI.
3. Get the current logging level of the specific package or class.
4. Enter a package name (for example, `org.apache.hadoop.ipc`) in the **Log** textbox and click on the **Get Log Level** button. You will get an output as shown in the following screenshot:

5. Enter the package name and logging level, and then click on the **Set Log Level** button to set the package's logging level (for example, DEBUG).

6. You will get an output page, as shown in the following screenshot, that shows **Effective level: DEBUG**, which means that the package's logging level has been changed to DEBUG:

7. Now you should be able to check the debug log in the region server's logfile, as follows:

```
2012-02-10 22:14:42,878 DEBUG org.apache.hadoop.ipc.HBaseClient:
IPC Client (47) connection to ip-10-176-201-128.us-west-
1.compute.internal/10.176.201.128:60000 from hadoop sendi
2012-02-10 22:14:42,879 DEBUG org.apache.hadoop.ipc.HBaseClient:
IPC Client (47) connection to ip-10-176-201-128.us-west-1.compute.
internal/10.176.201.128:60000 from hadoop got v
2012-02-10 22:14:42,880 DEBUG org.apache.hadoop.ipc.RPCEngine:
Call: regionServerReport 2
```

How it works...

Hadoop has its own online logging change facility. It is possible to get or set a Hadoop daemon's logging level from its web UI. This is useful to debug a production cluster that does not allow restarting.

HBase simply inherits this facility from Hadoop. To enable the DEBUG-level logging of a specific HBase daemon on a particular region server, we locate the region server's web UI and then show its log level page. On this page, we can get or set a particular Java package's logging level.

In our demonstration, we have set the HBase IPC (`org.apache.hadoop.ipc`) package's logging level to DEBUG. As a result, the HRegionServer daemon starts writing its IPC debug information to its logfile.

A Hadoop/HBase daemon may generate a huge amount of debug logs in a short time. Do not forget to set it back to the INFO level, soon after you have got enough debug information.

There's more...

We can also get/set the logging level with the `hadoop daemonlog` command. The following command gets the IPC log level of the HMaster daemon running on localhost:

```
$ $HADOOP_HOME/bin/hadoop daemonlog -getlevel localhost:60010
org.apache.hadoop.ipc

Connecting to
http://localhost:60010/logLevel?log=org.apache.hadoop.ipc

Submitted Log Name: org.apache.hadoop.ipc

Log Class: org.apache.commons.logging.impl.Log4JLogger

Effective level: INFO
```

Executing `hadoop daemonlog` without an argument prints the command's usage.

```
$ $HADOOP_HOME/bin/hadoop daemonlog

USAGES:

java org.apache.hadoop.log.LogLevel -getlevel <host:port><name>

java org.apache.hadoop.log.LogLevel -setlevel
<host:port><name><level>
```

Graceful node decommissioning

We will describe how to stop a region server gracefully in this recipe.

It is possible to simply invoke the following command to stop the RegionServer daemon on a region server:

```
hadoop@slave1$ $HBASE_HOME/bin/hbase-daemon.sh stop regionserver
```

However, this approach has the disadvantage that regions deployed on the stopped region server will go offline for a while during the stopping process. In production, especially for clusters handling online requests, it is expected to gracefully stop a region server to minimize the region's offline time.

We will describe how HBase supports its graceful node decommissioning feature in this recipe.

Getting ready

Start your HBase cluster and log into the master node as the user (the hadoop user in our demonstration) who starts the cluster.

How to do it...

The instructions to gracefully decommission a region server are as follows:

1. Gracefully stop a region server by invoking the following command:

```
hadoop@master1$ $HBASE_HOME/bin/graceful_stop.sh ip-10-160-226-
84.us-west-1.compute.internal
Disabling balancer!
HBase Shell; enter 'help<RETURN>' for list of supported commands.
Type "exit<RETURN>" to leave the HBase Shell
Version 0.92.0, r1231986, Tue Jan 17 02:30:24 UTC 2012


balance_switch false
true


0 row(s) in 1.3370 seconds


Unloading ip-10-160-226-84.us-west-1.compute.internal region(s)
12/01/31 23:32:16 INFO region_mover: Moving 2 region(s) from ip-
10-160-226-84.us-west-1.compute.internal,60020,1328020203720
during this cycle
12/01/31 23:32:16 INFO region_mover: Moving region
5740a39d9eaa59c4175487c14e0a272a (0 of 2) to server=ip-10-161-83-
13.us-west-1.compute.internal,60020,1328013827479
12/01/31 23:32:17 INFO region_mover: Moving region
f6a1084fc7534c15696f4baa4abf61ce (1 of 2) to server=ip-10-161-83-
13.us-west-1.compute.internal,60020,1328013827479
12/01/31 23:32:18 INFO region_mover: Wrote list of moved regions
to /tmp/ip-10-160-226-84.us-west-1.compute.internal
Unloaded ip-10-160-226-84.us-west-1.compute.internal region(s)
ip-10-160-226-84.us-west-1.compute.internal: stopping
regionserver...
```

2. As the `graceful_stop.sh` script will turn off HBase's load balancing before it actually stops the region server daemon, explicitly enable it again if needed:

```
hadoop@master1$ echo 'balance_switch true' | $HBASE_HOME/bin/hbase shell

HBase Shell; enter 'help<RETURN>' for list of supported commands.

Type "exit<RETURN>" to leave the HBase Shell

Version 0.92.0, r1231986, Tue Jan 17 02:30:24 UTC 2012


balance_switch true

false

0 row(s) in 1.4450 seconds
```

How it works...

Stopping a region server is a region server-centric operation. It closes the regions deployed on the region server and stops itself. The master only learns of the region server's disappearance via the removal of the region server's znode in ZooKeeper, which is invoked by the region server as the last thing it does on its way out. There is a large window of unavailability while the closes are going on and until the master learns of the region server's removal. So to minimize this window, we use a graceful shutdown. It moves the regions off the region server one at a time (gracefully).

The `graceful_stop.sh` script moves regions off a region server and then stops it. As regions are firstly moved to other region servers, the region offline time is avoided during the stopping process.

Before moving the regions deployed on the specific region server, the script will turn off the cluster's load balancer first. This is important because the balancer might balance regions in the cluster at the same time the `graceful_stop.sh` script is moving regions. We must avoid this situation by turning off the balancer.

As you can see from the output of step 1, after the load balancer is turned off, the script moved two regions from the specified server to other region servers, then stopped the region server at last.

As the `graceful_stop.sh` script turned off the load balancer, you might want to turn it on again after the node decommission. That's what we did in step 2.

Make sure to pass the exact hostname shown on the HBase web UI to `graceful_stop.sh`, or it will not actually move the regions gracefully to other region servers.

The full usage of the `graceful_stop.sh` script is shown as follows:

```
./graceful_stop.sh
Usage: graceful_stop.sh [--config <conf-dir>] [--restart] [--
 reload] [--thrift] [--rest] <hostname>
 thrift       If we should stop/start thrift before/after the hbase
 stop/start
 rest         If we should stop/start rest before/after the hbase
 stop/start
 restart      If we should restart after graceful stop
 reload       Move offloaded regions back on to the stopped server
 debug        Display extra debug logging
 hostname     Hostname of server we are to stop
```

There's more...

You may have noticed that the `graceful_stop.sh` script has the `restart` and `reload` options. These options are used to rolling restart an HBase cluster. We will describe it in the *Rolling restart* recipe later.

See also

In this chapter:

  ▸   *Rolling restart*

Adding nodes to the cluster

One of the most important HBase features is that it is extremely scalable. HBase lineally scales out by adding nodes to the cluster. It is easy to start at a small cluster and scale it out when your service and data grows. Adding a region server to an HBase cluster would be an important maintenance task for administrators.

An HBase cluster can only have one active master node. However, we can add a backup master node to the cluster to make the HBase master **highly available** (**HA**).

In this recipe, we will describe how to add a backup master node to an HBase cluster. We will also describe adding region servers to a cluster after that.

Getting ready

Download and install HBase on the new master or region server first. Make sure the HBase configuration on that node is synced with other nodes in the cluster.

A region server usually runs on the same DataNode/TaskTracker of Hadoop. You might want to install Hadoop and start DataNode and TaskTracker on that node too.

We assume that you have got all Hadoop/HBase directories, configurations, and OS/user settings ready on that new node. Refer to *Chapter 1, Setting Up HBase Cluster* for details of these initial setups.

How to do it...

The instructions to add a backup master node to the cluster are as follows:

1. Start the HBase master daemon on the backup master node:

   ```
   hadoop@master2$ $HBASE_HOME/bin/hbase-daemon.sh start master
   ```

   From the master log, you will find that the newly started master is waiting to become the next active master:

   ```
   org.apache.hadoop.hbase.master.ActiveMasterManager: Another master
   is the active master, ip-10-176-201-128.us-west-
   1.compute.internal,60000,1328878644330; waiting to become the next
   active master
   ```

2. Add the new region server's hostname into the `regionservers` file, under the `$HBASE_HOME/conf` directory. For example, to add "`slave4`" to the cluster, we invoke the following command:

   ```
   hadoop@master1$ echo "slave4" >> $HBASE_HOME/conf/regionservers
   ```

3. Sync the modified `regionservers` file across the cluster.

4. Log in to the new server and start the region server daemon there:

   ```
   hadoop@slave4$ $HBASE_HOME/bin/hbase-daemon.sh start regionserver
   ```

5. Optionally, trigger a load balancer manually from HBase Shell to move some regions to the new region server. You can also wait for the next run of the balancer, which runs every five minutes by default.

   ```
   hbase> balance_switch true
   hbase> balancer
   ```

How it works...

In step 1, we simply started the HBase master daemon on the backup master node. HBase uses ZooKeeper to coordinate master election. All master nodes compete for creating a /hbase/master znode in ZooKeeper. The node which won the election (created the znode successfully) becomes the active master for the cluster. As now there is already a master present, the new master node goes into idle mode and waits to become the next active master if the current one is down.

To add a region server, first we added its hostname to the regionservers file in step 2. Next time we start the cluster, the region server daemon will be started automatically on that node.

As we do not restart the cluster, we manually started the region server daemon on the new node in step 4. The region server will query ZooKeeper to find and join the cluster.

Step 5 is optional. As the new region server has fewer regions deployed on it, we can trigger a load balancing explicitly to move some regions to it. The balancer runs every five minutes by default, so we can also just wait for the next run of the balancer.

There's more...

We can also start backup masters at the cluster's start time through the following steps:

1. Add backup master nodes to the conf/backup-masters file:

   ```
   hadoop@master1$ echo "master2" >> $HBASE_HOME/conf/backup-masters
   ```

2. Sync the backup-masters file across the cluster.

3. Start HBase normally; you will find that a backup HBase master will be started at the backup master node:

   ```
   hadoop@master1$ $HBASE_HOME/bin/start-hbase.sh
   starting master, logging to /usr/local/hbase/logs/hbase-hadoop-master-master1.out
   slave2: starting regionserver, logging to
   /usr/local/hbase/logs/hbase-hadoop-regionserver-slave2.out
   slave1: starting regionserver, logging to
   /usr/local/hbase/logs/hbase-hadoop-regionserver-slave1.out
   slave3: starting regionserver, logging to
   /usr/local/hbase/logs/hbase-hadoop-regionserver-slave3.out
   master2: starting master, logging to /usr/local/hbase/logs/hbase-hadoop-master-master2.out
   ```

❏ The master log on the backup master indicates that it is a backup master:

```
hadoop@master2$ tail /usr/local/hbase/logs/hbase-hadoop-
master-master2.log

2012-02-10 23:12:07,016 INFO
org.apache.hadoop.hbase.master.ActiveMasterManager: Another
master is the active master, ip-10-176-201-128.us-west-
1.compute.internal,60000,1328883123244; waiting to become
the next active master
```

Rolling restart

You might want to invoke a rolling restart when upgrading to a new HBase version, or when you want to apply some configuration changes. As described in the *Graceful node decommissioning* recipe, a rolling restart minimizes downtime because we only take a single region offline at a time rather than a whole cluster. A rolling restart keeps the region distribution the same as what it was before the restart. This is important to retain data locality.

New HBase versions are not always backward compatible. You can invoke a rolling restart to upgrade minor releases (for example, from 0.92.1 to 0.92.2), but not across major versions (for example, from 0.92.x to 0.94.x) because the protocol has changed between these versions. This will change in HBase 0.96 when you will be able to have old clients talk to new servers and vice versa.

Please check the following link for details about upgrading from one version to another:

`http://hbase.apache.org/book.html#upgrading`

A rolling restart contains steps involving restarting the master, gracefully restarting region servers, and finally checking the data consistency after the restart. We will describe these steps in this recipe.

Getting ready

Start your HBase cluster. Log into the master node as the user who started the cluster.

How to do it...

The instructions to rolling restart an HBase cluster are as follows:

1. Run `hbck` to ensure that the cluster is consistent:

   ```
   hadoop@master1$ $HBASE_HOME/bin/hbase hbck
   0 inconsistencies detected.
   Status: OK
   ```

2. Restart the master daemon:

   ```
   hadoop@master1$ $HBASE_HOME/bin/hbase-daemon.sh stop master
   hadoop@master1$ $HBASE_HOME/bin/hbase-daemon.sh start master
   ```

3. Disable the load balancer:

   ```
   hadoop@master1$ echo 'balance_switch false' |
   $HBASE_HOME/bin/hbase shell
   balance_switch false
   true
   0 row(s) in 1.1680 seconds
   ```

4. Create a `rolling-restart-rs.sh` script, shown as follows:

   ```
   $ vi rolling-restart-rs.sh
   #!/bin/bash
   HBASE_HOME=/usr/local/hbase/current

   zparent=`$HBASE_HOME/bin/hbase org.apache.hadoop.hbase.util.
   HBaseConfTool zookeeper.znode.parent`
   if [ "$zparent" == "null" ]; then
       zparent="/hbase"
   fi

   online_regionservers=`$HBASE_HOME/bin/hbase zkcli ls $zparent/rs
   2>&1 | tail -1 | sed "s/\[//" | sed "s/\]//"`
   for rs in $online_regionservers
   do
       rs_parts=(${rs//,/ })
       hostname=${rs_parts[0]}
       echo "Gracefully restarting: $hostname"
       $HBASE_HOME/bin/graceful_stop.sh --restart --reload  --debug
       $hostname
       sleep 1
   done
   ```

5. Make the script executable, and then execute it to gracefully restart each region server daemon in the cluster. You will get the following output:

```
hadoop@master1$ chmod +x rolling-restart-rs.sh
hadoop@master1$ ./rolling-restart-rs.sh
Gracefully restarting: ip-10-160-41-210.us-west-1.compute.internal
Disabling balancer!
HBase Shell; enter 'help<RETURN>' for list of supported commands.
Type "exit<RETURN>" to leave the HBase Shell
Version 0.92.0, r1231986, Tue Jan 17 02:30:24 UTC 2012

balance_switch false
false
0 row(s) in 1.2060 seconds

Unloading ip-10-160-41-210.us-west-1.compute.internal region(s)
Unloaded ip-10-160-41-210.us-west-1.compute.internal region(s)
ip-10-160-41-210.us-west-1.compute.internal: stopping
regionserver...
ip-10-160-41-210.us-west-1.compute.internal: starting
regionserver, logging to /usr/local/hbase/logs/hbase-hadoop-
regionserver-slave1.out
Reloading ip-10-160-41-210.us-west-1.compute.internal region(s)
Reloaded ip-10-160-41-210.us-west-1.compute.internal region(s)

Gracefully restarting: ip-10-166-109-91.us-west-1.compute.internal
...
Gracefully restarting: ip-10-176-79-57.us-west-1.compute.internal
...
Reloaded ip-10-176-79-57.us-west-1.compute.internal region(s)
```

6. Enable the load balancer again:

```
hadoop@master1$ echo 'balance_switch true' | $HBASE_HOME/bin/hbase
shell
balance_switch true
false
0 row(s) in 1.1730 seconds
```

7. Run hbck again to ensure that the cluster is consistent:

```
hadoop@master1$ $HBASE_HOME/bin/hbase hbck
```

How it works...

In step 1, we ran the `hbck` command to ensure that the cluster is consistent before the restart. After that we restarted the master daemon in step 2.

In step 3, before restarting the region servers, we turned off the balancer to avoid the situation in which balancing happens during the restart process.

The `rolling-restart-rs.sh` script we created in step 4 gets the root znode in ZooKeeper (`zparent`), first by invoking the `org.apache.hadoop.hbase.util.HBaseConfTool` class from the `hbase` command. `HBaseConfTool` is a Java class used to get the runtime HBase configurations. Passing `zookeeper.znode.parent` to it returns the `zparent` setting if set. If `zparent` is not set, we use the default `/hbase` value.

Each online region server has its znode under `$zparent/rs` in ZooKeeper. We use this to get the list of online region servers by invoking the `hbase zkcli ls` command. The return value is a string that contains space separated online region servers, such as `[region_server1,port,startcode region_server2,port,startcode region_server3,port,startcode]`. We did not fetch the region server list from the `conf/regionservers` file. This is because, in some environments such as a cluster using its own DNS service in Amazon EC2, the hostname in the file may be different from what is was given by HBase. The `graceful_stop.sh` script only accepts the hostname used in HBase, which is shown on the HBase web UI.

For each region server in the list, we invoke the `graceful_stop.sh` command passing the `--restart --reload --debug` options, and the server's hostname to gracefully restart the region server on that node.

As you can see from the output of step 5, for each online region server, the `rolling-restart-rs.sh` script moves regions off the region server one at a time, restarts them, and then reloads the moved regions back to the region server.

After all the region servers have been gracefully restarted, we enable the load balancer to its state again before restarting in step 6.

Finally in step 7, we executed `hbck` again to ensure that the cluster is running consistently.

There's more...

Notice that there is a `rolling-restart.sh` script in the `$HBASE_HOME/bin` directory. We did not use this script because we wanted to gracefully restart our region servers, which was not implemented in the script.

There is a patch that makes `rolling-restart.sh` behave in the same manner as previously described in this recipe. The patch is scheduled for version 0.96. You can check it at `https://issues.apache.org/jira/browse/HBASE-5314` for details.

Simple script for managing HBase processes

When the nodes in the cluster keep growing, you might want to find tools to show and manage the HBase-related processes running in the cluster. As the `hadoop` user is configured to be able to SSH from the master node to each slave node in the cluster without a password, it is easy for us to write a simple script to achieve this task with SSH login for every node and show/manage the running HBase processes on that node.

As Hadoop/HBase processes run in a **Java Virtual Machine** (**JVM**), our task is to manage these Java processes in the cluster.

In this recipe, we will create a simple script to show all the running Java processes owned by the `hadoop` user in an HBase cluster.

Getting ready

Start your HBase cluster. Log in to the master node as the user who started the cluster.

We assume that you are running HDFS and HBase as the same user (the `hadoop` user here).

How to do it...

The instructions to create a simple script to manage HBase processes are as follows:

1. Create a `cluster-jps.sh` script, shown as follows:

   $ vi cluster-jps.sh

   ```
   #!/bin/bash
   # Show all running Java processes on region servers. Must run on
   master using HBase owner user.

   JAVA_HOME=/usr/local/jdk1.6
   HBASE_HOME=/usr/local/hbase/current
   IFS=$'\n'

   printf "+-------------------------------+----------+--------------
   -----+\n"
   printf "|%-30s|%-10s|%-20s|\n" " HOST" " PID" " PROCESS"
   ```

```
printf "+---------------------------------+----------+--------------
-----+\n"
process_count=0
rs_count=0
for rs in `cat $HBASE_HOME/conf/regionservers`
do
    i=1
    for process in `ssh $rs "$JAVA_HOME/bin/jps" | grep -v Jps`
    do
        process_parts=(${process/ /$'\n'})
        pid=${process_parts[0]}
        pname=${process_parts[1]}
        if [ $i -eq 1 ]; then
            host="$rs"
        else
            host=" "
        fi
        printf "|%-30s|%-10s|%-20s|\n" " $host" " $pid" " $pname"

        i=`expr $i + 1`
        process_count=`expr $process_count + 1`
    done
    rs_count=`expr $rs_count + 1`
    printf "+---------------------------------+----------+-----------
---------+\n"
done
echo -e "$process_count running Java processes on $rs_count region
 servers.\n"
```

2. Run the script as the user who started Hadoop/HBase on the master node:

   hadoop@master1$ chmod +x cluster-jps.sh

   hadoop@master1$ ./cluster-jps.sh

3. You will get an output as shown in the following screenshot:

4. To show the master processes on the master node, invoke the following command:

```
hadoop@master1$ $JAVA_HOME/bin/jps
3005 Jps
1680 QuorumPeerMain
1781 HMaster
1538 NameNode
```

How it works...

In this script, we will get the region server list from the `conf/regionservers` file. Then for each region server, SSH log into the server and run the `jps` command on it. `Jps` is a command shipped along with the JDK installation to show running Java processes owned by the user. The most basic information we need, the **process ID** (**PID**) and name of each Java process, is contained in the output of the `jps` command.

The rest of the script just gathers the `jps` command output from each node and shows the result in a human-friendly format.

As we did in step 4, we can also use the `jps` command to show Java processes running on the master node. We skipped the logic that shows the master's Java processes, in this script.

As described in the *Setting up Nagios to monitor HBase processes* recipe of *Chapter 5, Monitoring and Diagnosis*, you will need to make sure these Java processes are monitored carefully.

Simple script for making deployment easier

There are many ways to deploy your HBase to the cluster. As Hadoop and HBase are written in Java, most of the deployment is done by simply copying all the files to the nodes in the cluster.

The simplest way is to use a script-based approach to sync HBase installation and configurations across the cluster. It may not be as cool compared to other modern deployment management tools, but it works well for small or even medium-sized clusters.

In this recipe, we will create a simple script to sync an HBase installation from its master node to all region servers in the cluster. This approach can be used to deploy Hadoop as well.

Getting ready

Log in to the master node as the user who starts the cluster. We assume that you have set up a non-password SSH from the master node to the region servers, for the user.

How to do it...

The instructions to create a simple script to make HBase deployment easier are as follows:

1. Create a `cluster-deploy.sh` script, shown as follows:

   ```
   $ vi cluster-deploy.sh
   ```

   ```bash
   #!/bin/bash
   # Sync HBASE_HOME across the cluster. Must run on master using
   HBase owner user.

   HBASE_HOME=/usr/local/hbase/current

   for rs in `cat $HBASE_HOME/conf/regionservers`
   do
       echo "Deploying HBase to $rs:"
       rsync -avz --delete --exclude=logs $HBASE_HOME/
       $rs:$HBASE_HOME/
       echo
       sleep 1
   done

   echo "Done"
   ```

2. Run the script as the user who starts Hadoop/HBase on the master node:

   ```
   hadoop@master1$ chmod +x cluster-deploy.sh
   hadoop@master1$ ./cluster-deploy.sh
   Deploying HBase to slave1:
   sending incremental file list
   ./
   conf/
   conf/hbase-site.xml

   sent 40023 bytes  received 259 bytes  80564.00 bytes/sec
   total size is 55576486  speedup is 1379.69

   Deploying HBase to slave2:
   ...

   Deploying HBase to slave3:
   ...

   Done
   ```

How it works...

The script uses the fact that all region servers are listed in the `conf/regionservers` file. It reads every region server's hostname from the file, and then invokes the `rsync` command to sync the HBase installation directory from master node to that region server. We add the `--delete` option to the `rsync` command because we want to remove unnecessary files from the region server.

To use this script, make some HBase configuration changes on the master node, and then run the script with the HBase owner user.

There's more...

When the cluster becomes larger, you might want to automate the deployment as much as possible, such as OS and user settings for a new node, fetching and deploying the package, and setting files from a central version managed configuration center.

You might want to try Puppet or Chef for these kinds of deployment tasks. There are some examples of Puppet and Chef configurations for HBase available on the Internet, the URLs of which are as follows:

- ▶ Puppet recipe: `http://hstack.org/hstack-automated-deployment-using-puppet/`

- ▶ Chef cookbook: `https://github.com/ueshin/chef-cookbooks`

Another tool you might want to give a try is Apache Bigtop, which can be found at the following location:

`http://incubator.apache.org/bigtop/`

Bigtop is a project for the development of packaging and tests of the Hadoop ecosystem. It is not yet ready for prime time, but it is a great tool for easily building and deploying Hadoop and HBase.

Kerberos authentication for Hadoop and HBase

Security support has been added to the recently released Hadoop 1.0 and HBase 0.92. With security enabled, only authenticated users can access a Hadoop and HBase cluster. The authentication is provided by a separate authentication service managed by trusted administrators. This makes HBase a considerable option to store sensitive, big data such as financial data.

Hadoop relies on the Kerberos authentication service for its security support. A secure HBase must run on HDFS with security support, so HBase also relies on Kerberos to provide it with security support.

The following is the description of Kerberos on Wikipedia:

> *Kerberos is a computer network authentication protocol which works on the basis of "tickets" to allow nodes communicating over a non-secure network to prove their identity to one another in a secure manner.*

The most widely used Kerberos implementation is MIT Kerberos. We will describe how to install and set up MIT Kerberos in this recipe. The installation includes setting up a Kerberos admin server and a **Key Distribution Center** (**KDC**).

Getting ready

You will need a Linux server to install MIT Kerberos. Make sure you have root privileges on that server. We assume that the hostname of the server is `master2` in this recipe.

Create the Kerberos logging directory on the server in advance, using the following command:

```
$ sudo mkdir /var/log/kerberos
```

How to do it...

The instructions to install MIT Kerberos are as follows:

1. Install the Kerberos admin server and KDC:

   ```
   hac@master2$ sudo apt-get install krb5-{admin-server,kdc}
   ```

   During the installation, you will be asked to enter your default realm name. The standard name for a Kerberos realm is your domain name in uppercase. As we use `hbase-admin-cookbook.com` as our domain in this book, we will choose `HBASE-ADMIN-COOKBOOK.COM` for the realm name, as shown in the following screenshot:

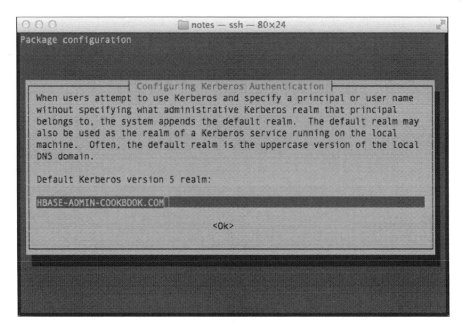

The installation will also ask you to enter the Kerberos server and administrative server. Enter the fully qualified domain name of your server here. In our demonstration, it is `master2.hbase-admin-cookbook.com`.

2. Create a realm using the following command:

   hac@master2$ sudo krb5_newrealm

 The command will ask for the master password. Enter your password and do not forget it.

3. Configure Kerberos by editing the `krb5.conf` file, shown as follows:

   hac@master2$ sudo vi /etc/krb5.conf

   ```
   [realms]
       HBASE-ADMIN-COOKBOOK.COM = {
           kdc = master2.hbase-admin-cookbook.com
           admin_server = master2.hbase-admin-cookbook.com
           default_domain = hbase-admin-cookbook.com
       }

   [domain_realm]
   .hbase-admin-cookbook.com = HBASE-ADMIN-COOKBOOK.COM
   hbase-admin-cookbook.com = HBASE-ADMIN-COOKBOOK.COM
   ```

```
[logging]
    kdc = FILE:/var/log/kerberos/krb5kdc.log
    admin_server = FILE:/var/log/kerberos/kadmin.log
    default = FILE:/var/log/kerberos/krb5lib.log
```

4. Grant full privileges to admin users by uncommenting the following line in the `kadm5.acl` file:

   hac@master2$ sudo vi /etc/krb5kdc/kadm5.acl

   */admin *

5. Restart the Kerberos admin server and KDC to apply the changes:

   hac@master2$ sudo invoke-rc.d krb5-admin-server restart

   hac@master2$ sudo invoke-rc.d krb5-kdc restart

6. Test the installation and configuration in the `kadmin.local` console:

   hac@master2$ sudo kadmin.local

   Authenticating as principal root/admin@HBASE-ADMIN-COOKBOOK.COM with password.

   kadmin.local: listprincs

   K/M@HBASE-ADMIN-COOKBOOK.COM

   kadmin/admin@HBASE-ADMIN-COOKBOOK.COM

   kadmin/changepw@HBASE-ADMIN-COOKBOOK.COM

   kadmin/history@HBASE-ADMIN-COOKBOOK.COM

   kadmin/ip-10-174-14-251.us-west-1.compute.internal@HBASE-ADMIN-COOKBOOK.COM

   krbtgt/HBASE-ADMIN-COOKBOOK.COM@HBASE-ADMIN-COOKBOOK.COM

7. Create a principal with administrative privileges:

   kadmin.local: addprinc root/admin

   WARNING: no policy specified for root/admin@HBASE-ADMIN-COOKBOOK.COM; defaulting to no policy

   Enter password for principal "root/admin@HBASE-ADMIN-COOKBOOK.COM":

   Re-enter password for principal "root/admin@HBASE-ADMIN-COOKBOOK.COM":

   Principal "root/admin@HBASE-ADMIN-COOKBOOK.COM" created.

8. Add a test user account (a "principal") to Kerberos:

   kadmin.local: addprinc hac

9. Quit the `kadmin.local` console and test the authentication for the test user by obtaining a Kerberos ticket:

```
kadmin.local: quit

hac@master2$ klist -5

klist: No credentials cache found (ticket cache
FILE:/tmp/krb5cc_1002)

hac@master2$ kinit

Password for hac@HBASE-ADMIN-COOKBOOK.COM:

hac@master2$ klist -5

Ticket cache: FILE:/tmp/krb5cc_1002

Default principal: hac@HBASE-ADMIN-COOKBOOK.COM


Valid starting       Expires             Service principal

02/05/12 11:48:49   02/05/12 21:48:49   krbtgt/HBASE-ADMIN-
COOKBOOK.COM@HBASE-ADMIN-COOKBOOK.COM

renew until 02/06/12 11:48:46
```

10. Terminate the cached ticket using the following commands:

```
hac@master2$ kdestroy

hac@master2$ klist -5

klist: No credentials cache found (ticket cache
FILE:/tmp/krb5cc_1002)
```

11. Delete the test user account using the following commands:

```
hac@master2$ sudo kadmin.local

kadmin.local:  delprinc hac
```

How it works...

We installed our Kerberos admin server and KDC on the same `master2` server. We set HBASE-ADMIN-COOKBOOK.COM as our default realm during the installation. The realm was actually created in step 2, using the `krb5_newrealm` command.

In step 3, we configured Kerberos's realm, domain, and log settings in the `/etc/krb5.conf` file. We granted full privileges to admin users in step 4. After that, we restarted Kerberos to apply the changes.

To test the installation and configuration, we entered Kerberos' `kadmin.local` console in step 6. `kadmin.local` is a prompt console for operating Kerberos. Only a `root` user on the Kerberos admin server can enter the `kadmin.local` console and execute Kerberos admin commands there.

We also ran the `listprincs` command to show the initial principals for Kerberos in step 6. A unique identity (user, host, and so on) in Kerberos is called a **principal**. A principal has a format of `primary/instance@REALM`.

In step 7, we added an admin user (the `root` user) to Kerberos. By entering its Kerberos password (not the OS password), the `root` user from a Kerberos client will be able to execute Kerberos's admin commands via the `kadmin` console. The `kadmin` console is similar to `kadmin.local`, but can be entered from other Kerberos clients using an admin user. It is useful when you need to grant admin users, but do not want them to have root access to the Kerberos admin server.

We also added a test principal for our `hac` user in step 8 and tested its authentication from step 9 to step 11.

Kerberos users need a ticket to access Kerberos's authenticated services. A ticket is issued with a **Ticket Granting Ticket** (**TGT**), which is issued by the KDC. To gain a TGT, users are asked to provide their Kerberos password to prove their identity. A Kerberos TGT can be cached and will get expired after the configured time.

In step 9, we have shown the `hac` user's cached TGTs using the `klist` command. The result is empty, which is what we expected. Then we requested a TGT using the `kinit` command. After that, the `klist` command shows the cached TGT and its expiration date. The cached TGT was removed with the `kdestroy` command in step 10.

There's more...

We did a basic Kerberos setup in this recipe. We will configure HDFS and HBase to use this Kerberos installation to provide security support in the following two recipes. The details of Kerberos are out of the scope of this book. Refer to the following URL for further information:

> ▶ *Kerberos: The Network Authentication Protocol* at `http://web.mit.edu/Kerberos/`

See also

In this chapter:

> ▶ *Configuring HDFS security with Kerberos*
> ▶ *HBase security configuration*

Configuring HDFS security with Kerberos

Newer releases of Hadoop (0.20.203 and above) support an optional Kerberos authentication of clients. This security support includes secure HDFS and secure MapReduce configurations.

The motivation for Hadoop security is not to defend against hackers, as all large Hadoop clusters are behind firewalls that only allow employees to access them. Its purpose is simply to allow storing sensitive data such as financial data on a shared cluster.

Prior releases of Hadoop already had file ownership and permissions in HDFS; the limitation was that they had no mechanisms for verifying user identity. With this Kerberos security support, user identities are verified by Kerberos, and only authenticated users are allowed to access the HDFS cluster.

As a secure HBase access is expected to be running on top of a secured HDFS cluster, setting up HDFS security is a prerequisite for HBase security configuration. In this recipe, we will focus on how to configure HDFS security with Kerberos.

Getting ready

We assume that you have a working **Kerberos Key Distribution Center** (**KDC**) and have realm set up. For more information about installing and configuring Kerberos, see the *Kerberos authentication for Hadoop and HBase* recipe in this chapter.

We assume that the `root` user on every node has administrative privileges in Kerberos. With this assumption, we will use the `kadmin` console to execute the Kerberos admin commands. If this assumption is not true, you will need to operate Kerberos via the `kadmin.local` console on the Kerberos admin server.

On every node of the cluster, create a directory to store the Kerberos keytab file, using the following command:

```
$sudo mkdir /etc/hadoop
```

Shut down your cluster before executing the steps discussed in this recipe.

How to do it...

To configure HDFS security with Kerberos, execute the following steps on *every node of the cluster*:

1. Install the Kerberos client software:

   ```
   $ sudo apt-get install krb5-{config,user} libpam-krb5
   ```

2. Enter the `kadmin` console using the following command:

```
$ sudo kadmin
```

3. Add the `hadoop` user principal to Kerberos. Replace the hostname part (`ip-10-168-46-11.us-west-1.compute.internal`) of the principal with your host's **fully qualified domain name (FQDN)**:

```
kadmin: addprinc -randkey hadoop/ip-10-168-46-11.us-west-1.compute.internal
```

4. Add the host principal to Kerberos. Replace the hostname part of the principal with your host's FQDN:

```
kadmin: addprinc -randkey host/ip-10-168-46-11.us-west-1.compute.internal
```

5. Create a keytab file using the following command:

```
kadmin: ktadd -k /etc/hadoop/hadoop.keytab -norandkey hadoop/ip-10-168-46-11.us-west-1.compute.internal host/ip-10-168-46-11.us-west-1.compute.internal
```

6. Quit from the `kadmin` console, and confirm if the keytab file has been created correctly:

```
kadmin: quit
```

```
$ klist -e -k -t /etc/hadoop/hadoop.keytab

Keytab name: WRFILE:/etc/hadoop/hadoop.keytab

KVNO Timestamp         Principal
---- ---------------- -----------------------------------------
     ------------
5 02/05/12 16:03:34 hadoop/ip-10-168-46-11.us-west-1.compute.internal@HBASE-ADMIN-COOKBOOK.COM (AES-256 CTS mode with 96-bit SHA-1 HMAC)

5 02/05/12 16:03:34 hadoop/ip-10-168-46-11.us-west-1.compute.internal@HBASE-ADMIN-COOKBOOK.COM (ArcFour with HMAC/md5)

5 02/05/12 16:03:34 hadoop/ip-10-168-46-11.us-west-1.compute.internal@HBASE-ADMIN-COOKBOOK.COM (Triple DES cbc mode with HMAC/sha1)

5 02/05/12 16:03:34 hadoop/ip-10-168-46-11.us-west-1.compute.internal@HBASE-ADMIN-COOKBOOK.COM (DES cbc mode with CRC-32)

5 02/05/12 16:03:34 host/ip-10-168-46-11.us-west-1.compute.internal@HBASE-ADMIN-COOKBOOK.COM (AES-256 CTS mode with 96-bit SHA-1 HMAC)
```

```
5 02/05/12 16:03:34 host/ip-10-168-46-11.us-west-
1.compute.internal@HBASE-ADMIN-COOKBOOK.COM (ArcFour with
HMAC/md5)

5 02/05/12 16:03:34 host/ip-10-168-46-11.us-west-
1.compute.internal@HBASE-ADMIN-COOKBOOK.COM (Triple DES cbc mode
with HMAC/sha1)

5 02/05/12 16:03:34 host/ip-10-168-46-11.us-west-
1.compute.internal@HBASE-ADMIN-COOKBOOK.COM (DES cbc mode with
CRC-32)
```

7. Make sure the keytab file is only readable by the `hadoop` user:

    ```
    $ sudo chown hadoop:hadoop /etc/hadoop/hadoop.keytab
    $ sudo chmod 400 /etc/hadoop/hadoop.keytab
    ```

8. Download the "**Java Cryptography Extension** (**JCE**) Unlimited Strength Jurisdiction Policy Files 6" from the following URL:

    ```
    http://www.oracle.com/technetwork/java/javase/downloads/index.
    html
    ```

    Install it by following the `README` file present in the downloaded file.

9. Enable Hadoop security by adding the following configurations to the `core-site.xml` file:

    ```
    $ vi $HADOOP_HOME/conf/core-site.xml
    ```

    ```
    <property>
      <name>hadoop.security.authentication</name>
      <value>kerberos</value>
    </property>

    <property>
      <name>hadoop.security.authorization</name>
      <value>true</value>
    </property>
    ```

10. Enable HDFS security by adding the following configuration to the `hdfs-site.xml` file:

    ```
    $ vi $HADOOP_HOME/conf/hdfs-site.xml
    ```

    ```
    <property>
      <name>dfs.block.access.token.enable</name>
      <value>true</value>
    </property>
    ```

11. Add the NameNode security configurations to the `hdfs-site.xml` file:

```
$ vi $HADOOP_HOME/conf/hdfs-site.xml

<property>
  <name>dfs.https.address</name>
  <value>${your_namenode_host}:50470</value>
</property>
<property>
  <name>dfs.https.port</name>
  <value>50470</value>
</property>
<property>
  <name>dfs.namenode.keytab.file</name>
  <value>/etc/hadoop/hadoop.keytab</value>
</property>
<property>
  <name>dfs.namenode.kerberos.principal</name>
  <value>hadoop/_HOST@HBASE-ADMIN-COOKBOOK.COM</value>
</property>
<property>
  <name>dfs.namenode.kerberos.https.principal</name>
  <value>host/_HOST@HBASE-ADMIN-COOKBOOK.COM</value>
</property>
```

12. Add the DataNode security configurations to the `hdfs-site.xml` file:

```
$ vi $HADOOP_HOME/conf/hdfs-site.xml

<property>
  <name>dfs.datanode.data.dir.perm</name>
  <value>700</value>
</property>
<!-- secure setup requires privileged ports -->
<property>
  <name>dfs.datanode.address</name>
  <value>0.0.0.0:1004</value>
</property>
<property>
  <name>dfs.datanode.http.address</name>
  <value>0.0.0.0:1006</value>
</property>
<property>
  <name>dfs.datanode.keytab.file</name>
  <value>/etc/hadoop/hadoop.keytab</value>
</property>
<property>
```

```
   <name>dfs.datanode.kerberos.principal</name>
   <value>hadoop/_HOST@HBASE-ADMIN-COOKBOOK.COM</value>
</property>
<property>
   <name>dfs.datanode.kerberos.https.principal</name>
   <value>host/_HOST@HBASE-ADMIN-COOKBOOK.COM</value>
</property>
```

13. Start the NameNode daemon on the master node:

    hadoop@master1$ $HADOOP_HOME/bin/hadoop-daemon.sh start namenode

    You will find logs like the following in the NameNode logfile:

    ```
    2012-02-05 20:26:48,642 INFO org.apache.hadoop.security.
    UserGroupInformation: Login successful for user hadoop/ip-10-168-
    46-11.us-west-1.compute.internal@HBASE-ADMIN-COOKBOOK.COM

    2012-02-05 20:37:19,397 INFO org.apache.hadoop.security.
    UserGroupInformation: Login successful for user host/ip-10-168-46-
    11.us-west-1.compute.internal@HBASE-ADMIN-COOKBOOK.COM
    2012-02-05 20:37:19,694 INFO org.apache.hadoop.http.HttpServer:
    Added global filtersafety (class=org.apache.hadoop.http.
    HttpServer$QuotingInputFilter)
    2012-02-05 20:37:19,705 INFO org.apache.hadoop.http.HttpServer:
    dfs.webhdfs.enabled = false
    2012-02-05 20:37:19,714 INFO org.apache.hadoop.http.HttpServer:
    Adding Kerberos filter to getDelegationToken
    2012-02-05 20:37:19,714 INFO org.apache.hadoop.http.HttpServer:
    Adding Kerberos filter to renewDelegationToken
    2012-02-05 20:37:19,716 INFO org.apache.hadoop.http.HttpServer:
    Adding Kerberos filter to cancelDelegationToken
    2012-02-05 20:37:19,717 INFO org.apache.hadoop.http.HttpServer:
    Adding Kerberos filter to fsck
    2012-02-05 20:37:19,718 INFO org.apache.hadoop.http.HttpServer:
    Adding Kerberos filter to getimage
    ```

    The following steps are for DataNode nodes only:

14. Change the data store directory permission to only readable by its owner:

    $ chmod -R 700 /usr/local/hadoop/var/dfs/data

15. Change the log directory owner to the hadoop user:

    $ chown -R hadoop:hadoop $HADOOP_HOME/logs

16. Configure the Hadoop secure DataNode user by adding the following command to the
    hadoop-env.sh file:

    $ vi conf/hadoop-env.sh

    HADOOP_SECURE_DN_USER=hadoop

17. For 32-bit systems *only*, build `jsvc` from source, and then replace the `commons-daemon` JAR file in the Hadoop `lib` directory, as described in the following steps:

    i. From Apache Commons Daemon download URL (`http://commons.apache.org/daemon/download_daemon.cgi`), download the `jsvc` source (`commons-daemon-1.x.y-native-src.tar.gz`), and build `jsvc` following the `README` file present in the tarball. Then, copy the built `jsvc` binary file to the `$HADOOP_HOME/libexec/jsvc.i386` file.

    ii. Also, download the Commons Daemon JAR file (`commons-daemon-1.x.y-bin.tar.gz`) with the same version of `jsvc`. Decompress it and replace `$HADOOP_HOME/lib/commons-daemon-1.0.1.jar` with the downloaded JAR file.

18. Start DataNode with the `root` user:

    ```
    $ sudo $HADOOP_HOME/bin/hadoop-daemon.sh start datanode
    ```

    You should be able to find logs if everything is configured well, which are shown as follows:

    ```
    2012-02-05 21:46:02,925 INFO org.apache.hadoop.security.
    UserGroupInformation: Login successful for user hadoop/ip-10-168-
    106-166.us-west-1.compute.internal@HBASE-ADMIN-COOKBOOK.COM using
    keytab file /etc/hadoop/hadoop.keytab
    ```

    After all DataNodes in the cluster have been started, test our secure HDFS using the following instructions:

19. Test the secure HDFS from its admin web page. Click on the **Browse the filesystem** link; an error will show on the screen, as seen in the following screenshot:

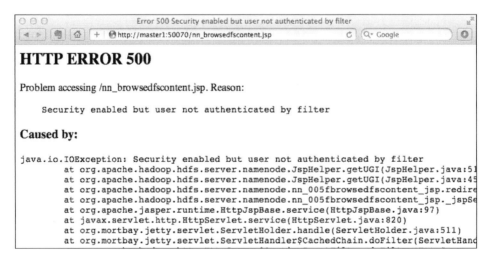

20. Test the secure HDFS from the command line on your client node:

```
hac@client1$ $HADOOP_HOME/bin/hadoop fs -ls /

12/02/05 23:00:50 ERROR security.UserGroupInformation:
PriviledgedActionException as:hac
cause:javax.security.sasl.SaslException: GSS initiate failed
[Caused by GSSException: No valid credentials provided (Mechanism
level: Failed to find any Kerberos tgt)]

12/02/05 23:00:50 WARN ipc.Client: Exception encountered while
connecting to the server : javax.security.sasl.SaslException: GSS
initiate failed [Caused by GSSException: No valid credentials
provided (Mechanism level: Failed to find any Kerberos tgt)]

12/02/05 23:00:50 ERROR security.UserGroupInformation:
PriviledgedActionException as:hac cause:java.io.IOException:
javax.security.sasl.SaslException: GSS initiate failed [Caused by
GSSException: No valid credentials provided (Mechanism level:
Failed to find any Kerberos tgt)]

Bad connection to FS. command aborted. exception: Call to ip-10-
168-46-11.us-west-1.compute.internal/10.168.46.11:8020 failed on
local exception: java.io.IOException:
javax.security.sasl.SaslException: GSS initiate failed [Caused by
GSSException: No valid credentials provided (Mechanism level:
Failed to find any Kerberos tgt)]
```

21. Authenticate a user to access the secure HDFS from the kadmin console:

```
hac@client1$ sudo kadmin

kadmin: addprinc hac/ip-10-160-34-143.us-west-1.compute.internal


kadmin: quit
```

22. Obtain a Kerberos ticket for the user with the following command:

```
hac@client1$ kinit hac/ip-10-160-34-143.us-west-1.compute.internal

Password for hac/ip-10-160-34-143.us-west-
1.compute.internal@HBASE-ADMIN-COOKBOOK.COM:
```

23. Test the authentication from the command line on your client node again:

```
hac@client1$ $HADOOP_HOME/bin/hadoop fs -ls /

Found 6 items

drwxr-xr-x   - hadoop supergroup          0 2012-01-08 08:09
/backup

drwxr-xr-x   - hadoop supergroup          0 2012-02-04 21:29
/hbase
```

```
drwxr-xr-x   - hadoop supergroup            0 2011-11-24 17:13
/hbase-b
drwxrwxrwx   - hadoop supergroup            0 2012-01-08 22:47 /tmp
drwxr-xr-x   - hadoop supergroup            0 2012-01-03 22:12 /user
drwxr-xr-x   - hadoop supergroup            0 2012-01-25 11:08 /usr
```

How it works...

First of all, we installed the Kerberos client software on each HDFS node. After that, we entered the `kadmin` console to add Kerberos principals for the `hadoop` user of that node, and for the node itself. As we will only use these principals from their keytab files, we added the `-randkey` option to the `addprinc` command.

As we will only set up HDFS security in this recipe, we are using the `hadoop` user here. If you will also enable secure MapReduce, we recommend you use different users for HDFS and MapReduce, for example the `hdfs` and `mapreduce` users respectively.

Another point here is to add different principals for the `hadoop` user on each node. Although it is possible to add a single principal in Kerberos for the `hadoop` user on all nodes, this is not recommended. Because in this case, as the cluster will send many authentication requests to the same principal (`hadoop@YOUR_REALM.COM`), Kerberos might handle this as an attack and fail to authenticate.

In step 5, we created the keytab file (`/etc/hadoop/hadoop.keytab`) for the principals we added in the previous steps. A **keytab** is a file containing pairs of Kerberos principals and encrypted keys. Using this file, Hadoop can log in to Kerberos without being prompted for a password.

After confirming the keytab file in step 6, we made it only readable by the `hadoop` user in step 7.

Tickets are encrypted by default, using the AES-256 encryption. This requires "**Java Cryptography Extension** (**JCE**) Unlimited Strength Jurisdiction Policy Files 6" to be installed on all HDFS nodes and clients. That's what we did in step 8.

After enabling Hadoop and HDFS security in steps 9 and 10, we configured Kerberos security on NameNode in step 11. We set the keytab file path and principals in this step. The `_HOST` setting value will be replaced with the hostname of the node, at runtime.

DataNode security settings were added in step 12. For the `dfs.datanode.address` and `dfs.datanode.http.address` settings, note that a secure setup requires privileged ports (ports below 1024).

As you can see from the output of step 13, if everything was configured well, the `hadoop` user and the master node will get authenticated by Kerberos during the NameNode starting process.

For the DataNode node, we firstly changed the data store directory to only readable by the `hadoop` user in step 14.

A secure DataNode must be started by the `root` user and run by the `hadoop` user. This is configured in step 16 by adding the `HADOOP_SECURE_DN_USER=hadoop` setting to the `hadoop-env.sh` file.

Step 17 is necessary for 32-bit systems only. This is simply because the 32-bit `jsvc` binary file was not included in the current Hadoop release's tarball.

After all the DataNodes in the cluster have been started by the `root` user, we are now able to test the secured HDFS from its web UI and from the command-line interface as well.

As you can see from steps 19 and 20, non-authenticated users could not access the secured HDFS neither from the web UI nor the command line. This was what we had expected. Identities including components of HDFS itself, and clients, must be authenticated by Kerberos before they are able to communicate with other identities in the realm.

In step 21, we added a test principal for the `hac` user on our HDFS client node. After obtaining a Kerberos ticket (authenticated) in step 22, the user was able to access the secured HDFS successfully.

There's more...

We just discussed the most basic HDFS security configuration. As the scope of the book is limited, we have omitted some steps here, including:

- SecondaryNameNode security
- MapReduce security
- WebHDFS security if WebHDFS is enabled
- User accounts and groups
- Directories ownership on HDFS and the local filesystem
- The verification of DataNodes' identities to clients (HDFS-1150)

HBase security configuration

As HBase becomes more and more popular, different users and groups may store more data in a shared HBase cluster. You might not like all users having full permission to every HBase table. This adds risks to your data, for example, security risks or missed data operation.

Newer HBase releases (0.92 and above) have Kerberos-based security support. With this, user identities are verified by Kerberos, and only authenticated users are allowed to access data in a secured HBase cluster.

We will describe how to configure secure client access to HBase in this recipe.

Getting ready

Make sure you are using the security-enabled HBase release. If you are downloading from the official HBase site, the filename should look like `hbase-0.92.1-security.tar.gz`.

We assume that you have a working **Kerberos Key Distribution Center** (**KDC**) and have realm set up. For more information about installing and configuring Kerberos, see the *Kerberos authentication for Hadoop and HBase* recipe in this chapter.

As a secure HBase access is expected to be running on top of a secured HDFS cluster, you will also need to set up HDFS security in advance. Refer to the *Configuring HDFS security with Kerberos* recipe in this chapter, for details.

As we have used the same user (the `hadoop` user) to run HDFS and HBase in this book, we are able to share the keytab files. Generate the HBase owner's own keytab file if you are using a different user for HDFS and HBase.

How to do it...

The instructions to configure HBase security are as follows:

1. On every node in the cluster, add the following, most basic configuration to the `hbase-site.xml` file:

    ```
    $ vi $HBASE_HOME/conf/hbase-site.xml
    <property>
      <name>hbase.regionserver.kerberos.principal</name>
      <value>hadoop/_HOST@HBASE-ADMIN-COOKBOOK.COM</value>
    </property>
    <property>
      <name>hbase.regionserver.keytab.file</name>
      <value>/etc/hadoop/hadoop.keytab</value>
    </property>
    <property>
      <name>hbase.master.kerberos.principal</name>
      <value>hadoop/_HOST@HBASE-ADMIN-COOKBOOK.COM</value></property>
    <property>
      <name>hbase.master.keytab.file</name>
      <value>/etc/hadoop/hadoop.keytab</value>
    </property>
    ```

2. On every server node in the cluster, add the following configuration to the `hbase-site.xml` file:

    ```
    $ vi $HBASE_HOME/conf/hbase-site.xml
    <property>
    ```

```
  <name>hbase.security.authentication</name>
  <value>kerberos</value>
</property>
<property>
  <name>hbase.security.authorization</name>
  <value>true</value>
</property>
<property>
  <name>hbase.rpc.engine</name>
  <value>org.apache.hadoop.hbase.ipc.SecureRpcEngine</value>
</property>
<property>
  <name>hbase.coprocessor.region.classes</name>
  <value>org.apache.hadoop.hbase.security.token.TokenProvider
    </value>
</property>
```

3. On every HBase client node, add the following configuration to the `hbase-site.xml` file:

    $ vi $HBASE_HOME/conf/hbase-site.xml

    ```
    <property>
      <name>hbase.security.authentication</name>
      <value>kerberos</value>
    </property>
    <property>
      <name>hbase.rpc.engine</name>
      <value>org.apache.hadoop.hbase.ipc.SecureRpcEngine</value>
    </property>
    ```

4. Start the master daemon on the master node:

    hadoop@master1$ $HBASE_HOME/bin/hbase-daemon.sh start master

    If everything is configured well, you will find logs in the HBase logfile on the master node, as follows:

    ```
    2012-02-06 00:06:57,524 INFO org.apache.hadoop.security.
    UserGroupInformation: Login successful for user hadoop/ip-10-168-
    46-11.us-west-1.compute.internal@HBASE-ADMIN-COOKBOOK.COM
    ```

5. Start the region server daemon on every region server node:

    hadoop@master1$ $HBASE_HOME/bin/hbase-daemons.sh start regionserver

You should be able to find logs in the HBase logfile on the master node, shown as follows:

```
2012-02-06 00:13:10,206 INFO SecurityLogger.org.apache.hadoop.
security.authorize.ServiceAuthorizationManager: Authorization
successfull for hadoop/ip-10-168-62-63.us-west-1.compute.internal@
HBASE-ADMIN-COOKBOOK.COM for protocol=interface org.apache.hadoop.
hbase.ipc.HMasterRegionInterface
```

And logs on region server, as follows:

```
2012-02-06 00:14:29,276 INFO SecurityLogger.org.apache.hadoop.
security.authorize.ServiceAuthorizationManager: Authorization
successfull for hadoop/ip-10-168-46-11.us-west-1.compute.internal@
HBASE-ADMIN-COOKBOOK.COM for protocol=interface org.apache.hadoop.
hbase.ipc.HMasterRegionInterface
```

6. Clear the Kerberos cache and test the secure HBase configuration on your client node.

```
hac@client1$ kdestory

hac@client1$ $HBASE_HOME/bin/hbase shell

hbase> count 'hly_temp'

12/02/06 00:21:37 ERROR security.UserGroupInformation:
PriviledgedActionException as:hac
cause:javax.security.sasl.SaslException: GSS initiate failed
[Caused by GSSException: No valid credentials provided (Mechanism
level: Failed to find any Kerberos tgt)]
```

7. Obtain a Kerberos ticket and test again:

```
hac@client1$ kinit hac/ip-10-160-34-143.us-west-1.compute.internal

hac@client1$ $HBASE_HOME/bin/hbase shell

hbase> count 'hly_temp'

...

Current count: 94000, row: USW000948470714
Current count: 95000, row: USW000949080410
95630 row(s) in 22.1700 seconds
```

How it works...

In step 1, we configured the Kerberos principal and its keytab file for the HBase master and region servers in the `hbase-site.xlm` file. It is the common configuration for both the server nodes and client nodes. Like the Hadoop security configuration, the `_HOST` setting value will be replaced with the hostname of the node at runtime.

Step 2 is for the server nodes only. We have enabled the HBase authentication and authorization in the configuration. We have set HBase to use the Kerberos authentication, and HBase coprocessors-based authorization. HBase coprocessors is a new feature in the 0.92 release, based on Google's BigTable coprocessors. It is an arbitrary code that runs at each region in the region server. An example usage of HBase Coprocessors is to implement access control for HBase tables.

On the client side in step 3, we only need to configure Kerberos's authentication.

As you can see from the logs of steps 4 and 5, the HBase master and region servers will get authenticated by Kerberos during the starting up process.

As shown in steps 6 and 7, non-authenticated users could not access the secured HBase. This was what we had expected. Identities, including server-side components and clients, must be authenticated by Kerberos before they are able to communicate with other identities in the realm.

There's more...

We have set up secure client access to HBase in this recipe. Besides that, you might also want to configure access control for the HBase tables. Using the previous setup, implement the following configurations to enable access control:

- Configure ZooKeeper security
- Enable the AccessController coprocessor
- Edit user permissions in HBase Shell

As the scope of the book is limited, we have omitted these configurations. Refer to the following URL for a detailed description:

```
https://issues.apache.org/jira/browse/HBASE-4990
```

7
Troubleshooting

In this chapter, we will cover:

- ▶ Troubleshooting tools
- ▶ Handling the XceiverCount error
- ▶ Handling the "too many open files" error
- ▶ Handling the "unable to create new native thread" error
- ▶ Handling the "HBase ignores HDFS client configuration" issue
- ▶ Handling the ZooKeeper client connection error
- ▶ Handling the ZooKeeper session expired error
- ▶ Handling the HBase startup error on EC2

Introduction

Everyone expects their HBase cluster to run smoothly and steadily, but the cluster does not work as expected sometimes, especially when a cluster has not been well configured. This chapter describes things you can do to troubleshoot a cluster that is running in an unexpected status.

Before you start troubleshooting a cluster, it is better to get familiar with the tools that will help us restore the cluster. Useful tools are as important as a deep knowledge of HBase and the cluster you are operating. We will introduce several recommended tools and their sample usage, in the first recipe.

Problems usually occur on a cluster that is missing the basic setup. If you encounter problems with your cluster, the first thing you should do is analyze the master log file, as the master acts as the coordinator service of the cluster. Hopefully, you will be able to identify the root cause of the error once you have found the WARN or ERROR level logs in the log file. The region server log file is another source you need to check. The region server log file usually contains load-related error logs, as region servers handle the actual data storing and accessing for the cluster.

HBase runs on the top of HDFS, and it relies on ZooKeeper as its coordination service. Sometimes, it is necessary to investigate the HDFS, MapReduce, and ZooKeeper logs, as well. All these log files are, by default, stored under the `logs` directory of the installation folder. Of course, it is configurable in the `log4j` property file.

If you find an error message, search the online resource at `http://search-hadoop.com/`; it is quite possible that this has been reported and discussed before. There is a great HBase community that you can always ask for help. However, before you ask, do not forget to subscribe first—`http://hbase.apache.org/mail-lists.html`.

In this chapter, we will look through several of the most confronted issues. We will describe the error messages of these issues, why they happened, and how to fix them with the troubleshooting tools.

Troubleshooting tools

In order to troubleshoot an HBase cluster, besides a solid knowledge of the cluster you are operating, the tools you use are also important. We would like to recommend the following troubleshooting tools:

- `ps`: This can be used to find the top process that used the most memory and CPU
- **ClusterSSH tool**: This tool is used to control multiple SSH sessions simultaneously
- `jps`: This tool shows the Java processes for the current user
- `jmap`: This tool prints the Java heap summary
- `jstat`: This is the Java Virtual Machine statistics monitoring tool
- `hbase hbck`: This tool is used for checking and repairing region consistency and table integrity
- `hadoop fsck`: This tool is used for checking HDFS consistency

We will describe sample usage of these tools, in this recipe.

Getting ready

Start your HBase cluster.

How to do it...

The following are the troubleshooting tools we will describe:

- ► ps: This tool is used to find the top processes that occupied large amounts of memory. The following command sorts the processes by memory usage, in descending order:

```
$ ps auxk -rss | less

USER         PID %CPU %MEM     VSZ    RSS TTY       STAT START    TIME
COMMAND

hadoop      1346  1.2   6.6 1222680 115096 ?        Sl   11:01    0:10
/usr/local/jdk1.6/bin/java -XX:OnOutOfMemoryError=kill -9 %p
-Xmx1000m -ea -XX:+UseConcMarkSweepGC -XX:+CMSIncrementalMode
-Dhbase.log.dir=/usr/local/hbase/logs

...

org.apache.hadoop.hbase.regionserver.HRegionServer start
```

- ► **ClusterSSH tool**: This tool is used to control multiple SSH sessions, simultaneously. In order to install ClusterSSH (cssh) on a Ubuntu desktop, run the following command:

```
$ sudo apt-get install clusterssh
```

There is also a ClusterSSH tool for Mac OS X called csshx. You can download csshx from http://code.google.com/p/csshx/. Start the ClusterSSH tool to monitor a small HBase cluster. For example, on Mac OS X, run the following command to start multiple SSH sessions on each node of the HBase cluster:

```
$ csshX --login hac master1 slave1 slave2 slave3
```

A master window (the second one in the following screenshot) will also be created. In the red master window, type the following to run the top command on every node:

```
$ top
```

You will get a screen similar to the following screenshot:

- ▶ `jps`: This tool shows the Java processes for the current user. To show the Java processes on a slave node for the `hadoop` user, run the following command:

  `hadoop@slave1$ $JAVA_HOME/bin/jps`

  `1254 DataNode`

  `2445 Child`

  `1970 TaskTracker`

  `2481 Jps`

  `1812 HRegionServer`

- ▶ `jmap`: This tool prints the Java heap summary. In order to print the aforementioned HRegionServer process' Java heap summary, use the following command:

  `hadoop@slave1$ $JAVA_HOME/bin/jmap -heap 1812`

  `Attaching to process ID 1812, please wait...`

  `Debugger attached successfully.`

  `Client compiler detected.`

  `JVM version is 20.4-b02`

  `using thread-local object allocation.`

  `Concurrent Mark-Sweep GC`

```
Heap Configuration:

   MinHeapFreeRatio = 40

   MaxHeapFreeRatio = 70

   MaxHeapSize      = 1048576000 (1000.0MB)

   NewSize          = 16777216 (16.0MB)

   MaxNewSize       = 16777216 (16.0MB)

   OldSize          = 50331648 (48.0MB)

   NewRatio         = 7

   SurvivorRatio    = 8

   PermSize         = 12582912 (12.0MB)

   MaxPermSize      = 67108864 (64.0MB)


Heap Usage:
New Generation (Eden + 1 Survivor Space):
   capacity = 15138816 (14.4375MB)

   used     = 6533712 (6.2310333251953125MB)

   free     = 8605104 (8.206466674804688MB)

   43.1586723823052% used

Eden Space:
   capacity = 13500416 (12.875MB)

   used     = 6514736 (6.2129364013671875MB)

   free     = 6985680 (6.6620635986328125MB)

   48.25581670964806% used

From Space:
   capacity = 1638400 (1.5625MB)

   used     = 18976 (0.018096923828125MB)

   free     = 1619424 (1.544403076171875MB)

   1.158203125% used

To Space:
   capacity = 1638400 (1.5625MB)

   used     = 0 (0.0MB)

   free     = 1638400 (1.5625MB)

   0.0% used

concurrent mark-sweep generation:
   capacity = 274624512 (261.90234375MB)

   used     = 68805464 (65.61800384521484MB)
```

```
free      = 205819048 (196.28433990478516MB)
25.05437824865393% used
Perm Generation:
capacity = 26222592 (25.0078125MB)
used      = 15656912 (14.931594848632812MB)
free      = 10565680 (10.076217651367188MB)
59.70772073180256% used
```

▶   jstat: This is the Java Virtual Machine statistics monitoring tool. Run the
    following command to show the summary of the garbage collection statistics of a
    HRegionServer process:

    hadoop@slave1$ jstat -gcutil 1812 1000

    The output looks as shown in the following screenshot:

```
hadoop@slave1 ~$ jstat -gcutil 1812 1000
  S0      S1      E      0      P      YGC     YGCT    FGC    FGCT    GCT
  0.00  100.00  26.19  51.31  59.75    133    7.461    48   0.857   8.319
  0.00  100.00  49.81  52.78  59.75    137    7.687    49   0.864   8.550
  0.00   25.34   0.00  54.38  59.75    141    7.872    49   0.864   8.735
100.00    0.00  73.15  55.99  59.75    144    7.918    49   0.864   8.781
 25.85    0.00  14.57  58.73  59.75    148    8.134    49   0.864   8.997
 69.59    0.00  26.53  59.60  59.75    150    8.163    49   0.864   9.026
  0.00   39.32  36.55  59.89  59.75    151    8.177    49   0.864   9.040
100.00    0.00  54.03  61.03  59.81    152    8.193    49   0.864   9.056
100.00    0.00  37.95  63.11  59.81    154    8.226    49   0.864   9.090
100.00    0.00  37.78  64.55  59.81    156    8.323    49   0.864   9.187
  0.00   98.16  32.18  66.44  59.81    159    8.349    49   0.864   9.213
```

How it works...

The ps command has a k option, which we can use to specify the sorting order. We pass the
-rss format specifier to this option. This causes the ps command to sort processes by their
resident set size, in descending order. We use this method to find the top process that used
the most memory.

The Cluster SSH tool is convenient for managing small clusters. You can use it to invoke the
same commands simultaneously on multiple servers. Just as we have earlier, we open one
session to the master and every slave node in the cluster. Then, we invoke the top command
on each server, via the master window. This acts as a simple monitoring system for the cluster.

jps is a small, hands-on tool to manage Java processes. It shows the Java processes for the
current user.

Step 4 shows the output of the `jps` command on a slave node running the DataNode, RegionServer, and TaskTracker daemons. Hadoop and HBase are written in Java; this makes `jps` a useful tool for us.

`jmap` is a tool to print the Java heap summary. As shown in step 5, we use the `jmap -heap <PID>` command to show the HRegionServer daemon's heap summary. `jmap` will print the heap configuration and usage of the HRegionServer daemon.

`jstat` is a tool to show the **Java Virtual Machine (JVM)** statistics monitoring data. In the example, `jstat` attaches to the HRegionServer (PID 1812)'s JVM, takes samples at 1000 millisecond intervals, and displays the output, as specified by the `-gcutil` option. The output shows that the young generation collection keeps occurring. For example, between the 4th and 5th samples, the collection took 0.216 (**8.134** to **7.918** in the **YGCT** column) seconds and promoted objects from the Eden space (**E**) to the old space (**O**), resulting in an increase of old space utilization from **55.99%** to **58.73%**. Before the collection, the survivor space (**S0**) was **100%** utilized, but after this collection it is only **25.85%** utilized.

See also

▸ *HBase hbck—checking the consistency of an HBase cluster* recipe, in *Chapter 3, Using Administration Tools*

▸ *Simple scripts to report status of the cluster* recipe, in *Chapter 5, Monitoring and Diagnosis*

Handling the XceiverCount error

In this recipe, we will describe how to troubleshoot the following XceiverCount error shown in the DataNode logs:

```
2012-02-18 17:08:10,695 ERROR org.apache.hadoop.hdfs.server.datanode.
DataNode: DatanodeRegistration(10.166.111.191:50010, storageID=
DS-2072496811-10.168.130.82-50010-1321345166369, infoPort=50075,
ipcPort=50020):DataXceiver
java.io.IOException: xceiverCount 257 exceeds the limit of concurrent
xcievers 256
    at org.apache.hadoop.hdfs.server.datanode.DataXceiver.run
      (DataXceiver.java:92)
    at java.lang.Thread.run(Thread.java:662)
```

Getting ready

Log in to your master node.

How to do it...

The following are the steps to fix the XceiverCount error:

1. Add the following snippet to the HDFS setting file (`hdfs-site.xml`):

```
hadoop@master1$ vi $HADOOP_HOME/conf/hdfs-site.xml

<property>
    <name>dfs.datanode.max.xcievers</name>
    <value>4096</value>
</property>
```

2. Sync the `hdfs-site.xml` file across the cluster:

```
hadoop@master1$ for slave in `cat $HADOOP_HOME/conf/slaves`
do
    rsync -avz $HADOOP_HOME/conf/ $slave:$HADOOP_HOME/conf/
done
```

3. Restart HDFS and HBase from the master node:

```
hadoop@master1$ $HBASE_HOME/bin/stop-hbase.sh
hadoop@master1$ $HADOOP_HOME/bin/stop-dfs.sh

hadoop@master1$ $HADOOP_HOME/bin/start-dfs.sh
hadoop@master1$ $HBASE_HOME/bin/start-hbase.sh
```

How it works...

The `dfs.datanode.max.xcievers` (yes, this is misspelled) setting defines an HDFS DataNode's upper bound on the number of files that it will serve at any given time. Its default value is `256`, which is too small to run HBase on HDFS. If your DataNode reaches this upper bound, you will see an error log in the DataNode logs notifying you that the Xciever count has been exceeded.

We recommend setting it to a much higher value, 4096 for example, on modern machines. After changing this setting, you will need to sync the modified `hdfs-site.xml` file across the cluster and then restart HDFS to apply the changes.

Handling the "too many open files" error

In this recipe, we will describe how to troubleshoot the error shown in the following DataNode logs:

```
2012-02-18 17:43:18,009 ERROR org.apache.hadoop.hdfs.server.datanode.
DataNode: DatanodeRegistration(10.166.111.191:50010, storageID=
DS-2072496811-10.168.130.82-50010-1321345166369, infoPort=50075,
ipcPort=50020):DataXceiver
```
**java.io.FileNotFoundException: /usr/local/hadoop/var/dfs/data/current/
subdir6/blk_-8839555124496884481 (Too many open files)**
```
    at java.io.RandomAccessFile.open(Native Method)
    at java.io.RandomAccessFile.<init>(RandomAccessFile.java:216)
    at org.apache.hadoop.hdfs.server.datanode.FSDataset.
getBlockInputStream(FSDataset.java:1068)
```

Getting ready

To fix this issue, you will need root privileges on every node of the cluster. We assume you use the hadoop user to start your HDFS cluster.

How to do it...

To fix the "too many open files" error, execute the following steps on every node of the cluster:

1. Increase the open file number of the hadoop user by adding the following properties to the /etc/security/limits.conf file:

    $ vi /etc/security/limits.conf
    ```
    hadoop soft nofile 65535
    hadoop hard nofile 65535
    ```

2. Add the following line to the /etc/pam.d/login file:

    $ vi /etc/pam.d/login
    ```
    session     required    pam_limits.so
    ```

3. Log out and then log in again as the hadoop user.

4. Confirm that the open file limit has been increased, by running the following command:

    $ ulimit -n

    65535

5. Restart HDFS and HBase from the master node:

```
hadoop@master1$ $HBASE_HOME/bin/stop-hbase.sh
hadoop@master1$ $HADOOP_HOME/bin/stop-dfs.sh

hadoop@master1$ $HADOOP_HOME/bin/start-dfs.sh
hadoop@master1$ $HBASE_HOME/bin/start-hbase.sh
```

How it works...

HBase is a database running on Hadoop, and just like the other databases, it keeps lots of files open at the same time. On the other hand, Linux limits the number of file descriptors that a process may open. The default limitation is 1024, which is too small for HBase. If the hadoop user's open file number exceeds this upper bound, you will see an error in the DataNode logs indicating that too many files are open.

To run HBase smoothly, you will need to increase the maximum number of open file descriptors for the user running HDFS and HBase; in our case, that is the hadoop user.

We set the hadoop user's open file limit in the /etc/security/limits.conf file, in step 1, and then modify the /etc/pam.d/login file in step 2, so that the change works next time the user logs in to the system. The soft limit (soft nofile) is the value that the OS kernel enforces for the number of open file descriptors. The hard limit (hard nofile) acts as a ceiling for the soft limit. ulimit is a program to set and show the limit of the use of system-wide resources for the current user. As you can see in step 4, the ulimit -n command shows the open file limit for the hadoop user.

Do not forget to restart the HDFS cluster to apply the changes.

There's more...

You may also want to know the current open file number of the hadoop user. In order to get this information, use the lsof command:

```
$ lsof -uhadoop | wc -l
```

See also

- ▶ *Changing the kernel settings* recipe, in *Chapter 1, Setting Up HBase Cluster*
- ▶ *Handling the "unable to create new native thread" error*, in this chapter

Handling the "unable to create new native thread" error

In this recipe, we will describe how to troubleshoot the error shown in the following RegionServer logs:

```
2012-02-18 18:46:04,907 WARN org.apache.hadoop.hdfs.DFSClient:
DataStreamer Exception: java.lang.OutOfMemoryError: unable to create
new native thread
    at java.lang.Thread.start0(Native Method)
    at java.lang.Thread.start(Thread.java:640)
    at org.apache.hadoop.hdfs.DFSClient$DFSOutputStream$DataStreamer.
run(DFSClient.java:2830)
```

Getting ready

To fix this error, you will need root privileges on every node of the cluster. We assume you use the `hadoop` user to start your HDFS and HBase clusters.

How to do it...

To fix the "unable to create new native thread" error, execute the following steps on every node of the cluster:

1. Increase the maximum number of processes of the `hadoop` user by adding the following properties to the `/etc/security/limits.conf` file:

   ```
   $ vi /etc/security/limits.conf
   hadoop soft nproc 32000
   hadoop hard nproc 32000
   ```

2. Add the following line to the `/etc/pam.d/login` file:

   ```
   $ vi /etc/pam.d/login
   session    required    pam_limits.so
   ```

3. Log out and then log in again as the `hadoop` user.

4. Make sure the open process limit has been increased, by running the following command:

   ```
   $ ulimit -u
   32000
   ```

5. Restart HDFS and HBase from the master node:

```
hadoop@master1$ $HBASE_HOME/bin/stop-hbase.sh
hadoop@master1$ $HADOOP_HOME/bin/stop-dfs.sh

hadoop@master1$ $HADOOP_HOME/bin/start-dfs.sh
hadoop@master1$ $HBASE_HOME/bin/start-hbase.sh
```

How it works...

Linux limits the number of processes that a user may execute simultaneously. In a high load HBase cluster, a low nproc setting could manifest as an OutOfMemoryError exception, as shown earlier. If the running process numbers of the hadoop user exceed the nproc limit, you will see an error in the RegionServer logs to the tune of "unable to create new native thread".

To run HBase smoothly, you will need to increase the nproc limit for the user who runs HDFS and HBase.

We set the hadoop user's nproc limit in the /etc/security/limits.conf file in step 1 and then modify the /etc/pam.d/login file in step 2, so that the change works the next time the user logs in to the system. The soft limit (soft nproc) is the value that the OS kernel enforces for the number of processes. The hard limit (hard nproc) acts as a ceiling for the soft limit.

After logging out, we log back in again and run the ulimit -u program, to show the limit of the current user's process number.

Finally, we restart HDFS and HBase to apply the changes.

There's more...

In order to view the current thread number of the hadoop user, type the following command:

```
$ ps -o pid,comm,user,thcount -u hadoop
  PID COMMAND        USER     THCNT
 1349 su             hadoop     1
 1350 bash           hadoop     1
 1429 java           hadoop    32
 1580 java           hadoop    14
 1690 java           hadoop    48
 1819 ps             hadoop     1
```

The THCNT column of the output is the thread number of each process by the hadoop user.

See also

▶   *Changing the kernel settings, Chapter 1, Setting Up HBase Cluster*

▶   *Handling the "too many open files" error*, in this chapter

Handling the "HBase ignores HDFS client configuration" issue

You may have noticed that HBase ignores your HDFS client configuration, for example the `dfs.replication` setting. In the following example, we have set a replication factor of 2 for our HDFS client:

```
$ grep -A 1 "dfs.replication" $HADOOP_HOME/conf/hdfs-site.xml
    <name>dfs.replication</name>
    <value>2</value>
```

However, the HBase files on HDFS show a factor of 3, which is the default replication factor of HDFS:

HDFS: /hbase/.logs/ip-10-166-107-209.us-west-1.compute.internal,60020,1329569291435

http://ip-10-168-223-58.us-west-1.compute.internal:50075/browseDirectory.jsp?dir=%2F

Contents of directory /hbase/.logs/ip-10-166-107-209.us-west-1.compute.internal,60020,1329569291435

Goto : /hbase/.logs/ip-10-1 [go]

Go to parent directory

Name	Type	Size	Replication	Block Size	Modification Time	Permission	Owner	Group
ip-10-166-107-209.us-west-1.compute.internal%2C60020%2C1329569291435.1329569296122	file	0 KB	3	64 MB	2012-02-18 21:48	rw-r--r--	hadoop	supergroup

This is not what we expected—the replication factor was expected to be 2, but the actual value is 3.

We will describe why this happens and how to fix it, in this recipe.

Getting ready

Log in to your master node as the user who starts HDFS and HBase. We assume you are using the `hadoop` user for HDFS and HBase.

How to do it...

The following are the steps to apply your HDFS client configurations to HBase:

1. Add a symbolic link of the HDFS setting file (`hdfs-site.xml`) under the HBase configuration directory:

   ```
   $ hadoop@master1$ ln -s $HADOOP_HOME/conf/hdfs-site.xml $HBASE_
   HOME/conf/hdfs-site.xml
   ```

2. Sync this change across the cluster:

   ```
   hadoop@master1$ for slave in `cat $HBASE_HOME/conf/regionservers`

   do

       rsync -avz $HBASE_HOME/conf/ $slave:$HBASE_HOME/conf/

   done
   ```

3. Restart HBase. Now, the newly created HBase files will have the HDFS client configurations. The actual replication factor value will be 2, as we expected:

   ```
   hadoop@master1$ $HBASE_HOME/bin/stop-hbase.sh


   hadoop@master1$ $HBASE_HOME/bin/start-hbase.sh
   ```

How it works...

HDFS client configuration is set in the `hdfs-site.xml` file. To apply the HDFS client configuration to HBase, we need to add the settings in this file, and add the `hdfs-site.xml` file to the HBase's classpath.. The easiest way to do this is to create a symbolic link of the `hdfs-site.xml` file under the HBase configuration directory and then sync it across the cluster.

Once HBase has been restarted, you will notice that the HDFS client configurations will be applied.

Handling the ZooKeeper client connection error

In this recipe, we will describe how to troubleshoot the ZooKeeper client connection error shown in the following RegionServer logs:

```
2012-02-19 15:17:06,199 WARN org.apache.zookeeper.ClientCnxn:
Session 0x0 for server ip-10-168-47-220.us-west-1.compute.internal
/10.168.47.220:2181, unexpected error, closing socket connection and
attempting reconnect
```

```
java.io.IOException: Connection reset by peer
    at sun.nio.ch.FileDispatcher.read0(Native Method)
    at sun.nio.ch.SocketDispatcher.read(SocketDispatcher.java:21)
    at sun.nio.ch.IOUtil.readIntoNativeBuffer(IOUtil.java:198)
    at sun.nio.ch.IOUtil.read(IOUtil.java:166)
    at sun.nio.ch.SocketChannelImpl.read(SocketChannelImpl.java:243)
    at org.apache.zookeeper.ClientCnxnSocketNIO.
doIO(ClientCnxnSocketNIO.java:66)
```

Getting ready

Log in to your ZooKeeper quorum nodes.

How to do it...

The following are the steps to fix the ZooKeeper client connection error:

1. Add the following to the ZooKeeper configuration file (zoo.cfg) on every ZooKeeper quorum node:

    $ vi $ZOOKEEPER_HOME/conf/zoo.cfg

    maxClientCnxns=60

2. Restart ZooKeeper to apply the changes:

    $ $ZOOKEEPER_HOME/bin/zkServer.sh stop

    $ $ZOOKEEPER_HOME/bin/zkServer.sh start

How it works...

This error usually occurs when running a MapReduce job over an HBase cluster. ZooKeeper has a maxClientCnxns setting to limit the number of concurrent connections that a single client may make to a single member of the ZooKeeper ensemble. Every region server is a ZooKeeper client; if a region server's concurrent connection number exceeds this maximum client connection limit, it will be not able to create a new connection to the ZooKeeper ensemble. That's why the aforementioned error occured.

To fix this error, we need to set a higher value to the maxClientCnxns setting and restart ZooKeeper for the changes to be applied.

There's more...

The default value for maxClientCnxns has been changed to 60, since ZooKeeper 3.4.0. It should work well for many applications.

To view the current number of connections from a client to a specific ZooKeeper quorum node, run the following command:

```
$ echo "cons" | nc localhost 2181 | grep "your.client.ip.address" | wc -1
```

Replace `localhost` with the hostname of your ZooKeeper quorum node, and the "`your. client.ip.address`" with your client's IP address.

Handling the ZooKeeper session expired error

In this recipe, we will describe how to troubleshoot the following ZooKeeper session expired error shown in the RegionServer logs:

```
2012-02-19 16:49:15,405 WARN org.apache.hadoop.hbase.regionserver.
HRegionServer: Failed deleting my ephemeral node
org.apache.zookeeper.KeeperException$SessionExpiredException:
KeeperErrorCode = Session expired for /hbase/rs/ip-10-168-37-91.us-
west-1.compute.internal,60020,1329635463251
    at org.apache.zookeeper.KeeperException.create(KeeperException.
java:127)
    at org.apache.zookeeper.KeeperException.create(KeeperException.
java:51)
    at org.apache.zookeeper.ZooKeeper.delete(ZooKeeper.java:868)
    at org.apache.hadoop.hbase.zookeeper.RecoverableZooKeeper.
delete(RecoverableZooKeeper.java:107)
```

This issue is critical, because master or region servers will shut themselves down if they lose connection to the ZooKeeper quorum.

Getting ready

Log in to the server where this error occurred.

How to do it...

The following are the steps to fix the ZooKeeper session expired issue:

1. Check `hbase-env.sh`; make sure you give plenty of RAM to the HBase daemons. The default of 1 GB won't be enough for heavy clusters:

   ```
   $ vi $HBASE_HOME/conf/hbase-env.sh

   export HBASE_HEAPSIZE=8000
   ```

2. Run the `vmstat` command to show the virtual memory statistics:

   ```
   $ vmstat 1
   ```

   ```
   procs ------------memory---------- ---swap-- -----io---- -system-- ----cpu----
    r  b   swpd   free   buff  cache   si   so    bi    bo   in   cs us sy id wa
    0  0      0 1357724  12656 155736    0    0    52     4   13   17  0  0 98  1
    7  1      0 1355760  12664 157208    0    0  1180     0  151  274  1  0 97  0
    3  0      0 1336956  12692 171836    0    0  8736    40 1157 1766 33 12  0  0
    4  2      0 1319704  12704 187180    0    0  8196  5584 1223 1618 32  9  0  0
   ```

   Check the **swap** columns called **si** (swap in) and **so** (swap out), and make sure you don't swap.

3. Use the `jstat` command to show the Java Garbage Collection (GC) statistics:

   ```
   $ jstat -gcutil <java_process_pid> 1000
   ```

   ```
    S0    S1     E      O      P      YGC    YGCT   FGC   FGCT    GCT
   6.42  0.00  77.46  45.22  60.00    24   0.344   12   0.279   0.622
   6.42  0.00  80.01  45.22  60.00    24   0.344   12   0.279   0.622
   6.42  0.00  80.70  45.22  60.00    24   0.344   12   0.279   0.622
   6.42  0.00  81.22  45.22  60.00    24   0.344   12   0.279   0.622
   6.42  0.00  81.71  45.22  60.00    24   0.344   12   0.279   0.622
   ```

   Check the **FGCT** column, and make sure RegionServer doesn't run into a long GC pause.

4. Use the `top` command to show CPU statistics. Make sure the RegionServer thread has plenty of CPU resources. MapReduce may use a lot of CPU power, causing the RegionServer to starve and run into a long GC pause.

5. Consider reducing the map/reduce slots number on the region server, if MapReduce consumes too much CPU resource. Adjust the following value:

   ```
   $ vi $HADOOP_HOME/conf/mapred-site.xml
   ```

   ```xml
   <property>
     <name>mapred.tasktracker.map.tasks.maximum</name>
     <value>2</value>
   </property>
   <property>
     <name>mapred.tasktracker.reduce.tasks.maximum</name>
     <value>1</value>
   </property>
   ```

6. Consider increasing the ZooKeeper session timeout by editing the `hbase-site.xml` file:

```
$ vi $HBASE_HOME/conf/hbase-site.xml

<property>
    <name>zookeeper.session.timeout</name>
    <value>120000</value>
</property>
```

7. Increase the ZooKeeper maximum session timeout on every ZooKeeper quorum node. Modify the `zoo.cfg` file to increase the `maxSessionTimeout` value:

```
$ vi $ZOOKEEPER_HOME/conf/zoo.cfg

maxSessionTimeout= 120000
```

8. Restart ZooKeeper on every ZooKeeper quorum node, if you made changes to the `zoo.cfg` file:

```
$ $ZOOKEEPER_HOME/bin/zkServer.sh stop
```

```
$ $ZOOKEEPER_HOME/bin/zkServer.sh start
```

9. Sync the files you modified across the cluster, and then restart your Hadoop/HBase cluster.

How it works...

This error often occurs on an overloaded HBase cluster. An HBase Master and RegionServer daemon acts as a ZooKeeper client; if the client cannot communicate with the ZooKeeper quorum in a configured time, the connection will time out and this error will occur.

The two most likely reasons why a ZooKeeper connection gets timed out are as follows:

► A long JVM GC pause

► The configured timeout time is too short

From steps 1 to 5, we try to find out whether a long GC caused the error or not. HBase needs plenty of RAM to run smoothly. The default size of 1 GB won't be enough for heavy clusters. So, change the value of `HBASE_HEAPSIZE` in the `hbase-env.sh` file to a higher one (for example, 8 GB), but lower than 16 GB. The reason we recommend setting the HBase heap size lower than 16 GB is, if we use a very big heap size here, the GC will take a very long time to complete, which is what we must avoid.

Make sure your RegionServer doesn't swap. The `vmstat` command can be used to see whether a swap happened or not. In step 2, we use the `vmstat` command to show virtual memory statistics in a 1-second interval. There is a `vm.swappiness` kernel setting you should change, to avoid swap. We will describe it in the *Setting vm.swappiness to 0 to avoid swap* recipe, in *Chapter 8, Basic Performance Tuning*.

`jstat` is a Java Virtual Machine statistics monitoring tool. We use the `-gcutil` option in step 3 to show the Java GC statistics for a specific Java process, in a 1-second interval. The **FGCT** column of the output is the total, full GC time; check this column to see whether a long GC pause happened or not.

Another reason for a long GC pause is that the RegionServer process may not have enough CPU resources. This is especially true when running heavy MapReduce jobs on an HBase cluster. In this case, if you are running heavy MapReduce jobs, use the MapReduce configurations `mapred. tasktracker.map.tasks.maximum` and `mapred.tasktracker.reduce.tasks. maximum`, to control the number of maps/reduces spawned simultaneously on a TaskTracker.

If you wish to increase the ZooKeeper session timeout, set `zookeeper.session.timeout` in the `hbase-site.xml` file, and `maxSessionTimeout` in the ZooKeeper configuration file (`zoo.cfg`). The `maxSessionTimeout` option is a ZooKeeper server-side configuration. It is an upper bound of a client session timeout, so its value must be bigger than the HBase `zookeeper.session.timeout` value.

 Note that setting a higher timeout means that the cluster will take at least that much time to failover a failed RegionServer. You will need to think about whether it is acceptable to your system or not.

See also

▸ *Troubleshooting tools*, in this chapter

▸ *Setting vm.swappiness to 0 to avoid swap* recipe, in *Chapter 8, Basic Performance Tuning*

Handling the HBase startup error on EC2

In this recipe, we will describe how to troubleshoot the HBase startup error shown in the following Master logs:

```
2011-12-10 14:04:57,422 ERROR org.apache.hadoop.hbase.HServerAddress:
Could not resolve the DNS name of ip-10-166-219-206.us-west-1.compute.
internal
2011-12-10 14:04:57,423 FATAL org.apache.hadoop.hbase.master.HMaster:
Unhandled exception. Starting shutdown.

java.lang.IllegalArgumentException: hostname can't be null
    at java.net.InetSocketAddress.<init>(InetSocketAddress.java:121)
    at org.apache.hadoop.hbase.HServerAddress.getResolvedAddress(HServ
erAddress.java:108)
    at org.apache.hadoop.hbase.HServerAddress.<init>(HServerAddress.
java:64)
```

This error usually happens after stopping and restarting EC2 instances. The reason is that HBase stores region locations in its "system" -ROOT- and .META. tables. The location information contains the internal EC2 DNS name in it. Stopping an EC2 instance will change this DNS name. Due to the DNS name change, HBase will not be able to resolve the old DNS name in its system table to the new one, thus causing the aforementioned error message.

In this recipe, we will describe how to fix this issue, so that you can feel free to stop/start your EC2 instances for HBase (if your HDFS saves data on the EC2 instance storage, you will need to save your data on other storages such as Amazon S3 before restarting an EC2 instance).

Getting ready

Make sure you have already set up your Amazon EC2 environment for HBase. If you haven't already, refer to the *Getting ready on Amazon EC2* recipe in *Chapter 1, Setting Up HBase Cluster,* for how to get ready on EC2 to run HBase on it.

You will need an account that has root privileges on every node of the cluster, to run the scripts we will create later.

How to do it...

The following are the steps to fix the HBase startup error on EC2:

1. Create a ec2-running-hosts.sh script, as shown in the following snippet:

```
$ vi ec2-running-hosts.sh

#!/bin/bash

ec2-describe-instances > /tmp/all-instances
ip_type=$1
if [ "$ip_type" == "private" ]; then
    addresses=`grep ^INSTANCE /tmp/all-instances | cut -f18`
elif [ "$ip_type" == "public" ]; then
    addresses=`grep ^INSTANCE /tmp/all-instances | cut -f17`
else
    echo "Usage: `basename $0` private|public"
    exit -1
fi
for address in $addresses
do
    instance_id=`grep $address /tmp/all-instances | cut -f2`
    dns=`grep $address /tmp/all-instances | cut -f5`
    host=`grep ^TAG /tmp/all-instances | grep $instance_id | cut
-f5`
```

```
    echo -e "${address}\t${dns}\t${host}"

done
```

2. Create an `update-ec2-hosts.sh` script as shown in the following snippet. Replace YOUR_PASSWORD in the script with the password of the account you are using to run the script:

$ vi update-ec2-hosts.sh

```
#!/bin/bash

if [ $# -lt 2 ]; then
    echo "Usage: `basename $0` host-file target-host"
    exit 1
fi
host_file=$1
target_host=$2

bin=`dirname $0`
bin=`cd $bin;pwd`

echo "updating hosts file on $target_host using $host_file"
# backup
ssh -f $target_host "cp /etc/hosts /tmp/hosts.org"

cp $bin/hosts.template /tmp/hosts.update
cat $host_file >> /tmp/hosts.update
scp /tmp/hosts.update $target_host:/tmp

# chmod 700 this file as we write password here
ssh -f -t -t -t $target_host "sudo -S cp /tmp/hosts.update /etc/
hosts <<EOF
YOUR_PASSWORD
EOF
"
echo "[done] update hosts file on $target_host"
```

3. Make sure the `update-ec2-hosts.sh` script is only readable by you:

$ chmod 700 update-ec2-hosts.sh

4. Copy your `/etc/hosts` file from your EC2 instance to the same directory as the `update-ec2-hosts.sh` script and rename it to `hosts.template`:

$ cp /etc/hosts hosts.template

5. Create an `update-ec2-private-hosts.sh` script with the following content. Replace the value of `NS_HOSTNAME` with the hostname of your name server:

```
$ vi update-ec2-private-hosts.sh
#!/bin/bash

bin=`dirname $0`
bin=`cd $bin;pwd`
NS_HOSTNAME="ns1"

$bin/ec2-running-hosts.sh private | tee /tmp/ec2-running-host

cp $bin/hosts.template /tmp/hosts.update
cat /tmp/ec2-running-host >> /tmp/hosts.update

while read line
do
    host=`echo "$line" | cut -f3`
    if [ "$host" == "$NS_HOSTNAME" ]; then
        # do not update name server
        continue
    fi
    echo
    echo "Updating $host"

    bash $bin/update-ec2-hosts.sh "/tmp/ec2-running-host" "$host"
    sleep 1
done < /tmp/ec2-running-host
```

6. Create an `update-ec2-hmaster-hosts.sh` script, as shown in the following snippet. Replace the value of `HMASTER_HOSTNAME` and `RS_HOSTNAMES` with the hostname of the Master and RegionServer nodes, respectively:

```
$ vi update-ec2-hmaster-hosts.sh
#!/bin/bash
bin=`dirname $0`
bin=`cd $bin;pwd`

IFS_BAK=$IFS
IFS="
"
HMASTER_HOSTNAME="master1"
RS_HOSTNAMES="slave[123]"

scp $HMASTER_HOSTNAME:/tmp/hosts.org /tmp
```

```
scp $HMASTER_HOSTNAME:/etc/hosts /tmp

rm -f /tmp/hosts.done
while read line
do
    echo "$line" | egrep -q "$RS_HOSTNAMES"
    if [ $? -ne 0 ]; then
        echo -e "${line}" >> /tmp/hosts.done
    else
        slave=`echo "$line" | cut -f3`
        original_private_dns=`grep "$slave" /tmp/hosts.org | cut
-f2`
        echo -e "${line}\t${original_private_dns}" >> /tmp/hosts.
done
    fi
done < /tmp/hosts

bash $bin/update-ec2-hosts.sh "/tmp/hosts.done" "$HMASTER_
HOSTNAME"
```

7. Take the scripts created in the previous steps to your name server on EC2, and run the `update-ec2-private-hosts.sh` file from there:

   hac@ns1$ ./update-ec2-private-hosts.sh

   10.176.202.34 ip-10-176-202-34.us-west-1.compute.internal master1

   10.160.49.250 ip-10-160-49-250.us-west-1.compute.internal   ns1

   10.160.47.194 ip-10-160-47-194.us-west-1.compute.internal   slave1

   10.176.23.117 ip-10-176-23-117.us-west-1.compute.internal client1

   10.160.39.197 ip-10-160-39-197.us-west-1.compute.internal   slave2

   10.168.41.175 ip-10-168-41-175.us-west-1.compute.internal   slave3

   Updating master1

   updating hosts file on master1 using /tmp/ec2-running-host

   hosts.update
   100% 657   0.6KB/s   00:00

   [done] update hosts file on master1

   [sudo] password for hac:

   Updating slave1

   ...

   The `/etc/hosts` file on every node has been updated by the script, using EC2 API.

8. Run `update-ec2-hmaster-hosts.sh`, if `update-ec2-private-hosts.sh` has finished successfully:

```
hac@ns1$ ./update-ec2-hmaster-hosts.sh

hosts.org
100% 1457      1.4KB/s    00:00

hosts
100%  657      0.6KB/s    00:00

updating hosts file on master1 using /tmp/hosts.done

hosts.update
100% 1058      1.0KB/s    00:00

[done] update hosts file on master1
```

The old DNS entry of each slave node will be appended to the `/etc/hosts` file on the master node.

9. Run the following command to check the hosts file:

```
hac@master1$ grep "slave" /etc/hosts
```

The following screenshot shows the command's output:

```
hac@master1 ~$ grep "slave" /etc/hosts
10.160.47.194    ip-10-160-47-194.us-west-1.compute.internal    slave1  ip-10-160-113-205.us-west-1.compute.internal
10.160.39.197    ip-10-160-39-197.us-west-1.compute.internal    slave2  ip-10-168-55-126.us-west-1.compute.internal
10.168.41.175    ip-10-168-41-175.us-west-1.compute.internal    slave3  ip-10-176-21-234.us-west-1.compute.internal
```

Log in to your master node as the `hadoop` user and start HBase on this node:

```
hadoop@master1$ $HADOOP_HOME/bin/start-dfs.sh

starting namenode, logging to /usr/local/hadoop/logs/hadoop-hadoop-
namenode-master1.out

slave1: Warning: Permanently added the RSA host key for IP address
'10.160.47.194' to the list of known hosts.

slave2: Warning: Permanently added the RSA host key for IP address
'10.160.39.197' to the list of known hosts.

slave3: Warning: Permanently added the RSA host key for IP address
'10.168.41.175' to the list of known hosts.

slave1: starting datanode, logging to /usr/local/hadoop/logs/hadoop-
hadoop-datanode-slave1.out

slave3: starting datanode, logging to /usr/local/hadoop/logs/hadoop-
hadoop-datanode-slave3.out

slave2: starting datanode, logging to /usr/local/hadoop/logs/hadoop-
hadoop-datanode-slave2.out

hadoop@master1$ $ZOOKEEPER_HOME/bin/zkServer.sh start

JMX enabled by default
```

```
Using config: /usr/local/zookeeper/current/bin/../conf/zoo.cfg

Starting zookeeper ... STARTED

hadoop@master1$ $HBASE_HOME/bin/start-hbase.sh

starting master, logging to /usr/local/hbase/logs/hbase-hadoop-master-
master1.out

slave3: starting regionserver, logging to /usr/local/hbase/logs/hbase-
hadoop-regionserver-slave3.out

slave1: starting regionserver, logging to /usr/local/hbase/logs/hbase-
hadoop-regionserver-slave1.out

slave2: starting regionserver, logging to /usr/local/hbase/logs/hbase-
hadoop-regionserver-slave2.out
```

How it works...

As a simple solution, every time we stop and restart the instances before starting HBase, we update the `/etc/hosts` file on every node in the cluster and then append the old DNS entry of each slave node to the master node's `/etc/hosts` file. With this, HBase Master is able to resolve the old DNS entries in its system tables to the updated, new IP address and update them with the new DNS entries in the system tables, too.

In order to implement this idea, we create the `ec2-running-hosts.sh` script in step 1, and invoke the `ec2-describe-instances` EC2 API, to get information about all our running EC2 instances, and grep the IP address, DNS name, and user data (hostname) of each running instance. These are the new DNS entries we need to update to the `/etc/hosts` file of each node.

The `update-ec2-hosts.sh` script we have created in step 2, is a utility script to SSH into a particular server and overwrite the `/etc/hosts` file in that server, without human interaction. The script also backs up the original `/etc/hosts` file before overwriting it. We write the account's password in the script so that we don't need to enter it on every node. That's why it was noted in step 3, that the script should only readable to yourself.

The `update-ec2-private-hosts.sh` script created in step 5 makes the two scripts we created in the previous steps work together to get new DNS entries, appends them to a `hosts.template` file, and then uses the `hosts.template` file to overwrite the `/etc/hosts` file on every running EC2 instance, except the DNS name server.

The `update-ec2-hmaster-hosts.sh` script created in step 6 does the simple work of appending *a new IP address to an old DNS name* mapping for each slave node to the new `/etc/hosts` file, so that HBase Master can resolve old DNS entries stored in its system tables to the new IP addresses. After that, the script invokes `update-ec2-hosts.sh` to overwrite the `/etc/hosts` file on the master node, using the newly appended file.

After executing the `update-ec2-private-hosts.sh` and `update-ec2-hmaster-hosts.sh` scripts in order, we will now be able to start HDFS and HBase normally.

As you can see, these scripts are simple but useful, if you want to start your HBase EC2 instances only when you need to run HBase on them.

There's more...

You may also like to update the public DNS name of your EC2 instances to the /etc/hosts file on your local PC, so that you can access the HBase web UI from your web browser. The following are the steps to do this:

1. Create an update-ec2-public-hosts.sh script, as shown in the following snippet, and put it under the same directory as the scripts we created in the previous section:

```
$ vi update-ec2-public-hosts.sh

#!/bin/bash

bin=`dirname $0`
bin=`cd $bin;pwd`

$bin/ec2-running-hosts.sh public | tee /tmp/ec2-running-host

# backup
cp /etc/hosts /tmp/hosts.org

# update
cp $bin/hosts.local /tmp/hosts.update
cat /tmp/ec2-running-host >> /tmp/hosts.update

sudo cp /tmp/hosts.update /etc/hosts
echo "[done] update EC2 public hostname in hosts file"
```

2. Copy your /etc/hosts file to the same directory as the update-ec2-public-hosts.sh script, and rename it to hosts.local:

```
$ cp /etc/hosts hosts.local
```

3. Run the update-ec2-public-hosts.sh script on your local PC. The script will ask you to enter the password of your account, because it needs root privileges to update the /etc/hosts file:

```
184.72.22.179 ip-10-176-202-34.us-west-1.compute.internal
master1

...

184.169.243.211     ip-10-168-41-175.us-west-1.compute.internal
slave3

Password:

[done] update EC2 public hostname in hosts file
```

4. Now, open your web browser and enter the URL `http://master1:60010/master.jsp`. You will get the HBase web UI. Replace `master1` with your master node's hostname.

 Note that you will need a Mac OS X or Linux PC to use this script.

See also

▶   *Getting ready on Amazon EC2*, in *Chapter 1, Setting Up HBase Cluster*

8
Basic Performance Tuning

In this chapter, we will cover:

- ▶ Setting up Hadoop to spread disk I/O
- ▶ Using a network topology script to make the Hadoop rack-aware
- ▶ Mounting disks with `noatime` and `nodiratime`
- ▶ Setting `vm.swappiness` to 0 to avoid swap
- ▶ Java GC and HBase heap settings
- ▶ Using compression
- ▶ Managing compactions
- ▶ Managing a region split

Introduction

Performance is one of the most interesting characteristics of an HBase cluster's behavior. It is a challenging operation for administrators, because performance tuning requires deep understanding of not only HBase but also of Hadoop, **Java Virtual Machine Garbage Collection (JVM GC)**, and important tuning parameters of an operating system.

The structure of a typical HBase cluster is shown in the following diagram:

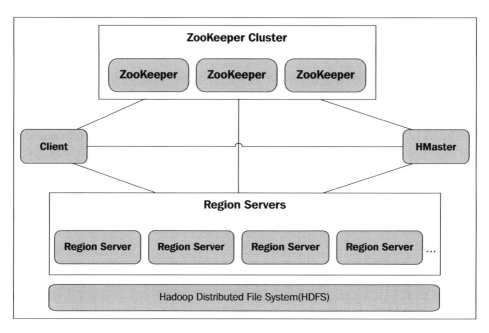

There are several components in the cluster—the ZooKeeper cluster, the HBase master node, region servers, the **Hadoop Distributed File System** (**HDFS**) and the HBase client.

The ZooKeeper cluster acts as a coordination service for the entire HBase cluster, handling master selection, root region server lookup, node registration, and so on. The master node does not do heavy tasks. Its job includes region allocation and failover, log splitting, and load balancing. Region servers hold the actual regions; they handle I/O requests to the hosting regions, flush the in-memory data store (MemStore) to HDFS, and split and compact regions. HDFS is the place where HBase stores its data files (StoreFile) and write ahead logs (WAL). We usually have an HBase region server running on the same machine as the HDFS DataNode, but it is not mandatory.

The HBase client provides APIs to access the HBase cluster. To communicate with the cluster, clients need to find the region server holding a specific row key range; this is called region lookups. HBase has two system tables to support region lookups—the -ROOT- table and the .META. table.

The -ROOT- table is used to refer to regions in the .META. table, while the .META. table holds references to all user regions. First, the clients query ZooKeeper to find the -ROOT- table location (the region server where it is deployed); they then query the -ROOT- table, and subsequently the .META. table, to find the region server holding a specific region. Clients also cache region locations to avoid querying ZooKeeper, -ROOT-, and .META. tables every time.

With this background knowledge, we will describe how to tune HBase to gain better performance, in this chapter.

Besides HBase itself, other tuning points include Hadoop configurations, the JVM garbage collection settings, and the OS kernel parameters. These are as important as tuning HBase itself. We will also include recipes to tune these configurations, in this chapter.

Setting up Hadoop to spread disk I/O

Modern servers usually have multiple disk devices to provide large storage capacities. These disks are usually configured as RAID arrays, as their factory settings. This is good for many cases but not for Hadoop.

The Hadoop slave node stores HDFS data blocks and MapReduce temporary files on its local disks. These local disk operations benefit from using multiple independent disks to spread disk I/O.

In this recipe, we will describe how to set up Hadoop to use multiple disks to spread its disk I/O.

Getting ready

We assume you have multiple disks for each DataNode node. These disks are in a **JBOD** (**Just a Bunch Of Disks**) or RAID0 configuration. Assume that the disks are mounted at `/mnt/d0`, `/mnt/d1`, ..., `/mnt/dn`, and the user who starts HDFS has write permission on each mount point.

How to do it...

In order to set up Hadoop to spread disk I/O, follow these instructions:

1. On each DataNode node, create directories on each disk for HDFS to store its data blocks:

    ```
    hadoop$ mkdir -p /mnt/d0/dfs/data
    hadoop$ mkdir -p /mnt/d1/dfs/data
    ...
    hadoop$ mkdir -p /mnt/dn/dfs/data
    ```

2. Add the following code to the HDFS configuration file (`hdfs-site.xml`):

    ```
    hadoop@master1$ vi $HADOOP_HOME/conf/hdfs-site.xml
    <property>
      <name>dfs.data.dir</name>
    ```

```
    <value>/mnt/d0/dfs/data,/mnt/d1/dfs/data,...,/mnt/dn/dfs/data
    </value>
</property>
```

3. Sync the modified `hdfs-site.xml` file across the cluster:

```
hadoop@master1$ for slave in `cat $HADOOP_HOME/conf/slaves`
do
    rsync -avz $HADOOP_HOME/conf/ $slave:$HADOOP_HOME/conf/
done
```

4. Restart HDFS:

```
hadoop@master1$ $HADOOP_HOME/bin/stop-dfs.sh
hadoop@master1$ $HADOOP_HOME/bin/start-dfs.sh
```

How it works...

We recommend JBOD or RAID0 for the DataNode disks, because you don't need the redundancy of RAID, as HDFS ensures its data redundancy using replication between nodes. So, there is no data loss when a single disk fails.

Which one to choose, JBOD or RAID0? You will theoretically get better performance from a JBOD configuration than from a RAID configuration. This is because, in a RAID configuration, you have to wait for the slowest disk in the array to complete before the entire write operation can complete, which makes the average I/O time equivalent to the slowest disk's I/O time. In a JBOD configuration, operations on a faster disk will complete independently of the slower ones, which makes the average I/O time faster than the slowest one. However, enterprise-class RAID cards might make big differences. You might want to benchmark your JBOD and RAID0 configurations before deciding which one to go with.

For both JBOD and RAID0 configurations, you will have the disks mounted at different paths. The key point here is to set the `dfs.data.dir` property to all the directories created on each disk. The `dfs.data.dir` property specifies where the DataNode should store its local blocks. By setting it to comma-separated multiple directories, DataNode stores its blocks across all the disks in round robin fashion. This causes Hadoop to efficiently spread disk I/O to all the disks.

Warning

Do not leave blanks between the directory paths in the `dfs.data.dir` property value, or it won't work as expected.

You will need to sync the changes across the cluster and restart HDFS to apply them.

There's more...

If you run MapReduce, as MapReduce stores its temporary files on TaskTracker's local file system, you might also like to set up MapReduce to spread its disk I/O:

1. On each TaskTracker node, create directories on each disk for MapReduce to store its intermediate data files:

    ```
    hadoop$ mkdir -p /mnt/d0/mapred/local
    hadoop$ mkdir -p /mnt/d1/mapred/local
    ...
    hadoop$ mkdir -p /mnt/dn/mapred/local
    ```

2. Add the following to MapReduce's configuration file (`mapred-site.xml`):

    ```
    hadoop@master1$ vi $HADOOP_HOME/conf/mapred-site.xml
    <property>
      <name>mapred.local.dir</name>
      <value>/mnt/d0/mapred/local,/mnt/d1/mapred/local,...,/mnt/dn/
    mapred/local
      </value>
    </property>
    ```

3. Sync the modified `mapred-site.xml` file across the cluster and restart MapReduce.

MapReduce generates a lot of temporary files on TaskTrackers' local disks during its execution. Like HDFS, setting up multiple directories on different disks helps spread MapReduce disk I/O significantly.

Using network topology script to make Hadoop rack-aware

Hadoop has the concept of "Rack Awareness". Administrators are able to define the rack of each DataNode in the cluster. Making Hadoop rack-aware is extremely important because:

- ▶ Rack awareness prevents data loss
- ▶ Rack awareness improves network performance

In this recipe, we will describe how to make Hadoop rack-aware and why it is important.

Getting ready

You will need to know the rack to which each of your slave nodes belongs. Log in to the master node as the user who started Hadoop.

How to do it...

The following steps describe how to make Hadoop rack-aware:

1. Create a `topology.sh` script and store it under the Hadoop configuration directory. Change the path for `topology.data`, in line 3, to fit your environment:

   hadoop@master1$ vi $HADOOP_HOME/conf/topology.sh

   ```
   while [ $# -gt 0 ] ; do
     nodeArg=$1
     exec< /usr/local/hadoop/current/conf/topology.data
     result=""
     while read line ; do
       ar=( $line )
       if [ "${ar[0]}" = "$nodeArg" ] ; then
         result="${ar[1]}"
       fi
     done
     shift
     if [ -z "$result" ] ; then
       echo -n "/default/rack "
     else
       echo -n "$result "
     fi
   done
   ```

   Don't forget to set the execute permission on the script file:

   hadoop@master1$ chmod +x $HADOOP_HOME/conf/topology.sh

2. Create a `topology.data` file, as shown in the following snippet; change the IP addresses and racks to fit your environment:

   hadoop@master1$ vi $HADOOP_HOME/conf/topology.data

   ```
   10.161.30.108      /dc1/rack1
   10.166.221.198     /dc1/rack2
   10.160.19.149      /dc1/rack3
   ```

3. Add the following to the Hadoop core configuration file (`core-site.xml`):

   hadoop@master1$ vi $HADOOP_HOME/conf/core-site.xml

   ```
   <property>
     <name>topology.script.file.name</name>
     <value>/usr/local/hadoop/current/conf/topology.sh</value>
   </property>
   ```

4. Sync the modified files across the cluster and restart HDFS and MapReduce.

5. Make sure HDFS is now rack-aware. If everything works well, you should be able to find something like the following snippet in your NameNode log file:

    ```
    2012-03-10 13:43:17,284 INFO org.apache.hadoop.net.
    NetworkTopology: Adding a new node: /dc1/rack3/10.160.19.149:50010

    2012-03-10 13:43:17,297 INFO org.apache.hadoop.net.
    NetworkTopology: Adding a new node: /dc1/rack1/10.161.30.108:50010

    2012-03-10 13:43:17,429 INFO org.apache.hadoop.
    net.NetworkTopology: Adding a new node: /dc1/
    rack2/10.166.221.198:50010
    ```

6. Make sure MapReduce is now rack-aware. If everything works well, you should be able to find something like the following snippet in your JobTracker log file:

    ```
    2012-03-10 13:50:38,341 INFO org.apache.hadoop.net.
    NetworkTopology: Adding a new node: /dc1/rack3/ip-10-160-19-149.
    us-west-1.compute.internal

    2012-03-10 13:50:38,485 INFO org.apache.hadoop.net.
    NetworkTopology: Adding a new node: /dc1/rack1/ip-10-161-30-108.
    us-west-1.compute.internal

    2012-03-10 13:50:38,569 INFO org.apache.hadoop.net.
    NetworkTopology: Adding a new node: /dc1/rack2/ip-10-166-221-198.
    us-west-1.compute.internal
    ```

How it works...

The following diagram shows the concept of Hadoop rack awareness:

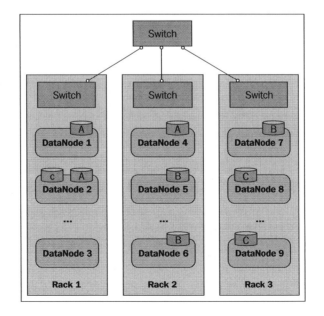

Each block of the HDFS files will be replicated to multiple DataNodes, to prevent loss of all the data copies due to failure of one machine. However, if all copies of data happen to be replicated on DataNodes in the same rack, and that rack fails, all the data copies will be lost. So to avoid this, the NameNode needs to know the network topology in order to use that information to make intelligent data replication.

As shown in the previous diagram, with the default replication factor of three, two data copies will be placed on the machines in the same rack, and another one will be put on a machine in a different rack. This ensures that a single rack failure won't result in the loss of all data copies.

Normally, two machines in the same rack have more bandwidth and lower latency between them than two machines in different racks. With the network topology information, Hadoop is able to maximize network performance by reading data from proper DataNodes. If data is available on the local machine, Hadoop will read data from it. If not, Hadoop will try reading data from a machine in the same rack, and if it is available on neither, data will be read from machines in different racks.

In step 1, we create a `topology.sh` script. The script takes DNS names as arguments and returns network topology (rack) names as the output. The mapping of DNS names to network topology is provided by the `topology.data` file, which was created in step 2. If an entry is not found in the `topology.data` file, the script returns `/default/rack` as a default rack name.

Note that we use IP addresses, and not hostnames in the `topology.data` file. There is a known bug that Hadoop does not correctly process hostnames that start with letters "a" to "f". Check HADOOP-6682 for more details: `https://issues.apache.org/jira/browse/HADOOP-6682`.

In step 3, we set the `topology.script.file.name` property in `core-site.xml`, telling Hadoop to invoke `topology.sh` to resolve DNS names to network topology names.

After restarting Hadoop, as shown in the logs of steps 5 and 6, HDFS and MapReduce add the correct rack name as a prefix to the DNS name of slave nodes. This indicates that the HDFS and MapReduce rack awareness work well with the aforementioned settings.

Mounting disks with noatime and nodiratime

If you are mounting disks purely for Hadoop and you use ext3 or ext4, or the XFS file system, we recommend that you mount the disks with the `noatime` and `nodiratime` attributes.

If you mount the disks as `noatime`, the access timestamps are not updated when a file is read on the filesystem. In the case of the `nodiratime` attribute, mounting disks does not update the directory inode access times on the filesystem. As there is no more disk I/O for updating the access timestamps, this speeds up filesystem reads.

In this recipe, we will describe why the `noatime` and `nodiratime` options are recommended for Hadoop, and how to mount disks with `noatime` and `nodiratime`.

Getting ready

You will need root privileges on your slave nodes. We assume you have two disks for only Hadoop—`/dev/xvdc` and `/dev/xvdd`. The two disks are mounted at `/mnt/is1` and `/mnt/is2`, respectively. Also, we assume you are using the ext3 filesystem.

How to do it...

To mount disks with `noatime` and `nodiratime`, execute the following instructions on every slave node in the cluster:

1. Add the following to the `/etc/fstab` file:

   ```
   $ sudo vi /etc/fstab
   /dev/xvdc    /mnt/is1    ext3 defaults,noatime,nodiratime  0  0
   /dev/xvdd    /mnt/is2    ext3 defaults,noatime,nodiratime  0  0
   ```

2. Unmount the disks and mount them again to apply the changes:

   ```
   $ sudo umount /dev/xvdc
   $ sudo umount /dev/xvdd


   $ sudo mount /dev/xvdc
   $ sudo mount /dev/xvdd
   ```

3. Check that the mount options have been applied:

   ```
   $ mount
   /dev/xvdc on /mnt/is1 type ext3 (rw,noatime,nodiratime)
   /dev/xvdd on /mnt/is2 type ext3 (rw,noatime,nodiratime)
   ```

How it works...

As Hadoop (HDFS) manages the metadata (inode) of its filesystem with NameNode, any access time information kept by Hadoop is independent of the `atime` attribute of individual blocks. So, the access timestamps in DataNode's local filesystem makes no sense here. That's why we recommend that you mount disks with `noatime` and `nodiratime`, if the disks are used purely for Hadoop. Mounting disks with `noatime` and `nodiratime` saves the write I/O every time a local file is accessed.

These options are set in the `/etc/fstab` file. Do not forget to unmount and mount the disks again, for the changes to be applied.

With these options enabled, an improvement in the performance of the HDFS read is expected. As HBase stores its data on HDFS, the HBase read performance is also expected to improve.

There's more...

Another method for optimization is to reduce the percentage of reserved blocks of the ext3 or ext4 filesystems. By default, some of the filesystem blocks are reserved for use by privileged processes. This is to avoid situations wherein user processes fill up the disk spaces that are required by the system daemons, in order to keep working. This is very important for the disks hosting the operating system but less useful for the disks only used by Hadoop.

Usually these Hadoop-only disks have a very large storage space. Reducing the percentage of the reserved blocks can add quite a few storage capacities to the HDFS cluster. Normally, the default percentage of reserved blocks is 5%. It can be reduced to 1%.

Warning:
Do not reduce the reserved blocks on the disks hosting the operating system.

To achieve this, run the following command on each disk of each slave node in the cluster:

```
$ sudo tune2fs -m 1 /dev/xvdc
tune2fs 1.41.12 (17-May-2010)
Setting reserved blocks percentage to 1% (1100915 blocks)
```

Setting vm.swappiness to 0 to avoid swap

Linux moves the memory pages that have not been accessed for some time to the swap space, even if there is enough free memory available. This is called swap out. On the other hand, reading swapped out data from the swap space to memory is called swap in. Swapping is necessary in many situations, but as **Java Virtual Machine** (**JVM**) does not behave well under swapping, HBase may run into trouble if swapped. The ZooKeeper session expiring is a typical problem that may be introduced by a swap.

In this recipe, we will describe how to tune the Linux vm.swappiness parameter to avoid swap.

Getting ready

Make sure you have root privileges on your nodes in the cluster.

How to do it...

To tune the Linux parameter to avoid swapping, invoke the following on each node in the cluster:

1. Execute the following command to set `vm.swappiness` to `0`:

```
root# sysctl -w vm.swappiness=0
vm.swappiness = 0
```

   This change will persist until the next reboot of the server.

2. Add the following to the `/etc/sysctl.conf` file, so that the setting will be enabled whenever the system boots:

```
root# echo "vm.swappiness = 0" >> /etc/sysctl.conf
```

How it works...

The `vm.swappiness` parameter can be used to define how aggressively memory pages are swapped to disk. It accepts any value from `0` to `100`—a low value means that the kernel will be less likely to swap, whereas a higher value will make the kernel swap out applications more often. The default value is `60`.

We set `vm.swappiness` to `0` in step 1, which will cause the kernel to avoid swapping processes out of physical memory for as long as possible. This is good for HBase, because HBase processes consume a large amount of memory. A higher `vm.swappiness` value will make HBase swap a lot and encounter very slow garbage collection. This is likely to result in the RegionServer process being killed off, as the ZooKeeper session times out. We recommend that you set it to `0` or any other low number (for example, `10`) and observe the state of swapping.

Note that the value set by the `sysctl` command only persists until the next reboot of the server. You need to set `vm.swappiness` in the `/etc/sysctl.conf` file, so that the setting is enabled whenever the system reboots.

See also

▶ *Changing the kernel settings* recipe, *Chapter 1, Setting Up HBase Cluster*

Java GC and HBase heap settings

As HBase runs within JVM, the JVM **Garbage Collection** (**GC**) settings are very important for HBase to run smoothly, with high performance. In addition to the general guideline for configuring HBase heap settings, it's also important to have the HBase processes output their GC logs and then tune the JVM settings based on the GC logs' output.

We will describe the most important HBase JVM heap settings as well as how to enable and understand GC logging, in this recipe. We will also cover some general guidelines to tune Java GC settings for HBase.

Getting ready

Log in to your HBase region server.

How to do it...

The following are the recommended Java GC and HBase heap settings:

1. Give HBase enough heap size by editing the `hbase-env.sh` file. For example, the following snippet configures a 8000-MB heap size for HBase:

   ```
   $ vi $HBASE_HOME/conf/hbase-env.sh
   export HBASE_HEAPSIZE=8000
   ```

2. Enable GC logging by using the following command:

   ```
   $ vi $HBASE_HOME/conf/hbase-env.sh
   export HBASE_OPTS="$HBASE_OPTS -verbose:gc -XX:+PrintGCDetails
   -XX:+PrintGCTimeStamps -Xloggc:/usr/local/hbase/logs/gc-hbase.log"
   ```

3. Add the following code to start the **Concurrent-Mark-Sweep GC** (**CMS**) earlier than the default:

   ```
   $ vi $HBASE_HOME/conf/hbase-env.sh
   export HBASE_OPTS=
     "$HBASE_OPTS -XX:CMSInitiatingOccupancyFraction=60"
   ```

4. Sync the changes across the cluster and restart HBase.

5. Check that the GC logs were output to the specified log file (`/usr/local/hbase/logs/gc-hbase.log`).

The GC log looks like the following screenshot:

```
1430.648: [GC 1430.648: [DefNew: 14783K->1599K(14784K), 0.0764200 secs] 118614K->110202K(187836K) icms_dc=11 , 0.0766
1431.357: [GC [1 CMS-initial-mark: 108602K(173052K)] 116079K(187836K), 0.0100050 secs] [Times: user=0.01 sys=0.00, re
1431.406: [CMS-concurrent-mark-start]
1431.989: [GC 1431.989: [DefNew: 14783K->1599K(14784K), 0.1053170 secs] 123386K->115016K(187836K) icms_dc=17 , 0.1054
1433.232: [GC 1433.232: [DefNew: 14783K->1599K(14784K), 0.0947460 secs] 128200K->117896K(187836K) icms_dc=17 , 0.0950
1434.848: [GC 1434.848: [DefNew: 14783K->1600K(14784K), 0.1114330 secs] 131080K->123922K(187836K) icms_dc=22 , 0.1116
1436.799: [GC 1436.799: [DefNew: 14784K->1599K(14784K), 0.0995270 secs] 137106K->129940K(187836K) icms_dc=22 , 0.0996
1437.903: [CMS-concurrent-mark: 1.944/6.496 secs] [Times: user=2.81 sys=0.14, real=6.50 secs]
1437.903: [CMS-concurrent-preclean-start]
1438.106: [CMS-concurrent-preclean: 0.157/0.203 secs] [Times: user=0.08 sys=0.02, real=0.20 secs]
1438.106: [CMS-concurrent-abortable-preclean-start]
1438.767: [GC 1438.767: [DefNew: 14783K->1599K(14784K), 0.0849710 secs] 143124K->133747K(187836K) icms_dc=22 , 0.0851
1440.449: [GC 1440.449: [DefNew: 14783K->1600K(14784K), 0.0842540 secs] 146931K->138415K(187836K) icms_dc=22 , 0.0844
1441.396: [CMS-concurrent-abortable-preclean: 0.374/3.290 secs] [Times: user=1.20 sys=0.07, real=3.29 secs]
1441.435: [GC[YG occupancy: 9417 K (14784 K)]1441.435: [Rescan (non-parallel) 1441.435: [grey object rescan, 0.000456
s]1441.476: [weak refs processing, 0.0000200 secs] [1 CMS-remark: 136815K(173052K)] 146232K(187836K), 0.0413960 secs]
1441.482: [CMS-concurrent-sweep-start]
1441.999: [GC 1441.999: [DefNew: 14639K->1600K(14784K), 0.0268920 secs] 151401K->141237K(187836K) icms_dc=22 , 0.0270
1443.189: [GC 1443.189: [DefNew: 14784K->1600K(14784K), 0.0656800 secs] 154013K->146727K(187836K) icms_dc=22 , 0.0658
1444.362: [GC 1444.362: [DefNew: 14784K->1599K(14784K), 0.0553500 secs] 155810K->148619K(187836K) icms_dc=22 , 0.0555
1444.928: [CMS-concurrent-sweep: 0.531/3.446 secs] [Times: user=1.53 sys=0.08, real=3.44 secs]
```

How it works...

In step 1, we configure the HBase heap memory size. By default, HBase uses a heap size of 1GB, which is too low for modern machines. A heap size of more than 4GB is good for HBase, while our recommendation is 8GB or larger, but under 16GB.

In step 2, we enable the JVM logging. With that setting, you will get a region server's JVM logs, similar to what we have shown in step 5. Basic knowledge about JVM memory allocation and garbage collection is required to understand the log output. The following is a diagram of the JVM generational garbage collection system:

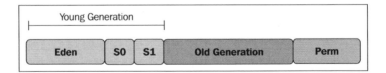

There are three heap generations: the **Perm** (or Permanent) generation, the **Old Generation** (or Tenured) generation, and the **Young Generation**. The young generation section consists of three separate spaces: the **Eden** space and two survivor spaces, **S0** and **S1**.

Usually, objects are allocated in the **Eden** space of the young generation. If an allocation fails (the **Eden** is full), all Java threads are halted and a young generation GC (Minor GC) is invoked. All surviving objects in the young generation (**Eden** and **S0** space) are copied to the **S1** space. If the **S1** space is full, objects are copied (promoted) to the old generation. The old generation is collected (Major/Full GC) when a promotion fails. The permanent and old generations are usually collected together. The permanent generation is used to hold class and method definitions for objects.

Back to our sample in step 5, the minor GC output for the aformentioned options is produced in the following form:

```
<timestamp>: [GC [<collector>: <starting occupancy1> -> <ending
occupancy1>, <pause time1> secs] <starting occupancy3> -> <ending
occupancy3>, <pause time3> secs] [Times: <user time> <system time>, <real
time>]
```

In this output:

- `<timestamp>` is the times at which the GCs happen, relative to the start of the application.

- `<collector>` is an internal name for the collector used in the minor collection.

- `<starting occupancy1>` is the occupancy of the young generation before the collection.

- `<ending occupancy1>` is the occupancy of the young generation after the collection.

- `<pause time1>` is the pause time in seconds for the minor collection.

- `<starting occupancy3>` is the occupancy of the entire heap before the collection.

- `<ending occupancy3>` is the occupancy of the entire heap after the collection.

- `<pause time3>` is the pause time for the entire garbage collection. This would include the time for a major collection.

- `[Time:]` explains the time spend in GC collection, user time, system time, and real time.

The first line of our output in step 5 indicates a minor GC, which pauses the JVM for 0.0764200 seconds. It has reduced the young generation space from about 14.8MB to 1.6MB.

Following that, we see the CMS GC logs. HBase uses CMS GC as its default garbage collector for the old generation.

CMS GC performs the following steps:

1. Initial mark
2. Concurrent marking
3. Remark
4. Concurrent sweeping

CMS halts the application's threads only during the initial mark and remark phases. During the concurrent marking and sweeping phases, the CMS thread runs along with the application's threads.

The second line in the example indicates that the CMS initial mark took 0.0100050 seconds and the concurrent marking has taken 6.496 seconds. Note that it is a concurrent marking; Java was not paused.

There is a pause at the line that starts with `1441.435: [GC[YG occupancy: …]` in the earlier screenshot of the GC log. The pause here is 0.0413960 seconds to remark the heap. After that, you can see the sweep starts. The CMS sweep took 3.446 seconds, but the heap size didn't change that much (it kept on occupying about 150MB) here.

The tuning point here is to keep all these pauses low. To keep the pauses low, you may need to adjust the young generation space's size via the `-XX:NewSize` and `-XX:MaxNewSize` JVM flags, to set them to relative small values (for example, up to several hundred MB). If the server has more CPU power, we recommend using the Parallel New Collector by setting the `-XX:+UseParNewGC` option. You may also want to tune the parallel GC thread number for the young generation, via the `-XX:ParallelGCThreads` JVM flag.

We recommend adding the aforementioned settings to the `HBASE_REGIONSERVER_OPTS` variable, instead of the `HBASE_OPTS` variable in the `hbase-env.sh` file. The `HBASE_REGIONSERVER_OPTS` variable only affects the region server processes, which is good, because the HBase master neither handles heavy tasks nor participates in the data process.

For the old generation, the concurrent collection (CMS) generally cannot be sped up, but it can be started earlier. CMS starts running when the percentage of allocated space in the old generation crosses a threshold. This threshold is automatically calculated by the collector. For some situations, especially during loading, if the CMS starts too late, HBase may run into full garbage collection. To avoid this, we recommend setting the `-XX:CMSInitiatingOccupancyFraction` JVM flag to explicitly specify at what percentage the CMS should be started, as what we did in step 3. Starting at 60 or 70 percent is a good practice. When using CMS for an old generation, the default young generation GC will be set to the Parallel New Collector.

There's more...

If you are using an HBase version prior to 0.92, consider enabling the MemStore-Local Allocation Buffer to prevent old generation heap fragmentation under heavy write loads:

```
$ vi $HBASE_HOME/conf/hbase-site.xml
  <property>
    <name>hbase.hregion.memstore.mslab.enabled</name>
    <value>true</value>
  </property>
```

This feature is enabled by default in HBase 0.92.

▶ *Setting up Ganglia to monitor an HBase cluster* recipe, in *Chapter 5, Monitoring and Diagnosis*

Using compression

One of the most important features of HBase is the use of data compression. It's important because:

▶ Compression reduces the number of bytes written to/read from HDFS

▶ Saves disk usage

▶ Improves the efficiency of network bandwidth when getting data from a remote server

HBase supports the GZip and LZO codec. Our suggestion is to use the LZO compression algorithm because of its fast data decompression and low CPU usage. As a better compression ratio is preferred for the system, you should consider GZip.

Unfortunately, HBase cannot ship with LZO because of a license issue. HBase is Apache-licensed, whereas LZO is GPL-licensed. Therefore, we need to install LZO ourselves. We will use the hadoop-lzo library, which brings splittable LZO compression to Hadoop.

In this recipe, we will describe how to install LZO and how to configure HBase to use LZO compression.

Getting ready

Make sure Java is installed on the machine on which hadoop-lzo is to be built.

Apache Ant is required to build hadoop-lzo from source. Install Ant by running the following command:

```
$ sudo apt-get -y install ant
```

All nodes in the cluster need to have native LZO library installed. You can install it by using the following command:

```
$ sudo apt-get -y install liblzo2-dev
```

How to do it...

We will use the hadoop-lzo library to add LZO compression support to HBase:

1. Get the latest hadoop-lzo source from `https://github.com/toddlipcon/hadoop-lzo`.

2. Build the native and Java hadoop-lzo libraries from source. Depending on your OS, you should either choose to build 32-bit or 64-bit binaries. For example, to build 32-bit binaries, run the following commands:

```
$ export JAVA_HOME="/usr/local/jdk1.6"

$ export CFLAGS="-m32"

$ export CXXFLAGS="-m32"

$ cd hadoop-lzo

$ ant compile-native

$ ant jar
```

These commands will create the `hadoop-lzo/build/native` directory and the `hadoop-lzo/build/hadoop-lzo-x.y.z.jar` file. In order to build 64-bit binaries, just change the value of CFLAGS and CXXFLAGS to `-m64`.

3. Copy the built libraries to the `$HBASE_HOME/lib` and `$HBASE_HOME/lib/native` directories on your master node:

```
hadoop@master1$ cp hadoop-lzo/build/hadoop-lzo-x.y.z.jar $HBASE_
HOME/lib

hadoop@master1$ mkdir $HBASE_HOME/lib/native/Linux-i386-32

hadoop@master1$ cp hadoop-lzo/build/native/Linux-i386-32/lib/*
$HBASE_HOME/lib/native/Linux-i386-32/
```

For a 64-bit OS, change `Linux-i386-32` (in the previous step) to `Linux-amd64-64`.

4. Add the configuration of `hbase.regionserver.codecs` to your `hbase-site.xml` file:

```
hadoop@master1$ vi $HBASE_HOME/conf/hbase-site.xml

<property>
  <name>hbase.regionserver.codecs</name>
  <value>lzo,gz</value>
</property>
```

5. Sync the `$HBASE_HOME/conf` and `$HBASE_HOME/lib` directories across the cluster.

6. HBase ships with a tool to test whether compression is set up properly. Use this tool to test the LZO setup on each node of the cluster. If everything is configured accurately, you will get the SUCCESS output:

```
hadoop@client1$ $HBASE_HOME/bin/hbase org.apache.hadoop.hbase.
util.CompressionTest /tmp/lzotest lzo

12/03/11 11:01:08 INFO hfile.CacheConfig: Allocating LruBlockCache
with maximum size 249.6m
```

```
12/03/11 11:01:08 INFO lzo.GPLNativeCodeLoader: Loaded native gpl
library

12/03/11 11:01:08 INFO lzo.LzoCodec: Successfully loaded &
initialized native-lzo library [hadoop-lzo rev Unknown build
revision]

12/03/11 11:01:08 INFO compress.CodecPool: Got brand-new
compressor

12/03/11 11:01:18 INFO compress.CodecPool: Got brand-new
decompressor

SUCCESS
```

7. Test the configuration by creating a table with LZO compression, and verify it in HBase Shell:

```
$ hbase> create 't1', {NAME => 'cf1', COMPRESSION => 'LZO'}

$ hbase> describe 't1'

DESCRIPTION
ENABLED
 {NAME => 't1', FAMILIES => [{NAME => 'cf1', BLOOMFILTER =>
'NONE', true

  REPLICATION_SCOPE => '0', VERSIONS => '3', COMPRESSION => 'LZO',

 MIN_VERSIONS => '0', TTL => '2147483647', BLOCKSIZE => '65536',
IN

 _MEMORY => 'false', BLOCKCACHE => 'true'}]}

1 row(s) in 0.0790 seconds
```

How it works...

We built the hadoop-lzo Java and native libraries and installed them under the $HBASE_HOME/lib and $HBASE_HOME/lib/native directories, respectively. By adding LZO compression support, HBase StoreFiles (HFiles) will use LZO compression on blocks as they are written. HBase uses the native LZO library to perform the compression, while the native library is loaded by HBase via the hadoop-lzo Java library that we built.

In order to avoid starting a node with any codec missing or misinstalled, we add LZO to the hbase.regionserver.codecs setting in the hbase-site.xml file. This setting will cause a failed startup of a region server if LZO is not installed properly. If you see logs such as "Could not load native gpl library", there is an issue with the LZO installation. In order to fix it, make sure that the native LZO libraries are installed and the path is configured properly.

A compression algorithm is specified on a per-column family basis. As shown in step 7, we create a table, t1, with a single column family, cf1, which uses LZO compression on it.

Although it adds a read-time penalty as the data blocks probably is decompressed when reading, LZO is fast enough as a real-time compression library. We recommend using LZO as the default compression algorithm in production HBase.

There's more...

Another compression option is to use the recently released Snappy compression library and Hadoop Snappy integration. As the setup is basically the same as what we did before, we will skip the details. Check the following URL to know how to add Snappy compression to HBase:

```
http://hbase.apache.org/book.html#snappy.compression
```

Managing compactions

An HBase table has the following physical storage structure:

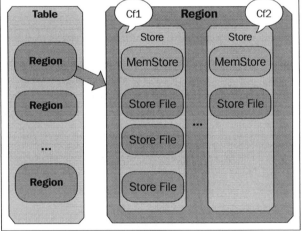

It consists of multiple regions. While a region may have several Stores, each holds a single column family. An edit first writes to the hosting region store's in-memory space, which is called MemStore. When the size of MemStore reaches a threshold, it is flushed to StoreFiles on HDFS.

As data increases, there may be many StoreFiles on HDFS, which is not good for its performance. Thus, HBase will automatically pick up a couple of the smaller StoreFiles and rewrite them into a bigger one. This process is called minor compaction. For certain situations, or when triggered by a configured interval (once a day by default), major compaction runs automatically. Major compaction will drop the deleted or expired cells and rewrite all the StoreFiles in the Store into a single StoreFile; this usually improves the performance.

However, as major compaction rewrites all of the Stores' data, lots of disk I/O and network traffic might occur during the process. This is not acceptable on a heavy load system. You might want to run it at a lower load time of your system.

In this recipe, we will describe how to turn off this automatic major compaction feature, and run it manually.

Getting ready

Log in to your HBase master server as the user who starts the cluster.

How to do it...

The following steps describe how to disable automatic major compaction:

1. Add the following to `hbase-site.xml` file:

   ```
   $ vi $HBASE_HOME/conf/hbase-site.xml

   <property>
     <name>hbase.hregion.majorcompaction</name>
     <value>0</value>
   </property>
   ```

2. Sync the changes across the cluster and restart HBase.

3. With the aforementioned setting, automatic major compaction will be disabled; you will now need to run it explicitly.

4. In order to manually run a major compaction on a particular region through HBase Shell, run the following command:

   ```
   $ echo "major_compact 'hly_temp,,1327118470453.5ef67f6d2a792fb0bd7
   37863dc00b6a7.'" | $HBASE_HOME/bin/hbase shell

   HBase Shell; enter 'help<RETURN>' for list of supported commands.

   Type "exit<RETURN>" to leave the HBase Shell

   Version 0.92.0, r1231986, Tue Jan 17 02:30:24 UTC 2012


   major_compact 'hly_temp,,1327118470453.5ef67f6d2a792fb0bd737863dc0
   0b6a7.'

   0 row(s) in 1.7070 seconds
   ```

How it works...

The `hbase.hregion.majorcompaction` property specifies the time (in milliseconds) between major compactions of all the StoreFiles in a region. The default value is `86400000`, which means once a day. We set it to `0` in step 1 to disable the automatic major compaction. This will prevent a major compaction from running during a heavy load time, for example when the MapReduce jobs are running over the HBase cluster.

On the other hand, major compaction is required to help performance. In step 4, we've shown an example of how to manually trigger a major compaction on a particular region, via HBase Shell. In this example, we have passed a region name to the `major_compact` command to invoke the major compaction only on a single region. It is also possible to run major compaction on all regions of a table, by passing the table name to the command. The `major_compact` command queues the specified tables or regions for major compaction; this will be executed in the background by the region server hosting them.

As we mentioned earlier, you might want to execute major compaction manually only during a low load time. This can be done easily by invoking the `major_compact` command from a cron job.

There's more...

Another approach to invoke major compaction is to use the `majorCompact` API provided by the `org.apache.hadoop.hbase.client.HBaseAdmin` class. It is easy to call this API in Java, thus you can manage complex major compaction scheduling from Java.

Managing a region split

Usually an HBase table starts with a single region. However, as data keeps growing and the region reaches its configured maximum size, it is automatically split into two halves, so that they can handle more data. The following diagram shows an HBase region splitting:

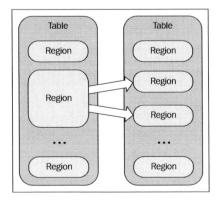

This is the default behavior of HBase region splitting. This mechanism works well for many cases, however there are situations wherein it encounters problems, such as the split/compaction storms issue.

With a roughly uniform data distribution and growth, eventually all the regions in the table will need to be split at the same time. Immediately following a split, compactions will run on the daughter regions to rewrite their data into separate files. This causes a large amount of disk I/O and network traffic.

In order to avoid this situation, you can turn off automatic splitting and manually invoke it. As you can control at what time to invoke the splitting, it helps spread the I/O load. Another advantage is that, manually splitting lets you have better control of the regions, which helps you trace and fix region-related issues.

In this recipe, we will describe how to turn off automatic region splitting and invoke it manually.

Getting ready

Log in to your HBase master server as the user who starts the cluster.

How to do it...

To turn off automatic region splitting and invoke it manually, follow these steps:

1. Add the following to the `hbase-site.xml` file:

   ```
   $ vi $HBASE_HOME/conf/hbase-site.xml

   <property>
     <name>hbase.hregion.max.filesize</name>
     <value>107374182400</value>
   </property>
   ```

2. Sync the changes across the cluster and restart HBase.

3. With the aforementioned setting, region splitting will not happen until a region's size reaches the configured 100GB threshold. You will need to explicitly trigger it on selected regions.

4. To run a region split through HBase Shell, use the following command:

   ```
   $ echo "split 'hly_temp,,1327118470453.5ef67f6d2a792fb0bd737863dc0
   0b6a7.'" | $HBASE_HOME/bin/hbase shell

   HBase Shell; enter 'help<RETURN>' for list of supported commands.
   Type "exit<RETURN>" to leave the HBase Shell
   Version 0.92.0, r1231986, Tue Jan 17 02:30:24 UTC 2012

   split 'hly_temp,,1327118470453.5ef67f6d2a792fb0bd737863dc00b6a7.'
   0 row(s) in 1.6810 seconds
   ```

How it works...

The `hbase.hregion.max.filesize` property specifies the maximum region size in *bytes*. By default, the value is 1GB (256MB for versions prior to HBase 0.92), which means that when a region exceeds this size, it is split into two. We set this maximum region size to 100GB in step 1, which is a very high number.

As splitting won't happen until regions reach the 100GB upper boundary, we need to invoke it explicitly. In step 4, we invoke splitting on a specified region via HBase Shell, using the `split` command.

Do not forget to split large regions. A region is the basic unit of data distribution and balancing in HBase. Regions should be split into proper size and at low load time.

On the other hand, too much splitting is not good. Having too many regions on a region server lowers its performance.

You might also want to trigger major compaction and balancing, after manually splitting regions.

There's more...

The setting that we set previously causes the entire cluster to have a default maximum region size of 100GB. Besides changing the entire cluster, it is also possible to specify the `MAX_FILESIZE` property on a column family basis, when creating a table:

```
$ hbase> create 't1', {NAME => 'cf1', MAX_FILESIZE => '107374182400'}
```

Like major compaction, you can also use the `split` API provided by the `org.apache. hadoop.hbase.client.HBaseAdmin` Java class.

See also

▶ *Precreating regions using your own algorithm* recipe, *Chapter 9, Advanced Configurations and Tuning*

9
Advanced Configurations and Tuning

In this chapter, we will cover:

- ▸ Benchmarking HBase cluster with YCSB
- ▸ Increasing region server handler count
- ▸ Precreating regions using your own algorithm
- ▸ Avoiding update blocking on write-heavy clusters
- ▸ Tuning memory size for MemStores
- ▸ Client side tuning for low latency systems
- ▸ Configuring block cache for column families
- ▸ Increasing block cache size on read-heavy clusters
- ▸ Client side scanner setting
- ▸ Tuning block size to improve seek performance
- ▸ Enabling Bloom Filter to improve the overall throughput

Introduction

This is another chapter about performance tuning. In *Chapter 8, Basic Performance Tuning,* we described some recipes to tune Hadoop, OS settings, Java, and HBase itself to improve the overall performance of the HBase cluster. Those are general improvements for many use cases. In this chapter, we will describe more "specific" recipes; some of them are for write-heavy clusters, while some are aimed to improve read performance of the cluster.

Before tuning a HBase cluster, you will need to know how its performance is. Therefore, we will start by introducing how to use **Yahoo! Cloud Serving Benchmark (YCSB)** to measure (benchmark) performance of a HBase cluster.

In the recipe *Precreating regions before moving data into HBase* in *Chapter 2*, we introduced how to use HBase's `RegionSplitter` utility to create a table with precreated regions to improve data loading speed. While `RegionSplitter` by default precreate regions with MD5 number boundaries, for situations where row keys cannot be represented as an MD5 number, we need to use other splitting algorithm. We will describe an approach to precreate regions with any boundaries you would like to specify.

There are basically two load type HBase clusters, the write-heavy cluster and the read-heavy cluster. Each type has different tuning options. Many tuning options are trade-off between write performance and read performance. We will have several recipes describing how to tune HBase cluster to gain better write performance; meanwhile, we will also introduce recipes to tune read-heavy HBase cluster. These recipes include server-side configuration tuning, client-side setting, and table schema selection.

There are no tuning that works for all situations. You need to think carefully about the performance requirements of your system, and tune your cluster to gain the best balance between write and read performance.

We assume you have basic knowledge about HBase architecture and have done general tunings for your cluster. You can refer to *Chapter 8, Basic Performance Tuning* for HBase architecture and basic HBase tuning.

Benchmarking HBase cluster with YCSB

Measuring the performance of a HBase cluster, or benchmarking the cluster, is as important as tuning the cluster itself. The performance characteristics of a HBase cluster that we should measure include at least the following:

- Overall throughput (operations per second) of the cluster
- Average latency (average time per operation) of the cluster

▶ Minimum latency

▶ Maximum latency

▶ Distribution of operation latencies

YCSB is a great tool to benchmark performance of HBase clusters. YCSB supports running variable load tests in parallel, to evaluate the insert, update, delete, and read performance of the system. Therefore, you can use YCSB to benchmark for both write-heavy and read-heavy HBase clusters. The record count to load, operations to perform, proportion of read and write, and many other properties are configurable for each test, so it is easy to use YCSB to test different load scenarios of the cluster.

YCSB can also be used to evaluate the performance of many other different key-value stores. A common use of YCSB is to benchmark multiple systems and compare their performance.

In this recipe, we will describe how to install YCSB and use it to test write-heavy and read-heavy HBase clusters.

Getting ready

Start your HBase cluster and log in to your HBase client node.

How to do it...

The following steps need to be followed to benchmark your HBase cluster with YCSB:

1. Download YCSB on your HBase client node and decompress it:

   ```
   $ wget https://github.com/downloads/brianfrankcooper/YCSB/ycsb-
   0.1.4.tar.gz
   $ tar xfvz ycsb-0.1.4.tar.gz
   $ cd ycsb-0.1.4
   ```

2. Add the HBase configuration file (hbase-site.xml) to YCSB HBase binding's classpath:

   ```
   $ rm hbase-binding/conf/hbase-site.xml
   $ ln -s $HBASE_HOME/conf/hbase-site.xml hbase-binding/conf/hbase-
   site.xml
   ```

   Only for HBase 0.92, add the HBase JAR file to YCSB HBase binding's classpath:

   ```
   $ cp $HBASE_HOME/hbase-0.92.0.jar hbase-binding/lib
   ```

   Only for HBase 0.92, add the ZooKeeper JAR file to YCSB HBase binding's classpath:

   ```
   $ cp $ZOOKEEPER_HOME/zookeeper-3.4.2.jar hbase-binding/lib
   ```

3. Create a test table in HBase:

```
$ $HBASE_HOME/bin/hbase shell

hbase> create 'usertable', {NAME => 'f1', VERSIONS => '1',
COMPRESSION => 'LZO'}
```

4. Invoke a write-heavy benchmark:

```
$ bin/ycsb load hbase -P workloads/workloada -p columnfamily=f1 -p
recordcount=1000000 -p threadcount=4 -s | tee -a workloada.dat

YCSB Client 0.1

Command line: -db com.yahoo.ycsb.db.HBaseClient -P workloads/
workloada -p columnfamily=f1 -p recordcount=1000000 -p
threadcount=4 -s -load

Loading workload...

Starting test.

 0 sec: 0 operations;

 10 sec: 49028 operations; 4902.8 current ops/sec; [INSERT
AverageLatency(us)=759.91]

 20 sec: 98060 operations; 4899.28 current ops/sec; [INSERT
AverageLatency(us)=777.67]

 ...

 160 sec: 641498 operations; 0 current ops/sec;

 170 sec: 641498 operations; 0 current ops/sec;

 180 sec: 682358 operations; 4086 current ops/sec; [INSERT
AverageLatency(us)=2850.51]

 ...

 240 sec: 1000000 operations; 4721.1 current ops/sec; [INSERT
AverageLatency(us)=525.48]

 240 sec: 1000000 operations; 0 current ops/sec;

[OVERALL], RunTime(ms), 240132.0

[OVERALL], Throughput(ops/sec), 4164.376259723818

[INSERT], Operations, 1000000

[INSERT], AverageLatency(us), 935.844141

[INSERT], MinLatency(us), 10

[INSERT], MaxLatency(us), 26530269

[INSERT], 95thPercentileLatency(ms), 0

[INSERT], 99thPercentileLatency(ms), 0

[INSERT], Return=0, 1000000

[INSERT], 0, 999296

[INSERT], 1, 42
```

```
...
[INSERT], 999, 0
[INSERT], >1000, 240
```

5. Invoke a read-heavy benchmark:

```
bin/ycsb run hbase -P workloads/workloadb -p columnfamily=f1 -p
recordcount=1000000 -p operationcount=100000 -p threadcount=4 -s |
tee -a workloadb.dat

YCSB Client 0.1

Command line: -db com.yahoo.ycsb.db.HBaseClient -P workloads/
workloadb -p columnfamily=f1 -p recordcount=1000000 -p
threadcount=4 -s -t

Loading workload...

Starting test.

 0 sec: 0 operations;

 10 sec: 11651 operations; 1165.1 current ops/sec; [UPDATE
AverageLatency(us)=95.15] [READ AverageLatency(us)=3576.62]

 20 sec: 26265 operations; 1461.25 current ops/sec; [UPDATE
AverageLatency(us)=43.71] [READ AverageLatency(us)=2877.47]

 ...

 60 sec: 100000 operations; 544.22 current ops/sec; [UPDATE
AverageLatency(us)=25.15] [READ AverageLatency(us)=3139.45]

[OVERALL], RunTime(ms), 60740.0

[OVERALL], Throughput(ops/sec), 1646.3615409944023

[UPDATE], Operations, 5082

[UPDATE], AverageLatency(us), 45.35615899252263

[UPDATE], MinLatency(us), 12

[UPDATE], MaxLatency(us), 6155

[UPDATE], 95thPercentileLatency(ms), 0

[UPDATE], 99thPercentileLatency(ms), 0

[UPDATE], Return=0, 5082

[UPDATE], 0, 5080

[UPDATE], 1, 1

[UPDATE], 2, 0

[UPDATE], 3, 0

...

[UPDATE], >1000, 0

[READ], Operations, 94918
```

```
[READ], AverageLatency(us), 2529.312764702164
[READ], MinLatency(us), 369
[READ], MaxLatency(us), 484754
[READ], 95thPercentileLatency(ms), 8
[READ], 99thPercentileLatency(ms), 13
[READ], Return=0, 94918
[READ], 0, 31180
[READ], 1, 21938
[READ], 2, 18331
[READ], 3, 10227
...
```

How it works...

The latest YCSB version at the time of writing is 0.1.4. This version has the precompiled HBase binding. To use YCSB HBase binding, we added a link of our HBase cluster's configuration file (hbase-site.xml) to the `hbase-binding/conf` folder under YCSB installation. This tells YCSB the connection information of our HBase cluster.

As the YCSB 0.1.4 tarball is built with HBase 0.90.5, if you are using HBase 0.92 for your cluster, you need to update YCSB's HBase and ZooKeeper JAR files to the version your cluster is running, or you may get an error complaining `Not a host:port pair` in the output. To achieve this, just copy the HBase and ZooKeeper JAR files to the `hbase-binding/lib` folder under the YCSB installation.

Before running the load test, we need to create the test table in HBase at first. The test table's name is fixed: it must be `usertable`. We also need to create a column family for the table. In step 3, we created the `usertable` with a column family called `f1`, which has one version and LZO compression support.

After creating the test table, we can run a YCSB load test using the `ycsb` command. Executing the `ycsb` command without parameters will show the command usage.

```
$ bin/ycsb
Usage: bin/ycsb command database [options]

Commands:
    load        Execute the load phase
    run         Execute the transaction phase
    shell       Interactive mode
```

Databases:

    basic   https://github.com/brianfrankcooper/YCSB/tree/master/
basic

    cassandra-10 https://github.com/brianfrankcooper/YCSB/tree/master/
cassandra

    cassandra-7   https://github.com/brianfrankcooper/YCSB/tree/master/
cassandra

    cassandra-8   https://github.com/brianfrankcooper/YCSB/tree/master/
cassandra

    gemfire   https://github.com/brianfrankcooper/YCSB/tree/master/
gemfire

    hbase   https://github.com/brianfrankcooper/YCSB/tree/master/
hbase

    infinispan   https://github.com/brianfrankcooper/YCSB/tree/master/
infinispan

    jdbc   https://github.com/brianfrankcooper/YCSB/tree/master/
jdbc

    mapkeeper   https://github.com/brianfrankcooper/YCSB/tree/master/
mapkeeper

    mongodb   https://github.com/brianfrankcooper/YCSB/tree/master/
mongodb

    nosqldb   https://github.com/brianfrankcooper/YCSB/tree/master/
nosqldb

    redis   https://github.com/brianfrankcooper/YCSB/tree/master/
redis

    voldemort   https://github.com/brianfrankcooper/YCSB/tree/master/
voldemort

Options:

    -P file   Specify workload file

    -p key=value Override workload property

    -s   Print status to stderr

    -target n   Target ops/sec (default: unthrottled)

    -threads n   Number of client threads (default: 1)

Workload Files:

    There are various predefined workloads under workloads/ directory.

    See https://github.com/brianfrankcooper/YCSB/wiki/Core-Properties

    for the list of workload properties.

In step 4, we invoked a write-heavy test to load 1 million records into our test table in HBase. The test behavior is defined by Workload Files. The workloads specify the data that will be loaded into the table, and the operations that will be executed against the data. There are predefined workloads under YCSB's `workloads` directory. Here we chose `workloads/workloada` as our workload file. This is an update-heavy workload. We also overwrote the default record count of the workload by specifying `-p recordcount=1000000` on the command line. We invoked four client threads to run the test by passing `-p threadcount=4` to the command. The `-s` option makes YCSB report the status periodically to the output.

As you can see from the HBase web UI, YCSB started loading test data into the table we created previously in step 3:

The load test took 240132.0 milliseconds to complete, with an average throughput of 4164 operations per second. The output also reports the insert operation number, overall latency, and detailed latency. All the inserts were successfully completed (`Return=0`). Almost all of the inserts (999296) were completed in less than 1 ms, while 42 inserts were completed between 1 and 2 ms. There are also 240 inserts that took more than 1000 ms to complete. These inserts were probably being blocked for a while by the region servers due to high load.

We also invoked a read-heavy test in step 5. We performed 100,000 operations (`-p operationcount=100000`) over the test data, while 95% of the operations were reads (defined in `workloads/workloadb`). The test completed in 60740.0 ms; throughput was 1646 operations per second. As you can see, HBase writes are much faster than reads.

YCSB supports other useful properties such as reporting time series latencies. See the following for the list of workload properties:

```
https://github.com/brianfrankcooper/YCSB/wiki/Core-Properties
```

There's more...

HBase is shipped with its own performance evaluation (PE) tool which can be used to benchmark HBase, too. The following is the usage of the HBase PE tool:

```
$ $HBASE_HOME/bin/hbase org.apache.hadoop.hbase.PerformanceEvaluation
Usage: java org.apache.hadoop.hbase.PerformanceEvaluation \
  [--miniCluster] [--nomapred] [--rows=ROWS] <command> <nclients>


Options:
 miniCluster       Run the test on an HBaseMiniCluster
 nomapred          Run multiple clients using threads (rather than use
mapreduce)
 rows              Rows each client runs. Default: One million
 flushCommits      Used to determine if the test should flush the table.
Default: false
 writeToWAL        Set writeToWAL on puts. Default: True


Command:
 filterScan        Run scan test using a filter to find a specific row
based on its value (make sure to use --rows=20)
 randomRead        Run random read test
 randomSeekScan    Run random seek and scan 100 test
 randomWrite       Run random write test
 scan              Run scan test (read every row)
 scanRange10       Run random seek scan with both start and stop row (max
10 rows)
 scanRange100      Run random seek scan with both start and stop row (max
100 rows)
 scanRange1000     Run random seek scan with both start and stop row (max
1000 rows)
 scanRange10000    Run random seek scan with both start and stop row (max
10000 rows)
 sequentialRead    Run sequential read test
 sequentialWrite   Run sequential write test


Args:
 nclients          Integer. Required. Total number of clients (and
HRegionServers)
```

```
                    running: 1 <= value <= 500
```

Examples:

 To run a single evaluation client:

 $ bin/hbase org.apache.hadoop.hbase.PerformanceEvaluation
sequentialWrite 1

This is an example of using HBase PE to test sequential write performance:

```
$ $HBASE_HOME/bin/hbase org.apache.hadoop.hbase.PerformanceEvaluation
sequentialWrite 1

12/03/20 16:34:42 INFO hbase.PerformanceEvaluation: Start class org.
apache.hadoop.hbase.PerformanceEvaluation$SequentialWriteTest at offset 0
for 1048576 rows

12/03/20 16:34:50 INFO hbase.PerformanceEvaluation: 0/104857/1048576

12/03/20 16:34:57 INFO hbase.PerformanceEvaluation: 0/209714/1048576

...

12/03/20 16:36:11 INFO hbase.PerformanceEvaluation: Finished class org.
apache.hadoop.hbase.PerformanceEvaluation$SequentialWriteTest in 88730ms
at offset 0 for 1048576 rows
```

We use one client to sequentially write about 1 million rows (100 bytes per row) into our test table in the HBase cluster. The test took 88 seconds to finish. There is no need to specify a table and column family name, as the HBase PE tool will create a table called `TestTable` with a column family called `info` in its code.

> Note that you will need to execute the write tests before using PE to run read tests, as read tests use the data inserted by the write tests.

Increasing region server handler count

Region server keeps a number of running threads to answer incoming requests to user tables. To prevent region server running out of memory, this number is set to very low by default. For many situations, especially when you have lots of concurrent clients, you will need to increase this number to handle more requests.

We will describe how to tune the region server handler count in this recipe.

Getting ready

Log in to the master node as the user who starts HBase.

How to do it...

The following steps need to be followed to increase region server handler count:

1. On the master node, add the following to your `hbase-site.xml` file:

   hadoop@master1$ vi $HBASE_HOME/conf/hbase-site.xml

   ```
   <property>
     <name>hbase.regionserver.handler.count</name>
     <value>40</value>
   </property>
   ```

2. Sync the changes across the cluster:

   hadoop@master1$ for slave in `cat $HBASE_HOME/conf/regionservers`

   do

   rsync -avz $HBASE_HOME/conf/ $slave:$HBASE_HOME/conf/

   done

3. Restart HBase to have the changes applied.

How it works...

The `hbase.regionserver.handler.count` property controls the count of RPC listener threads. By default, the property is set to 10. This is a rather low value to prevent the region server running out of memory in some situations.

You should set it to a low value if your region server has low memory available. A low value is also good for handling requests which require lots of memory, such as putting a big value into HBase or scanning data with a large cache configuration. Setting `hbase.regionserver.handler.count` to high means more concurrent clients, which may consume too much memory in a region server, or even use up all the memory.

If your request requires only a litter memory, but needs high transactions per second (TPS), consider setting it to a bigger value so that a region server can handle more concurrent requests.

When tuning this value, we recommend you enable RPC-level logging, and monitor the memory usage of each RPC request and GC status.

You will need to sync the changes across the cluster and restart HBase to apply it.

See also

▶ *Enabling HBase RPC DEBUG-level logging* recipe, in *Chapter 6, Maintenance and Security*

Precreating regions using your own algorithm

When we create a table in HBase, the table starts with a single region. All data inserted into that table goes to the single region. As data keeps growing, when the size of the region reaches a threshold, *Region Splitting* happens. The single region is split into two halves so that the table can handle more data.

In a write-heavy HBase cluster, this approach has several issues that need to be fixed:

▸ The split/compaction storm issue.

As data grows uniformly, most of the regions are split at the same time, which causes huge disk I/O and network traffics.

▸ Load is not well balanced until enough regions have been split.

Especially right after the table is created, all requests go to the same region server where the first region is deployed.

The split/compaction issue has been discussed in the *Managing region split* recipe in *Chapter 8, Basic Performance Tuning.* by using a manually splitting approach. For the second issue, we introduced how to avoid it by previously creating regions at the table creation time, in the *Precreating regions before moving data into HBase* recipe in *Chapter 2*. We described how to use HBase `RegionSplitter` utility to precreate regions.

By default, the `RegionSplitter` utility uses MD5 algorithm to generate region starting keys of an MD5 checksum. Keys are in the range "00000000" to "7FFFFFFF". This works well for many cases; but there are situations where you might want to generate the keys using your own algorithm, so that the load is spread well among your cluster.

As HBase row key is fully controlled by applications which put data into HBase, for many situations, the range and distribution of row keys are predictable somehow. Thus it is possible to calculate the region splitting keys and use them to create presplit regions.

We will describe how to achieve this goal in this recipe. We will create a table with predefined regions, using regions' starting keys specified in a text file.

Getting ready

Log in to your HBase client node and create a `split-keys` file there. Put your region splitting keys into the file, one key per line. As an example, we assume the file contains the following keys:

```
$ cat split-keys
a0000
affff
b0000
bffff
```

How to do it...

Follow these instructions to precreate regions using your own algorithm:

1. Create a `FileSplitAlgorithm` Java class which implements the `org.apache.hadoop.hbase.util.RegionSplitter.SplitAlgorithm` interface:

   ```
   $ vi FileSplitAlgorithm.java
   import org.apache.hadoop.hbase.util.RegionSplitter.SplitAlgorithm;

   public class FileSplitAlgorithm implements SplitAlgorithm {
       public static final String SPLIT_KEY_FILE = "split-keys";
   }
   ```

2. Implement the `split()` method of the interface as follows:

   ```
   $ vi FileSplitAlgorithm.java
   @Override
   public byte[][] split(int numberOfSplits) {
       BufferedReader br = null;
       try {
           File keyFile = new File(SPLIT_KEY_FILE);
           if (!keyFile.exists()) {
               throw new FileNotFoundException("Splitting key file
   not found: " + SPLIT_KEY_FILE);
           }

           List<byte[]> regions = new ArrayList<byte[]> ();
           br = new BufferedReader(new FileReader(keyFile));
           String line;
           while ((line = br.readLine()) != null) {
               if (line.trim().length() > 0) {
                   regions.add(Bytes.toBytes(line));
   ```

```
                    }
                }
                return regions.toArray(new byte[0][]);

            } catch (IOException e) {
                throw new RuntimeException("Error reading splitting keys
        from " + SPLIT_KEY_FILE, e);
            } finally {
                if (br != null) {
                    try {
                        br.close();
                    } catch (IOException e) {
                        // ignore
                    }
                }
            }
        }
    }
```

3. There are several other methods of the interface we need to implement to compile the Java class. As we don't actually use them, just make an empty implementation to each of those methods, shown as follows (we skipped some methods here):

   ```
   $ vi FileSplitAlgorithm.java
   ```

   ```java
   @Override
   public byte[] firstRow() {
       return null;
   }

   @Override
   public byte[] lastRow() {
       return null;
   }
   ```

4. Compile the Java file:

   ```
   $ javac -classpath $HBASE_HOME/hbase-0.92.0.jar
   FileSplitAlgorithm.java
   ```

5. Copy the split-keys file which contains your splitting keys to the directory where FileSplitAlgorithm was compiled.

6. Run the following script to precreate regions at the table creation time:

   ```
   $ export HBASE_CLASSPATH=$HBASE_CLASSPATH:./
   ```

   ```
   $ $HBASE_HOME/bin/hbase org.apache.hadoop.hbase.util.
   RegionSplitter -D split.algorithm=FileSplitAlgorithm -c 2 -f f1
   test_table
   ```

```
12/03/25 08:09:42 DEBUG util.RegionSplitter: -D configuration
override: split.algorithm=FileSplitAlgorithm

12/03/25 08:09:42 DEBUG util.RegionSplitter: Creating table test_
table with 1 column families.  Presplitting to 2 regions

12/03/25 08:09:49 DEBUG util.RegionSplitter: Table created!
Waiting for regions to show online in META...

12/03/25 08:09:49 DEBUG util.RegionSplitter: Finished creating
table with 2 regions
```

7. Confirm that the table and predefined regions has been created correctly via the HBase web UI:

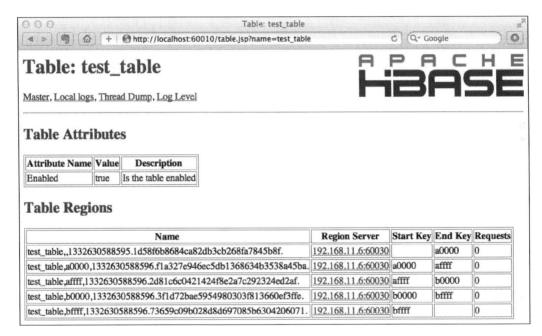

How it works...

HBase ships with a `RegionSplitter` utility class, which is used to:

- ► Create HBase tables with presplit regions
- ► Execute rolling split on all regions in an existing table
- ► Use customized algorithms to split regions

Our instructions are based on this utility class.

First, we created a `FileSplitAlgorithm` Java class implementing the `SplitAlgorithm` interface. `SplitAlgorithm` is a Java interface declared in the `RegionSplitter` class, used to define how `RegionSplitter` functions. We also defined a `SPLIT_KEY_FILE` constant in the `FileSplitAlgorithm` class to refer to the file which contains our region starting keys.

The `SplitAlgorithm` interface defines several methods that the implementation class needs to implement. To split regions at the time of table creation, we only need to implement the `split()` method like we did in step 2. This method is called by the `RegionSplitter` class to split an entire table. In our implementation, it reads split keys from the file we prepared, one key per line. Then, convert them to an array of `byte[]` representing the split keys for the initial regions of the table.

Other `SplitAlgorithm` interface methods are not necessary for our usage, so we just put empty implementation for those methods in step 3.

In step 4, we added the HBase jar to our classpath and then run the `javac` command to compile the Java code.

To use the class to split regions, we added our `FileSplitAlgorithm` class to `HBASE_CLASSPATH`, and then invoked the `RegionSplitter` utility with the following parameters:

- ▸ `-D split.algorithm=FileSplitAlgorithm`: The splitting algorithm.
- ▸ `-c 2`: Number of regions to split the table into; not used in our implementation.
- ▸ `-f f1`: Create a single column family named "f1".
- ▸ `test_table`: The name of the table to be created.

As you can see in step 7, the `test_table` is split into five regions separated by four split keys. The split keys are exactly what we put in the `split-keys` file.

Other table attributes are all with default values; you might want to change some of them by using the `alter` command via HBase Shell.

Note that even when regions are split previously, you will also need to design your row key at the application layer, to avoid writing too many sequential row keys to a single region. You need to choose your split algorithm carefully to fit your data access pattern.

There's more...

Another useful scenario of this approach is to speed up importing data into HBase from exported backup HBase tables.

As mentioned in the recipe *Backing up region starting keys* in *Chapter 4, Backing Up and Restoring HBase data*, you can backup your region starting keys via a simple script. With the `FileSplitAlgorithm` class, we can use those keys to previously restore the region boundaries of an HBase table, and then restore the data by importing from exported data files.

Compared to importing data from a single region, as regions are restored and balanced to many region servers firstly, the data restoring speed will be improved significantly.

See also

▸ *Managing region split* in *Chapter 8*

▸ *Precreating regions before moving data into HBase* in *Chapter 2*

▸ *Backing up region starting keys* in *Chapter 4*

Avoiding update blocking on write-heavy clusters

On a write-heavy HBase cluster, you may observe an unstable write speed. Most of the writes are very fast, while some are slow. For an online system, this unstable write speed is not acceptable even when average speed is very fast.

This situation is probably caused by the following two reasons:

▸ Split/compaction makes the cluster very high load

▸ Updates are blocked by region server

As we described in *Chapter 8, Basic Performance Tuning* you can avoid the split/compaction issues by disabling the automatic split/compaction and invoking them at low load time.

Grep your region server logs, if you find many messages saying "Blocking updates for ...", it is possible that many updates were blocked, and those updates might have poor response time.

To fix this issue, we need to tune both server side and client side configurations to gain a stable write speed. We will describe the most important server side tuning to avoid update blocking in this recipe.

Getting ready

Log in to your master node by the user who starts HBase.

How to do it...

To avoid update blocking, follow these steps:

1. Increase the `hbase.hregion.memstore.block.multiplier` property value in the `hbase-site.xml` file.

   ```
   $ vi $HBASE_HOME/conf/hbase-site.xml
   ```

   ```xml
   <property>
     <name>hbase.hregion.memstore.block.multiplier</name>
     <value>8</value>
   </property>
   ```

2. Increase the `hbase.hstore.blockingStoreFiles` property value in the `hbase-site.xml` file.

   ```
   $ vi $HBASE_HOME/conf/hbase-site.xml
   ```

   ```xml
   <property>
     <name>hbase.hstore.blockingStoreFiles</name>
     <value>20</value>
   </property>
   ```

3. Sync the changes across the cluster and restart HBase to apply the changes.

How it works...

This is the flow of HBase write operations:

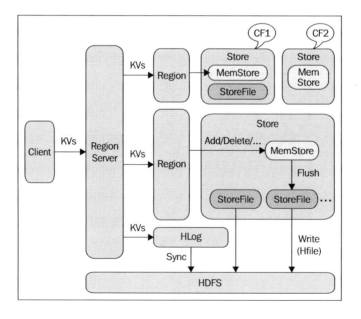

An edit first writes to RegionServer's **HLog** (Write Ahead Log), where the edit is persisted on **HDFS**. After that, the edit goes to the hosting HRegion, and then its column family HStore's in-memory space, which is called **MemStore**. When the size of **MemStore** reaches a threshold, it is flushed to a **StoreFile** on **HDFS**. StoreFiles save the data using the **HFile** file format internally.

HBase is a kind of Multiversion Concurrency Control (MVCC) architecture. To update/delete any old data, instead of overwriting it, HBase adds a newer version to the data. This makes HBase write very fast because all writes are sequential operations.

When there are many small StoreFiles on HDFS, HBase starts compaction to rewrite them into fewer but bigger ones. A region will be split into two halves if its size reaches a threshold.

To prevent long time compact/split and out of memory error, HBase blocks updates if a region's MemStore size reaches a threshold, which is defined by:

`hbase.hregion.memstore.flush.size` multiplied
`hbase.hregion.memstore.block.multiplier`

The `hbase.hregion.memstore.flush.size` property specifies the size at which MemStore will be flushed to disk. Its default value is 128MB (64MB in 0.90 release).

The `hbase.hregion.memstore.block.multiplier` property has a default value of 2, which means that if MemStore has 256MB (128 x 2) in size, updates will be blocked on that region. This value is too small in write-heavy clusters during spikes in update traffic, so we need to increase the blocking threshold.

We usually leave the `hbase.hregion.memstore.flush.size` property at its default value, and tune the `hbase.hregion.memstore.block.multiplier` property to a much bigger value like 8, to increase the MemStore blocking size, thus reducing the updates blocking count.

Note that increasing `hbase.hregion.memstore.block.multiplier` makes triggering a compact/split when flushing more likely, so tune it carefully.

Step 2 is for another blocking scenario. If any one **Store** has more than the `hbase.hstore.blockingStoreFiles` (7 by default) number of StoreFiles (one StoreFile per MemStore flushed), then updates are blocked for this region until a compaction is completed, or until `hbase.hstore.blockingWaitTime` (90 second by default) has been exceeded. We increased it to 20, which is a reasonably big value for write-heavy clusters. The side effects are that there will be more files to compact.

This tuning normally reduces the chances that updates blocking happens. While, as we just mentioned, it has side effects, too. We recommend you to tune these settings carefully, and watch writes throughputs and latencies during the tuning to find the best configuration values.

See also

▶ *Tuning memory size for MemStores*

Tuning memory size for MemStores

As we described in recipe *Avoiding update blocking on write-heavy clusters*, HBase write operations are applied in the hosting region's MemStore at first, and then flushed to HDFS to save memory space when MemStore size reaches a threshold. MemStore flush runs on background threads using a snapshot of the MemStore. Thus HBase keeps handling writes even when the MemStores are being flushed. This makes HBase writes very fast. If the write spike is so high that the MemStore flush cannot catch up, the speed writes fill MemStores and memory used by MemStores will keep growing. If the size of all MemStores in a region server reaches a configurable threshold, updates are blocked and flushes are forced.

We will describe how to tune this total MemStore memory size to avoid update blocking in this recipe.

Getting ready

Log in to your master node as the user who starts HBase.

How to do it...

The following steps need to be carried out to tune memory size for MemStores:

1. Increase the `hbase.regionserver.global.memstore.upperLimit` property value in the `hbase-site.xml` file:

    ```
    $ vi $HBASE_HOME/conf/hbase-site.xml

    <property>
      <name>hbase.regionserver.global.memstore.upperLimit</name>
      <value>0.45</value>
    </property>
    ```

2. Increase the `hbase.regionserver.global.memstore.lowerLimit` property value in the `hbase-site.xml` file:

    ```
    vi $HBASE_HOME/conf/hbase-site.xml

    <property>
      <name>hbase.regionserver.global.memstore.lowerLimit</name>
      <value>0.4</value>
    </property>
    ```

3. Sync the changes across the cluster and restart HBase to apply the changes.

How it works...

The `hbase.regionserver.global.memstore.upperLimit` property controls the maximum size of all MemStores in a region server, before new updates are blocked and flushes are forced. This is a configuration to prevent HBase from running out of memory by write spikes. By default, it is set to 0.4, which means 40% of region server heap size.

The default value works well for many cases. But, if you detected many log entries saying `Flush of region xxxx due to global heap pressure` in your region server logs, then you may need to tune this property to handle the high write rate.

The `hbase.regionserver.global.memstore.lowerLimit` property we tuned in step 2, specifies when MemStores are forced to flush, they keep flushing until the memory size occupied by MemStores is decreased to this mark. The default value is 35% of the region server heap size.

On write-heavy clusters, increasing these two values helps reduce the chances that updates are blocked due to MemStore size limiting. On the other hand, you will need to tune it carefully to avoid the situation of full garbage collection or out of memory error.

There's more...

Normally, read performance is not so important as writes on write-heavy clusters. Thus we can tune the cluster to optimize for writes. One of the optimizations is to reduce the memory space allocated to HBase block cache, and make the room for MemStores. See the recipe *Increasing block cache size on read-heavy clusters* for how to tune block cache size.

See also

- *Avoiding update blocking on write-heavy clusters*
- *Configuring block cache for column families*
- *Increasing block cache size on read-heavy clusters*

Client-side tuning for low latency systems

We have introduced several recipes to avoid server side blocking. Those recipes should help the cluster run stably and with high performance. Cluster throughput and average latency will be improved significantly by server-side tuning.

However, in low latency and real-time systems, just server-side tuning is not enough. Even if it only occurs slightly, long time pause is not acceptable in low latency systems.

There are client-side configurations we can tune to avoid long time pause. In this recipe, we will describe how to tune those configurations and how they work.

Getting ready

Log in to your HBase client node as the user who accesses HBase.

How to do it...

Follow these instructions to perform client side tuning for write-heavy clusters:

1. Reduce the `hbase.client.pause` property value in the `hbase-site.xml` file:

   ```
   $ vi $HBASE_HOME/conf/hbase-site.xml
   ```

   ```
   <property>
     <name>hbase.client.pause</name>
     <value>20</value>
   </property>
   ```

2. Tune the `hbase.client.retries.number` property value in the `hbase-site.xml` file:

   ```
   $ vi $HBASE_HOME/conf/hbase-site.xml
   ```

   ```
   <property>
     <name>hbase.client.retries.number</name>
     <value>11</value>
   </property>
   ```

3. Set `hbase.ipc.client.tcpnodelay` to `true` in the `hbase-site.xml` file:

   ```
   $ vi $HBASE_HOME/conf/hbase-site.xml
   ```

   ```
   <property>
     <name>hbase.ipc.client.tcpnodelay</name>
     <value>true</value>
   </property>
   ```

4. Reduce the `ipc.ping.interval` value in the `hbase-site.xml` file:

   ```
   $ vi $HBASE_HOME/conf/hbase-site.xml
   ```

   ```
   <property>
     <name>ipc.ping.interval</name>
     <value>4000</value>
   </property>
   ```

How it works...

The purpose of tuning the `hbase.client.pause` and `hbase.client.retries.number` properties in step 1 and 2, is to let clients retry quickly in a short time period if they failed to connect to the cluster.

The `hbase.client.pause` property controls how long the client should sleep between retries. Its default value is 1000 milliseconds (1 second). The `hbase.client.retries.number` property is used to specify the maximum number of retries. By default, its value is 10.

The sleep time between each retry is calculated with the following command:

```
pause_time = hbase.client.pause * RETRY_BACKOFF[retries]
```

Where `RETRY_BACKOFF` is a retry back off multiplier table, which has the following definition:

```
public static int RETRY_BACKOFF[] = { 1, 1, 1, 2, 2, 4, 4, 8, 16, 32
};
```

After retrying more than 10 times, HBase will always use the last multiplier (32) to calculate pause time.

As we configured 20ms as our pause time and maximum retry number of 11, we will have the following pause time between retries of connection to the cluster:

```
{ 20, 20, 20, 40, 40, 80, 80, 160, 320, 640, 640 }
```

This means the client will retry 11 times within 2060ms before it gives up connecting to the cluster.

In step 3, we set `hbase.ipc.client.tcpnodelay` to true. This setting disables *Nagle's Algorithm* for socket transmission between client and servers.

Nagle's Algorithm is a means to improve the efficiency of networks, by buffering a number of small outgoing messages, and sending them all at once. *Nagle's Algorithm* is enabled by default. Low latency systems should disable *Nagle's Algorithm* by setting `hbase.ipc.client.tcpnodelay` to `true`.

In step 4, we set `ipc.ping.interval` to 4000 milliseconds (4 seconds) so that we don't timeout during the socket transmission between client and servers. The default `ipc.ping.interval` is 1 minute, which is a little too long for low latency systems.

There's more...

You can also use the `org.apache.hadoop.hbase.HBaseConfiguration` class on your client code to overwrite the value of the preceding properties set in `hbase-site.xml`. The following sample code has the same effect as the settings of the previous steps 1 and 2:

```
Configuration conf = HBaseConfiguration.create();
conf.setInt("hbase.client.pause", 20);
conf.setInt("hbase.client.retries.number", 11);
HTable table = new HTable(conf, "tableName");
```

Configuring block cache for column families

HBase supports block cache to improve read performance. When performing a scan, if block cache is enabled and there is room remaining, data blocks read from StoreFiles on HDFS are cached in region server's Java heap space, so that next time, accessing data in the same block can be served by the cached block. Block cache helps in reducing disk I/O for retrieving data.

Block cache is configurable at table's column family level. Different column families can have different cache priorities or even disable the block cache. Applications leverage this cache mechanism to fit different data sizes and access patterns.

In this recipe, we will describe how to configure block cache for column families and tips to leverage HBase block cache.

Getting ready

Log in to your HBase client node.

How to do it...

The following steps need to be carried out to configure block cache at column family level:

1. Start HBase Shell:

    ```
    $ $HBASE_HOME/bin/hbase shell
    HBase Shell; enter 'help<RETURN>' for list of supported commands.
    Type "exit<RETURN>" to leave the HBase Shell
    Version 0.92.0, r1231986, Tue Jan 17 02:30:24 UTC 2012


    hbase(main):001:0>
    ```

2. Execute the following to create a table with three column families:

    ```
    hbase> create 'table1', {NAME => 'f1'}, {NAME => 'f2', IN_MEMORY
    => 'true'}, {NAME => 'f3', BLOCKCACHE => 'false'}

    0 row(s) in 1.0690 seconds
    ```

3. Show the properties of the table created previously:

    ```
    hbase> describe 'table1'
    DESCRIPTION
    ENABLED
     {NAME => 'table1', FAMILIES => [{NAME => 'f1', BLOOMFILTER =>
    'NONE', REPLICATION_SCOPE => '0', VERSIONS => '3',   true
      COMPRESSION => 'NONE', MIN_VERSIONS => '0', TTL => '2147483647',
    BLOCKSIZE => '65536', IN_MEMORY => 'false', BLOC
    ```

KCACHE => 'true'}, {**NAME => 'f2'**, BLOOMFILTER => 'NONE', REPLICATION_
SCOPE => '0', VERSIONS => '3', COMPRESSION =
 > 'NONE', MIN_VERSIONS => '0', TTL => '2147483647', BLOCKSIZE
=> '65536', **IN_MEMORY => 'true', BLOCKCACHE => 'true'**}, {**NAME => 'f3'**,
BLOOMFILTER => 'NONE', REPLICATION_SCOPE => '0', VERSIONS => '3',
COMPRESSION => 'NONE', MIN_
 VERSIONS => '0', TTL => '2147483647', BLOCKSIZE => '65536', **IN_**
MEMORY => 'false', BLOCKCACHE => 'false'}]}
1 row(s) in 0.0290 seconds

How it works...

We created a table (`table1`) with three column families, `f1`, `f2`, and `f3`. For family `f1`, we
didn't specify any properties, so all its properties were set to default. As shown in step 3, its
block cache is enabled (`BLOCKCACHE => 'true'`) and in memory is off (`IN_MEMORY =>
'false'`).

HBase block cache contains three levels of block priority: single, multiple, and in-memory
access. A block is added with an in-memory flag (this means HBase will try to keep that block
in memory more aggressively, but it is not guaranteed) if necessary, otherwise it becomes
a single access priority. Once a block is accessed again, it is marked as multiple access. As
shown in the following diagram, cache space for these three priorities is different; single and
in-memory are 25%, multiple access is 50% of total cache space, respectively:

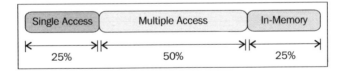

The column family `f2` we created above, was marked as in-memory enabled. Thus blocks
belonging to that family are cached with in-memory priority. For family `f3`, block cache is
disabled, which means the column family's data blocks will not be cached. Disabling block
cache is not recommended.

As data is cached per-block basis, it is very efficient to access data in the same block. This is
especially true for small size rows. Therefore, putting data which will be accessed at the same
time in the same column family is a good practice for table schema design. For example,
when using HBase to store web pages crawled from the Internet, it is good to have a `meta`
column family with in-memory enabled to hold metadata of a web page, and a `raw` column
family to store the raw content of the page.

There's more...

You can also change the block cache property for an existing column family by using the `alter` command via HBase Shell:

1. Disable the table you want to change:

   ```
   hbase> disable 'table1'

   0 row(s) in 7.0580 seconds
   ```

2. Change block size for the table using the `alter` command:

   ```
   hbase> alter 'table1', {NAME => 'f1', IN_MEMORY => 'true'}
   Updating all regions with the new schema...
   1/1 regions updated.
   Done.

   0 row(s) in 6.0990 seconds
   ```

3. Confirm your changes with the `describe` command:

   ```
   hbase> describe 'table1'
   DESCRIPTION
   ENABLED
    {NAME => 'table1', FAMILIES => [{NAME => 'f1', BLOOMFILTER =>
   'NONE', REPLICATION_SCOPE => '0', VERSIONS => '3',   false
    COMPRESSION => 'NONE', MIN_VERSIONS => '0', TTL => '2147483647',
   BLOCKSIZE => '65536', IN_MEMORY => 'true', BLOCK
    CACHE => 'true'}, {NAME => 'f2'...

   1 row(s) in 0.0300 seconds
   ```

4. Enable the table again:

   ```
   hbase> enable 'table1'

   0 row(s) in 2.0530 seconds
   ```

Here we just enabled in-memory for an existing column family `f1` in the table `table1`.

See also

▶ *Increasing block cache size on read-heavy clusters*

▶ *Client side scanner setting*

Increasing block cache size on read-heavy clusters

As described in recipe *Tuning memory size for MemStores* and *Configuring block cache for column families*, region server allocates a large amount of its Java heap space for MemStores to increase write performance. It also uses lots of the heap space to cache StoreFile blocks to improve read performance.

There is balance between write and read performance. While on read-heavy clusters, as read performance is more important, you might want to allocate more memory to block cache.

In this recipe, we will describe how to increase block cache size. We will also include tips for finding out whether block cache is enough or not.

Getting ready

Log in to your master node as the user who starts HBase.

How to do it...

The following steps need to be carried out to increase block cache size:

1. Increase the `hfile.block.cache.size` property value in the `hbase-site.xml` file:

    ```
    $ vi $HBASE_HOME/conf/hbase-site.xml

    <property>
      <name>hfile.block.cache.size</name>
      <value>0.3</value>
    </property>
    ```

2. Sync the changes across the cluster and restart HBase to apply the changes.

How it works...

The total block cache space of a region server is configured by the `hfile.block.cache.size` property. This property specifies the percentage of maximum region server heap to allocate for block cache. By default, it allocates 25% of the maximum heap size.

In step 1, we increased the total space for block cache to 30% of the maximum region server heap size. On read-heavy clusters, it is recommended to reduce the space for MemStores and allocate more memory to block cache. MemStores and block cache normally consume approximately 60%~70% of the maximum region server heap size. This is a reasonable value. The total value of MemStore upper limit and block cache should not be higher than this level except when you are absolutely sure it will be fine.

Another indicator to determine how much memory we should allocate for block cache is to check the region server metrics, either on Ganglia or the HBase web UI. For example, click the region server link on the HBase web UI; you will find the most important metrics of the region server:

HBase Region Server: ip-10-161-93-46.us-w...ompute.internal,60020,1333175315906:60020

http://ip-10-161-93-46.us-west-1.compute.internal   Google

Grammar   Google   Search Hadoop   Del   翻訳   YJ   goo   Wikipedia   Popular ▼   save-to-del   »

Attribute Name	Value	Description
HBase Version	0.92.0, r1231986	HBase version and revision
HBase Compiled	Tue Jan 17 02:30:24 UTC 2012, jenkins	When HBase version was compiled and by whom
Metrics	requestsPerSecond=0, numberOfOnlineRegions=3, numberOfStores=5, numberOfStorefiles=4, storefileIndexSizeMB=0, rootIndexSizeKB=48, totalStaticIndexSizeKB=32, totalStaticBloomSizeKB=0, memstoreSizeMB=0, readRequestsCount=19737, writeRequestsCount=0, compactionQueueSize=0, flushQueueSize=0, usedHeapMB=71, maxHeapMB=998, blockCacheSizeMB=49.46, blockCacheFreeMB=200.15, blockCacheCount=768, blockCacheHitCount=127, blockCacheMissCount=768, blockCacheEvictedCount=0, blockCacheHitRatio=14%, blockCacheHitCachingRatio=14%, hdfsBlocksLocalityIndex=100	RegionServer Metrics; file and heap sizes are in megabytes

Check the MemStore size, block cache size, hit ratio, and so forth on the page; you will find this information useful to help you tune the cluster. If block cache hit ratio is very low, you may need to review your table schema and data access pattern; put columns together if they are always accessed at the same time. Using Bloom Filter is another solution to increase block cache hit ratio. If you are encountering many block evictions, consider increasing the block cache size to fit more blocks.

See also

- ▸ *Tuning memory size for MemStores*
- ▸ *Configuring block cache for column families*
- ▸ *Enabling Bloom Filter to improve the overall throughput*

Client side scanner setting

To achieve better read performance, besides server side tuning, what's important is the scanner setting at client application side. Better client scanner setting makes the scan process much more efficient. By contrast, a badly configured scanner will not only slow down the scan itself, but also have a negative effect on the region server. So we need to configure the client side scanner settings carefully.

The most important scanner settings include scan caching, scan attribute selection, and scan block caching. We will describe how to configure these settings properly in this recipe.

Getting ready

Log in to your HBase client node by the user who accesses HBase.

How to do it...

The following steps need to be followed to change client side scanner settings:

1. To fetch more rows when calling the `next()` method on a scanner, increase the `hbase.client.scanner.caching` property value in the `hbase-site.xml` file:

   ```
   $ vi $HBASE_HOME/conf/hbase-site.xml

   <property>
     <name>hbase.client.scanner.caching</name>
     <value>500</value>
   </property>
   ```

2. Only fetch the columns you need by specifying the column families and qualifiers. Sample code looks like the following:

   ```
   Scan scan = new Scan();
   // your scan filtering code
   scan.addColumn(family1, qualifier1);
   scan.addColumn(family1, qualifier2);
   ```

3. To disable block cache for a particular scan, add the following to your code. Note that this does not disable block cache on the server side, but prevents the blocks scanned by the scanner to be cached.

   ```
   Scan scan = new Scan();
   // your scan filtering code
   scan.setCacheBlocks(false);
   ```

How it works...

In step 1, we changed scan caching to 500, which is much bigger than the default value of 1. This means the region server will transfer 500 rows at a time to the client to be processed. For some situations, such as running MapReduce to read data from HBase, setting this value to a bigger one makes the scan process much more efficient than the default. However, a higher caching value requires more memory to cache the rows for both the client and region server.

It also has the risk that the client may time out before it completes processing the date set and calls `next()` on the scanner. If the client process is fast, set caching higher. Otherwise, you will need to set it lower. We will introduce how to set per-scan basis caching in the *There's more...* section.

Step 2 shows the idea that if only a small subset of a column family is to be processed, then only the required data should be transferred to clients. This is especially important when large amounts of rows are to be processed (for example, during MapReduce). The overhead of non-need data transfer becomes a performance penalty over large datasets. Therefore, instead of using `scan.addFamily()`, which will return all columns in the column family to clients, we should call `scan.addColumn()` to specify only the columns we need.

A block will not be added to block cache if block cache is disabled on the scanner where the block is scanned. As we did in step 3, disabling block cache for a particular scan is sometimes very important. For example, when full scanning a table with MapReduce, you should disable block cache for the scan because all blocks in the table will be scanned, which fills up the block cache space with one time access blocks, and triggers a cache eviction process again and again.

From the HBase web UI, you will find two block cache hit ratio metrics: `blockCacheHitRatio` and `blockCacheHitCachingRatio`. Their difference is that, `blockCacheHitRatio` is the percentage of block cache hit count on the total request count, while `blockCacheHitCachingRatio` only includes the requests where cache was turned on. We can increase `blockCacheHitCachingRatio` by disabling block cache for some scans.

There's more...

We changed the `hbase.client.scanner.caching` property to `500` in `hbase-site.xml` in the previous section. All client sessions on that node will inherit this default caching row number after the change. However, you can also specify a per-scan basis caching rows by using the HBase client Scan API. The following code sets the scanner to fetch 1000 rows when `next()` is called:

```
Scan scan = new Scan();
// your scan filtering code
scan.setCaching(1000);
```

▶ *Client-side tuning for low latency systems*

Tuning block size to improve seek performance

HBase data are stored as StoreFile in the HFile format. StoreFiles are composed of HFile blocks. HFile block is the smallest unit of data that HBase reads from its StoreFiles. It is also the basic element that region server caches in the block cache.

The size of the HFile block is an important tuning parameter. To achieve better performance, we should select different block sizes, based on the average Key/Value size and disk I/O speed. Like block cache and Bloom Filter, HFile block size is also configurable at the column family level.

We will describe how to show the average Key/Value size and tune block size to improve seek performance in this recipe.

Getting ready

Log in to your HBase client node.

How to do it...

The following steps need to be carried out to tune block size to improve seek performance:

1. Use the following command to show the average Key/Value size in a HFile. Change the file path to fit your environment. HFiles for a particular column family are stored under `${hbase.rootdir}/table_name/region_name/column_family_name` on HDFS.

   ```
   $ $HBASE_HOME/bin/hbase org.apache.hadoop.hbase.io.hfile.
   HFile -m -f /hbase/hly_temp/0d1604971684462a2860d43e2715558d
   /n/1742023046455748097
   ```

   ```
   Block index size as per heapsize: 12240
   reader=/hbase/hly_temp/0d1604971684462a2860d43e2715558d
   /n/1742023046455748097, compression=lzo, inMemory=false,
   firstKey=USW000128350706/n:v01/1323026325955/Put,
   lastKey=USW000138830522/n:v24/1323026325955/Put, avgKeyLen=31,
   avgValueLen=4, entries=288024, length=2379789
   fileinfoOffset=2371102, dataIndexOffset=2371361,
   dataIndexCount=190, metaIndexOffset=0, metaIndexCount=0,
   totalBytes=12387203, entryCount=288024, version=1
   Fileinfo:
   ```

```
MAJOR_COMPACTION_KEY = \x00
MAX_SEQ_ID_KEY = 96573
TIMERANGE = 1323026325955....1323026325955
```
hfile.AVG_KEY_LEN = 31
hfile.AVG_VALUE_LEN = 4
```
hfile.COMPARATOR = org.apache.hadoop.hbase.KeyValue$KeyComparator
hfile.LASTKEY = \x00\x0FUSW000138830522\x01nv24\x00\x00\x014\x0A\
x83\xA1\xC3\x04
Could not get bloom data from meta block
```

2. Start HBase Shell:

    ```
    $ $HBASE_HOME/bin/hbase shell
    ```

3. Set block size for a particular column family via HBase Shell:

    ```
    hbase> create 'hly_temp', {NAME => 'n', BLOCKSIZE => '16384'}
    0 row(s) in 1.0530 seconds
    ```

4. Show the properties of the table created previously:

    ```
    hbase> describe 'hly_temp'
    DESCRIPTION
    ENABLED
     {NAME => 'hly_temp', FAMILIES => [{NAME => 'n', BLOOMFILTER =>
    'NONE', REPLICATION_SCOPE => '0', VERSIONS => '3',    true
     COMPRESSION => 'NONE', MIN_VERSIONS => '0', TTL => '2147483647',
    ```
    BLOCKSIZE => '16384'`, IN_MEMORY => 'false', BLOC`
    ```
     KCACHE => 'true'}]}

    1 row(s) in 0.0330 seconds
    ```

How it works...

First of all, we want to know the average Key/Value size of a particular column family. We invoked the HFile tool (`org.apache.hadoop.hbase.io.hfile.HFile` class) in step 1 to show the metadata of an HFile. As described in recipe *HFile tool, view textualized HFile content* in *Chapter 3*, with `-m` option, we can get metadata, including average Key/Value size, of an HFile file using this tool. In step 1, we passed the `-f` option and the file path to show a single HFile's metadata. If your table has only one column family, you can also use the `-r` option and a region name to show metadata of each HFile that belongs to that region. With this information, we are able to get the approximate average Key/Value size of a column family.

As you can see from the output of step 1, the average Key/Value size of the HFile is very small (35 bytes). For this case the average Key/Value size is very small (for example, 100 bytes); we should use small blocks (for example, 16KB) to avoid too many Key/Value pairs being stored in each block, which will increase the latency of in-block seek because the seeking operation always finds the key from the first Key/Value pair in sequence within a block.

We demonstrated how to configure a column family's block size via HBase Shell from step 2 to step 4. We created a `hly_temp` table, with a single column family 'n', and specified the column family's block size to 16384 bytes (16KB) in step 3. This is much smaller than the 64KB default block size.

Here we chose smaller block sizes for faster random access at the expense of larger block indices (more memory consumption). On the other hand, if average Key/Value is large, or slow disks cause bottlenecks, we should select a larger block size, so that a single disk I/O can fetch more data.

There's more...

You can also change block size for an existing column family by using the `alter` command from HBase Shell. This will be applied when creating new StoreFiles.

See also

- ▸ *HFile tool, view textualized HFile content* in *Chapter 3*

Enabling Bloom Filter to improve the overall throughput

HBase supports Bloom Filter to improve the overall throughput of the cluster. A HBase Bloom Filter is a space-efficient mechanism to test whether a StoreFile contains a specific row or row-col cell. Here are the details of Bloom Filter: `http://en.wikipedia.org/wiki/Bloom_filter`.

Without Bloom Filter, the only way to decide if a row key is contained in a StoreFile is to check the StoreFile's block index, which stores the start row key of each block in the StoreFile. It is very likely that the row key we are finding will drop in between two block start keys; if it does then HBase has to load the block and scan from the block's start key to figure out if that row key actually exists.

The problem here is that there will be a number of StoreFiles that exist before a major compaction aggregates them into a single one. Thus several StoreFiles may have some cells of the requested row key.

Think about the following example; it is an image showing how HBase stores data, block indices, and Bloom Filters in StoreFile:

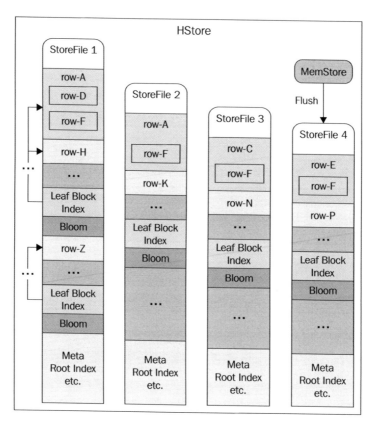

A single column family has four StoreFiles, which are created by MemStore flushes. The StoreFiles have similar spreads in row keys. Some row keys (for example, row-D) are localized to a few StoreFiles, while some (for example, row-F) are spread among many StoreFiles. Although only StoreFile 1 actually contains row-D, HBase also needs to load the first data block from StoreFiles 2 and 3 to figure out whether the block contains cells of row-D, because row-D drops in between the first data block. It would be better if there was a mechanism to tell HBase to skip loading StoreFiles 2 and 3.

This is a situation where Bloom Filter helps. Bloom Filter is used to reduce these unnecessary disk I/O, and thus improve the overall throughput of the cluster.

In this recipe, we will describe how to enable Bloom Filter for a column family, and tips to leverage HBase Bloom Filter to improve the overall throughput.

Getting ready

Log in to your HBase client node.

How to do it...

The following steps need to be carried out to enable Bloom Filter for a column family:

1. Start HBase Shell:

   ```
   $ $HBASE_HOME/bin/hbase shell
   HBase Shell; enter 'help<RETURN>' for list of supported commands.
   Type "exit<RETURN>" to leave the HBase Shell
   Version 0.92.0, r1231986, Tue Jan 17 02:30:24 UTC 2012


   hbase(main):001:0>
   ```

2. Execute the following to create a table with three column families:

   ```
   hbase> create 'table2', {NAME => 'f1'}, {NAME => 'f2', BLOOMFILTER
   => 'ROW'}, {NAME => 'f3', BLOOMFILTER => 'ROWCOL'}
   0 row(s) in 1.0690 seconds
   ```

3. Show the properties of the table created previously:

   ```
   hbase> describe 'table2'
   DESCRIPTION
   ENABLED
    {NAME => 'table2', FAMILIES => [{NAME => 'f1', BLOOMFILTER => 'NONE',
   REPLICATION_SCOPE => '0', VERSIONS => '3',   true
    COMPRESSION => 'NONE', MIN_VERSIONS => '0', TTL => '2147483647',
   BLOCKSIZE => '65536', IN_MEMORY => 'false', BLOC
     KCACHE => 'true'}, {NAME => 'f2', BLOOMFILTER => 'ROW', REPLICATION_
   SCOPE => '0', VERSIONS => '3', COMPRESSION =>
      'NONE', MIN_VERSIONS => '0', TTL => '2147483647', BLOCKSIZE =>
   '65536', IN_MEMORY => 'false', BLOCKCACHE => 'true'}, {NAME => 'f3',
   BLOOMFILTER => 'ROWCOL', REPLICATION_SCOPE => '0', VERSIONS => '3',
   COMPRESSION => 'NONE', MI
    N_VERSIONS => '0', TTL => '2147483647', BLOCKSIZE => '65536', IN_
   MEMORY => 'false', BLOCKCACHE => 'true'}]}
   1 row(s) in 0.0360 seconds
   ```

How it works...

We created a table (`table2`) with three column families, `f1`, `f2`, and `f3`. For family `f1`, we didn't specify any properties, so all its properties were set to default. As shown in step 3, its Bloom Filter is disabled (`BLOOMFILTER => 'NONE'`). We specified row level Bloom Filter for `f2` (`BLOOMFILTER => 'ROW'`), and row + column level Bloom Filter for `f3` (`BLOOMFILTER => 'ROWCOL'`).

If Bloom Filter is enabled, HBase will add Bloom Filter along with data blocks when creating a StoreFile. Bloom Filter is used to let HBase efficiently figure out whether a StoreFile contains a specific row or cell, without actually loading the file and scanning the block. Bloom Filter can be False Positives, which means a query returns `a row is contained in a file` but it is actually not. But False Negatives are not allowed for Bloom Filter, thus when a query returns `a row is not in a file`, the row will be definitely not in the file.

Normally, the error rate is 0.01 (configured by the `io.storefile.bloom.error.rate` setting), thus there is a 1% possibility that Bloom Filter will report that a StoreFile contains a row, but it is not true. Reducing the error rate requires more space to store Bloom Filter.

By default, Bloom Filter is disabled, which means HBase will not store Bloom Filter when creating StoreFiles. It is configurable at column family basis, to enable a row level or row + column level Bloom Filter. A row level Bloom Filter is used to test whether a row key is contained in a StoreFile, while a row + column Bloom Filter can tell HBase whether a StoreFile contains a specific cell. Row + column level Bloom Filter takes more disk space because cell entries are much bigger than row entries.

Even when Bloom Filter is enabled, you may not gain immediate performance on individual get operations, as HBase reads data in parallel, and the latency is bound by disk I/O speed. However, as the number of blocks loaded is greatly reduced, it improves the overall throughput significantly, especially in heavy load clusters.

Another advantage is that using Bloom Filter could improve block cache ratio. With Bloom Filter enabled, HBase can load fewer blocks to fetch the data that clients requested. Because unnecessary blocks are not loaded, blocks containing the data that clients actually request, have more chance to remain in the block cache. This improves read performance for the entire cluster.

The downside is, every entry in Bloom Filter uses about one byte storage. If you have small cells (for example, 20 bytes including the overhead of Key/Value information), then the Bloom Filter will be 1/20 of your file. On the other hand, if your average cell size is 1 KB, the Bloom Filter is about 1/1000 of your file in size. Assuming the StoreFile is 1 GB, then the filter needs only 1 MB on storage. Therefore, we would recommend you to disable Bloom Filter for small cell column families, and always enable it for medium or large cell families.

As we mentioned above, HBase supports row level and row + column level Bloom Filters. Which one to use, depends on your data access pattern. Returning to our example HStore, only a few StoreFiles hold `row-D`. This happens when cells of `row-D` are batch updated. If most of your cells in a row are updated together, row level filter is better. By contrast, like `row-F` in our example, if updates spread across many StoreFiles, and most StoreFiles contain parts of the row, then a row + column filter is recommended, as it is able to identify which StoreFile contains the exact parts of a row you requested.However, you also need to consider your data read pattern. It is obvious that row + column filter makes no sense if you always request the entire row. For example, to load the entire `row-F`, a region server will need to load all four StoreFiles anyway. When your read pattern is to load only a few columns of a row, for example, just the columns of `row-F` in StoreFile 4, then the row + column filter is useful, as the region server will skip loading the other StoreFiles.

> Note that HFile version 1, which is the default HFile format for releases prior to HBase 0.92, has a maximum number of elements a Bloom Filter can hold. This number is controlled by the `io.storefile.bloom.max.keys` property, and the default is 128M keys. If you have too many cells in your StoreFile, you might exceed this number. You will need to use a row level filter in order to reduce the key number in the Bloom Filter.

Bloom Filter is an efficient way to improve the overall performance of your cluster. The row level Bloom Filter works well for many cases; you should try it as your first choice, and consider the row + column Bloom Filter only when the row level filter does not fit your usage.

There's more...

You can also change the Bloom Filter property for existing tables' column families with the `alter` command via HBase Shell. It will be applied to StoreFiles created after the change.

Index

Thank you for buying
HBase Administration Cookbook

About Packt Publishing

Packt, pronounced 'packed', published its first book "*Mastering phpMyAdmin for Effective MySQL Management*" in April 2004 and subsequently continued to specialize in publishing highly focused books on specific technologies and solutions.

Our books and publications share the experiences of your fellow IT professionals in adapting and customizing today's systems, applications, and frameworks. Our solution based books give you the knowledge and power to customize the software and technologies you're using to get the job done. Packt books are more specific and less general than the IT books you have seen in the past. Our unique business model allows us to bring you more focused information, giving you more of what you need to know, and less of what you don't.

Packt is a modern, yet unique publishing company, which focuses on producing quality, cutting-edge books for communities of developers, administrators, and newbies alike. For more information, please visit our website: www.packtpub.com.

About Packt Open Source

In 2010, Packt launched two new brands, Packt Open Source and Packt Enterprise, in order to continue its focus on specialization. This book is part of the Packt Open Source brand, home to books published on software built around Open Source licences, and offering information to anybody from advanced developers to budding web designers. The Open Source brand also runs Packt's Open Source Royalty Scheme, by which Packt gives a royalty to each Open Source project about whose software a book is sold.

Writing for Packt

We welcome all inquiries from people who are interested in authoring. Book proposals should be sent to author@packtpub.com. If your book idea is still at an early stage and you would like to discuss it first before writing a formal book proposal, contact us; one of our commissioning editors will get in touch with you.

We're not just looking for published authors; if you have strong technical skills but no writing experience, our experienced editors can help you develop a writing career, or simply get some additional reward for your expertise.

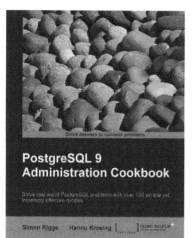

PostgreSQL 9 Administration Cookbook

ISBN: 978-1-849510-28-8   Paperback: 360 pages

Solve real-world PostgreSQL problems with over 100 simple yet incredibly effective recipes

1. Administer and maintain a healthy database

2. Monitor your database ensuring that it performs as quickly as possible

3. Tips for backup and recovery of your database

MySQL Admin Cookbook

ISBN: 978-1-847197-96-2   Paperback: 376 pages

99 great recipes for mastering MySQL configuration and administration

1. Set up MySQL to perform administrative tasks such as efficiently managing data and database schema, improving the performance of MySQL servers, and managing user credentials

2. Deal with typical performance bottlenecks and lock-contention problems

3. Restrict access sensibly and regain access to your database in case of loss of administrative user credentials

Please check **www.PacktPub.com** for information on our titles

[PACKT] open source*
PUBLISHING
community experience distilled

PostgreSQL 9.0 High Performance

ISBN: 978-1-849510-30-1   Paperback: 468 pages

Accelerate your PostgreSQL system and avoid the common pitfals that can slow it down

1. Learn the right techniques to obtain optimal PostgreSQL database performance, from initial design to routine maintenance

2. Discover the techniques used to scale successful database installations

3. Avoid the common pitfalls that can slow your system down

Cassandra High Performance Cookbook

ISBN: 978-1-849515-12-2   Paperback: 310 pages

Over 150 recipes to design and optimize large-scale Apache Cassandra deployments

1. Get the best out of Cassandra using this efficient recipe bank

2. Configure and tune Cassandra components to enhance performance

3. Deploy Cassandra in various environments and monitor its performance

4. Well illustrated, step-by-step recipes to make all tasks look easy!

Please check **www.PacktPub.com** for information on our titles

Made in the USA
Lexington, KY
17 September 2013